MW01679780

KEATING

Also by Edna Carew:

Fast Money
Fast Money 2
Language of Money
New Zealand's Money Revolution

KEATING

A Biography

EDNA CAREW

ALLEN & UNWIN
Sydney Wellington London Boston

© Edna Carew 1988
This book is copyright under the Berne Convention. No reproduction without permission. All rights reserved.

First published in 1988
Allen & Unwin Australia Pty Ltd
An Unwin Hyman company
8 Napier Street, North Sydney, NSW 2060 Australia

Allen & Unwin New Zealand Limited
60 Cambridge Terrace, Wellington, New Zealand

Unwin Hyman Limited
15–17 Broadwick Street, London W1V 1FP England

Unwin Hyman Inc.
8 Winchester Place, Winchester, Mass 01890 USA

National Library of Australia
Cataloguing-in-Publication entry:

Carew, Edna, 1949-
Keating, a biography.

Includes index.
ISBN 0 04 335059 3.

1. Keating, Paul, 1944- 2. Cabinet officers — Australia — Biography. 3. Legislators — Australia — Biography 4. Politicians — Australia — Biography. I. Title.

354.940672'092'4

Set in 11/12 Hyland by Love Computer Typesetting
Printed by Australian Print Group

Contents

To Hoffers
for his dry wit and excellent cooking —
and for quitting smoking.

Introduction

It is a measure of the interest he arouses that Paul Keating, still in his forties, has become the subject of a biography. A federal politician since the age of 25, and Australia's treasurer since 1983, he has made a vivid imprint on his country's financial system and structure. The image and thinking of the Australian Labor Party in the 1980s carries his brand. This mid-life account of a man whose career—whichever direction it takes—is far from over, explores the politician behind the moves, the passionately private person whose boots-and-all approach to political life has won him admirers and bitter detractors.

This book is not an 'authorised' account of Keating's life: he did not commission the biography. It was never suggested that he read the manuscript, nor has he requested to do so. He has co-operated, but not attempted to influence the content.

Acknowledgments

Many people—more than can be mentioned in this space—have willingly given me their co-operation during the time it took me to write this book. Their efforts have assisted in various ways—to round out a personal life story as well as to refine details in technical areas. Some prefer to remain anonymous. All have made a contribution.

This book would be a less complete and less authoritative account if Paul Keating had chosen not to lend some co-operation to the project. I much appreciate the time he, and Anita Keating, gave me. Likewise, I would like to thank Anne Keating for her help in providing childhood and family photographs which add substantially to the book. And I am grateful to Min Keating for allowing an author to plunder her cherished collection of family treasures. I hope she enjoys seeing them in print. Glenn A. Baker, Barry Brady, Mike Gavan and John Grayson have also generously provided photographic material.

Time constraints impose a cut-off point for research. There are others with whom I would like to have spoken. But I am especially grateful to those who interrupted busy schedules, often at short notice, to be interviewed. Special thanks go to Tony Cole, Fred Daly, Greg Keating, Paul Kelly, Susan Ryan, John Stroud and Barbara Ward.

And I thank the following for their time and thoughts: Percy Allan, Gil Appleton, Ron Barr, Kim Beazley snr, Kim Beazley jnr, Laurie Brereton, Moira and Mark Brophy, Rod Cameron, Edmund Campion, Bob Carr, Rod Cavalier, Mary and Greg Clout, Ron Dyer, Michael Egan, Mike Gavan, Margaret Gibb, John Grayson, Dierdre Grusovin, Richard Hall, Barry Hughes, Brother Michael Johnson, John Johnson, Bill Junor, Trish Kavanagh, Jan Kell, Ros Kelly, Glenda Korporaal, Mark Latham, John Leard, Graham Little, Father Michael

McCarthy, Jim McClelland, Leo McLeay, Peter McMahon, Ralph Marsh, John Martin, Bob McMullan, Fred Rizzo, Colleen Ryan, John Short, Bob Sorby, Megan Stoyles, Joan Taggart, John Tingle, Brian Toohey, Max Walsh, Tom Wheelwright, Gough Whitlam, Nicholas Whitlam. Others contributed their knowledge and experience to chapters dealing specifically with:

the accord: Simon Crean, Ross Gittins, Bill Kelty, Geoff McGill, Bill Russell, Pamela Williams, Ralph Willis.

ALP background and history: John Ducker, Michael Easson, Murray Goot, Stephen Loosely, Michael Sexton.

antiques: Bill Bradshaw, Leo Schofield.

Bankstown: John Engisch, Arthur Heiler, Ron Lockwood, George Williams.

finance, economics and tax: Richard Beetham, Warren Bird, Vern Christie, Alan Coates, David Collins, Ted Evans, Bernie Fraser, Peter Groenewegen, R.A. (Bob) Johnston, Peter Jonson, Chris Jordan, Ian McKenzie, David Morgan, John Phillips, Greg Smith, Tom Valentine, Bob White.

media legislation: Ken Archer, Fred Brenchley, Cass O'Connor, Max Powditch, Max Suich.

minerals and energy: Charles Copeman, Peter Dunn, Tom Fitzgerald, Sir Leslie Froggatt, Russ Fynmore, Gene Herbert, John McLeod, David McGarry, Murray McMillan, Paul Phillips.

rock 'n' roll: Glenn A. Baker, Barry Brady, Barry Connors.

My thanks go also to staff in Paul Keating's office, particularly Helen Ogston.

This is an appropriate opportunity to acknowledge those whose actions over the past ten years have brought me to the point where I could produce a book such as this. Ten years of writing involves a big cast but the key players include: Max Walsh, for inviting me to join the staff of the *Australian Financial Review* and enter the world of financial journalism; Geraldine Walsh, for introducing me to the publisher John Iremonger and setting in motion a fruitful relationship that has produced several books; John Iremonger for his support, particularly throughout this project. Last, but most important, John Hoffmann's careful editing and his steady hand with a corkscrew at the end of a long day's writing have been a constant comfort.

Edna Carew
Sydney 1988

Photographic acknowledgements

Roman numerals refer to the page numbers of the photographic sections lying between pages 112–13 and pages 144–5

i Min Keating
ii Min Keating
iii *top and left* Min Keating
above Mike Gavin
iv Barry Brady and Glenn A Baker
v Australian Labor Party
vi John Grayson
vii John Grayson
viii *top* Min Keating
bottom John Fairfax & Sons Limited
ix *top* Paul Keating
bottom John Fairfax & Sons Limited
x John Fairfax & Sons Limited
xi *top* Consolidated Press
bottom Photographer Rhonda Thwaite
xii Consolidated Press
xiii John Fairfax & Sons Limited
xiv John Fairfax & Sons Limited
xv *top* Paul Keating
bottom John Fairfax & Sons Limited
xvi John Fairfax & Sons Limited

A long way from Bankstown

Washington, September 1986: the world's top bankers, finance ministers and bureaucrats had gathered in the sultry heat of an Indian summer to attend the 41st annual meetings of the International Monetary Fund and the World Bank. Among them was Paul Keating, Australia's federal treasurer since March 1983. This was not the first IMF/World Bank talkfest Keating had attended, but it was the one at which he made his mark.

No shrinking violet on the domestic dais, Keating revels in taking the international stage. In 1986 he seized that opportunity. 'Do something, don't just talk,' he admonished the closed-door meeting of the interim committee of finance ministers, telling twenty-odd senior international economic dignitaries that they were 'long on rhetoric and short on action'. Abandoning his prepared text in favour of off-the-cuff invective—which is his forté—Keating lectured the group on the need for real progress in cutting back the US deficit, reducing protectionism and subsidisation, and fostering world trade. Keating's references to US policy-making as a 'pantomime' and to Germany and Japan as the 'play-it-safe club' met a mixed reception from his audience. Some were enraged; many representatives of smaller countries agreed with him. Keating railed against the US:

> I think we must face the fact that there is an absence of leadership in the United States at the administration and at the congress level.

> The administration says it wants a better budget deficit and the congress won't co-operate. It is a pantomime which is becoming very tiring for the rest of us to watch.

Bankstown, March 1988: Politics was the topic under discussion in the Cumberland Hotel, in this western suburb of Sydney, on Saturday 19 March 1988, the day on which the voters of New South Wales turned their Labor government out of office after twelve years. A trio of men, comfortably occupying a corner that seemed to be theirs by custom, drank schooners of beer and argued with mock aggressiveness about why the government could expect a hard time from the electorate. A bored barmaid muttered: 'God, not politics again,' and jokingly, vainly, ordered them to change the subject. One of the men had completed an early morning shift at a local polling booth, distributing how-to-vote leaflets. The government would not be spending any more money in Bankstown, he said. Why would a Labor government spend money in a safe Labor seat? The swinging seats were the ones that interested politicians. The name of Paul Keating, federal treasurer and federal member of parliament for Blaxland, the electorate which includes Bankstown, was mentioned. He was the federal member, they agreed, but he did not live among the people whom he represented.

Twenty, thirty years earlier, the Keating name was well-known in the bar of the Cumberland Hotel. Matt Keating, a boilermaker-turned-small-businessman, would be there on Saturday mornings, talking politics with his blue-collar mates. Irish, working-class, Catholic, Matt Keating was the epitome of Bankstown Labor.

The 1500-room Washington Sheraton is half a world away in distance from the Cumberland Hotel in Bankstown—and a world away in style. Paul Keating's career is the thread that makes the unlikely link between these two places.

The Sheraton stands in twelve acres of ground opposite leafy Rock Creek Park. For the past four decades, two years out of every three, it has hosted the annual meetings of the IMF and World Bank. The meetings last for four days. Preparation takes considerably longer as Sheraton staff make ready for the thousands of visiting dignitaries, install additional telephones, turn bedrooms into offices and gear up their restaurants to cater for international palates and preferences. Security is a prime concern. Another is the coffee supply—delegates to the IMF/World Bank conferences consume more coffee than any other group meeting at the Sheraton.

The 1986 series of meetings was officially opened by the US

President, Ronald Reagan, on Tuesday 2 October. But much of the important discussion had taken place during the preceding weekend at various interim committee meetings, as well as in the corridors and bars within reach of the labyrinthine convention centre. The meetings provide an annual opportunity for the international financial community to rub shoulders, renew acquaintanceships and establish useful contacts. Lunchtime receptions and evening cocktail parties are as important a part of the consultation as the high-level, closed-door discussions.

Keating did not travel to the US and the IMF meetings just to harangue foreign finance ministers—his overseas trips are deliberately slanted towards marketing, selling Australia as a sound place for the investment of foreign money. From the IMF meetings in Washington Keating flew to New York, where he addressed an investment banking seminar, before moving on for more meetings in London and Europe. And Keating is well-equipped to sell Australia. He is comfortable in New York's Wall Street and in the City of London. Lean and tall at almost six feet, invariably immaculately dressed in a dark, sober suit and white shirt, his black hair cut in a conservative short-back-and-sides fashion that, beyond some thinning at a receding hairline, has not changed over the years, he is a challenging figure.

Keating is a pragmatic product of the Right of the NSW ALP. The creed of the Right is to get things done, and that means having power. He has reached for power, and won it. In the process he has made acolytes and enemies—and he has affected the way that both see the Australian Labor Party.

1 A good Catholic boy

From a kid I was always out letter-boxing . . . I was interested in politics before I left school.

PAUL KEATING

IN JULY 1944 the International Monetary Fund was born in the town of Bretton Woods, New Hampshire, USA. It was the child of a meeting of the world's finest economic minds; an international symposium charged with finding a way to enable nations to grow and prosper in some semblance of economic harmony. Since then, the IMF has assembled every year, bringing together thousands of politicians, bankers and bureaucrats to examine the financial state of the world and, where it is possible, to pronounce on directions for growth and remedies for ailments. The IMF is history's most authoritative economic forum.

In that same year, on 18 January 1944, Paul John Keating was born in the suburb of Bankstown, New South Wales, in Australia, the first child of Matt and Min Keating. His parents were working-class. When Paul Keating left school, not yet fifteen, he knew nothing of economics. There was nothing to suggest that in 1986 he would be standing on a podium in Washington—on the international stage of the IMF—lecturing to the world's key financial decision-makers.

Bankstown in 1944 was a semi-rural area, 20 kilometres from the centre of Sydney. Keating was born during the lean years of World War II, when food and petrol rationing were the order of the day and blackouts ruled at night. Bankstown was yet to expand, as it did in the following years, under the effects of post-war revival and a resulting building boom. As the suburb grew it also radically altered in composition and appearance. The Bankstown into which the young Keating was born was almost entirely English-speaking and of Anglo-Celtic origin; the ethnic migration of later decades was yet to bring the flavour of Europe and Asia, the Vietnamese butcher, the croissant and hot bread shops, Asian restaurants and the mix of businesses that now make up the Mall and the Old Town Centre Plaza, the commercial heart of Keating's electorate.

When Paul Keating was a child, Bankstown was, he says, a 'villagey' sort of place. 'Everybody knew everybody then. Now it's part of the western suburbs but in those days there was a great sense of community—in Bankstown you felt like you belonged to some place.' Not all recollections of Bankstown in the 1950s agree with Keating's—the area was dubbed 'Gangstown' and the 'Little Chicago by the Georges River'. In 1955 Bankstown's local newspaper, the Torch, was burned down while its editor, Philip Engisch, was running a crusade against the graft and corruption in the area. Now the suburb is a city with a population of 250 000 and a respectability approaching staidness.

Childhood in the Bankstown 'village' was fairly ordinary. 'It was a pretty normal life, a pretty normal background,' Keating says. His boyhood pursuits were conventional—racing home-made billy-carts, riding his bike with his mates (kids got bikes later then, he points out, around eleven or twelve), going to the beach at Cronulla or Stanwell Park or swimming at the Bankstown Olympic pool. Keating recalls being trained by Don Talbot, better known as the trainer of the world-champion Konrad twins. Says Keating: 'They were keen as mustard, I wasn't.' His younger sister, Anne, says he was a 'normal larrikin kid'. He says: 'Where I lived was semi-rural in those days. We'd ride down to Bankstown airport, climb in and out of the old World War II planes, Hudson bombers and all that stuff. We'd ride through the bush, it was all bush in those days, ride out to Camden or the Warragamba dam, or even down to Wollongong, hang on to a truck on the Bulli pass—that's hard to conceive now.'

Keating says he had a good, secure family, which he believes helps a great deal, and refers to a survey carried out among members of parliament which revealed that they were mostly first-born children. Keating feels that is an interesting reflection of the investment by parents in their first child. In his view, the degree of confidence people get from their families carries them right through life. He is sure that this was true of his beginnings—a first-born child who was 'well set up'. He believes that 'gives you a place in the world'.

The Keating family illustrates the traditional pattern of Irish

Catholic life in Australia. On the minus side, this usually meant being immovably working class, starting out on life with inbuilt disadvantages, living in suburbs at the 'wrong' end of the city, marked out as Catholic in a predominantly Protestant culture. On the plus side there was tribal solidarity, loyalty that is demanded and given, the security of knowing one's base.

The three traditional adages of Catholic childhood were part of Keating's life: go to mass, join the union, support Labor. Father Michael McCarthy, who has known the Keating family since the 1960s when he lived in the Central Bankstown parish and who has baptised Paul and Anita Keating's children, describes Matt Keating as having had 'a lively faith'. Father McCarthy says the Bankstown community was one of 'good, honest souls, and Matt and Min were very much part of that milieu'. And Paul Keating's sense of self-worth, he says, reflects the influence of the family background. Matt Keating had grown up at a time when the church gave positive encouragement to the workers to join unions—otherwise, warned the priests, the unions would fall into the hands of the communists.

There is a tribal instinct in Irish Catholics. Keating says it is a system that 'breeds an interest in the social fabric—a honed-up sense of fairness that sticks with you'. He recalls going to church every Sunday; it was a part of life and a part of social life. 'After mass on Sunday you'd have groups of people standing there, hundreds of people, chatting for some 40 minutes. The same faces at school would turn up at church. It was a great sense of community. You weren't growing up anonymously.'

Certainly Keating is imbued with many of the characteristics associated with Irish-Catholic Australians, such as the passionate, fighting approach to issues. Susan Ryan, who until early 1988 was a minister in the Labor government, says: 'Paul Keating comes from that particular part of Australian society that has its roots in Irish Catholicism. It's a cultural imprint that goes well beyond where your grandparents actually came from.' Keating describes himself as 'a traditional Irish working-class person—philosophical, sentimental, emotional'.

The Keating family was far from affluent during the early years of Paul's life. Matt, Min and their four children—Paul, Lyn, Anne and Greg—lived in a twelve-square fibro house in Marshall Street, in the heart of Bankstown, until 1966. Then they sold and moved into the classier 'upper Bankstown' area of Condell Park, to a larger house in what had once been part of the bushland on which the young Paul rode his bike. Anne Keating says: 'It was a comfortable life. We never wanted for anything, but we were not indulged as kids.

It was a "no frills" childhood.' What the Keatings achieved in terms of improved life-style was earned by hard grind. By all accounts Matt Keating set his family an example of hard work and long hours.

All four Keating children have established themselves well. Lyn, next in age to Paul, was the first of the children to marry. She and her husband, Tony King, ran a property near Orange for some years before he accepted the post of secretary of the Australian Jockey Club and the family returned to Sydney. Anne Keating, ten years younger than her brother, trained as a teacher, lived in London for some years and went on to work with United Airlines. Greg, almost twelve years younger than Paul, qualified in law and is a senior partner with McClellands, the Sydney law firm founded by Jim McClelland, who turned to politics and was a minister in the Whitlam government.

The years separating Paul and Greg Keating represent more than a difference in age—during that decade, not only did the fortunes of the Keating family improve but times changed in a way that saw more school-leavers continue their studies at university. Education came to encompass more than a blackboard and a stick of chalk. Schools became more driven towards encouraging students into tertiary studies and developing professional skills. Even so, it was not until the 1970s and the Whitlam government that the costs of tertiary education were reduced in a way that helped a whole new stratum of society go to university.

When Paul Keating left De La Salle College, Bankstown, in November 1958, a couple of months short of his fifteenth birthday, there was little tradition of higher education. Keating says of that time: 'You just didn't know people who went to university.' It was not a matter of having an option; tertiary education was then priced out of reach of working-class families. The important goal was a secure job, and that meant going straight from school to a government agency or a bank. Being an accountant was the fashionable thing. He left school with the intermediate certificate, but subsequently went on to study at night, at Belmore Technical College, for what is now the higher school certificate.

Keating admits he was probably a bit bored with school, and at that stage too impatient to plough on to a tertiary course. According to Brother Michael Johnson, who was principal of De La Salle in 1958, the boys took their exams seriously in those days. Students' results were published in the newspapers, and the boys knew that family, friends and the world at large could scrutinise their success or failures. Keating was in a class of 28 boys who, according to Brother Johnson, were an unusually bright group, although they could be a wild lot, tough on their teachers. Keating came around tenth in the class. He enjoyed subjects such as maths, physics and chemistry. He did well in those but was less strong in literature and history, fields in which he is now much more interested. Brother Johnson remembers him as bright, but quiet in the classroom. There was no indication then of the drive and aggression that were to distinguish the adult Paul Keating. Two of his classmates, Fred Rizzo and Mike Gavan, remember Keating as being a bit more serious at times than the average kid who was interested in girls and cars.

Much of what was to influence Paul Keating's life was absorbed from his family, particularly from his father. Matt Keating was the first in a line of older mentors from whom the young Paul learned—a line that included names that have been both revered and reviled, such as Jack Lang, the old war-horse of Labor, and Rex Connor, Whitlam's minister for minerals and energy. Keating also had the encouragement and interest of local Labor figures, such as Wally Adnum and Vic Beavis. Beavis, who later directed his preselection and first election campaigns, was a close confidant and friend. Adnum, a local Bankstown identity, into his sixties when Keating was a young man, took an unusually close interest in someone he identified as having talent and promise. Matt Keating is remembered in his neighbourhood as a kind, tolerant, hard-working man, deeply interested in and involved in politics, someone with a good sense of humour and a flair for colourful expressions which his son inherited. Paul Keating has also inherited his mother's more fiery, volatile disposition. As he grows older Keating increasingly resembles his father; the intense, dark brown eyes are from his mother. Mother and son are both strong personalities, very close but known to have had their clashes. Keating's sister Anne says he is a 'good mix of both parents'.

Paul Keating's political consciousness was formed during the 1950s, the time of the great Labor split, when people's political and religious allegiances were very much part of life. Influenced and encouraged by his father, he was working with the Labor Party at the age of twelve, handing out leaflets at the hustings, and he joined the party when he left school. Given his background, there was only one political party that Keating could have considered joining—the Australian Labor Party. Keating talks of his burning desire to get into politics:

> From a kid I was always out letter-boxing. In the Labor Party, in the branch area, you get a little grid of streets where you do your part, and my father used to do his part and I'd do it mostly with him. I was

> interested in politics before I left school . . . from the age of twelve, I suppose, I knew what was what . . . I knew what party I liked and why I did.

Laurie Brereton, whose friendship with Keating goes back to their shared commitment in the 1960s to the Labor Youth Council, describes that political apprenticeship:

> Paul Keating grew up, as I grew up, in the Labor Party, and that was the first job you got, delivering dodgers. And the second job that you got was handing out how-to-vote forms on election days and the third job that you got was booth captain and you'd generally done all those by the time you were fourteen. And then you got to join the Labor Party when you were fifteen.

Paul Keating has inherited his father's admiration for self-made men. Matt Keating himself was one of that breed. He had little time for professionals and academics, regarding them as 'the pimple on the bum of society'. If Matt Keating had a philosophy of life, it was bedded in striving for excellence through hard work. When Paul Keating was born his father was one of 150 boilermakers working in the sprawling Chullora railway workshops in Sydney's west. Ralph Marsh, who worked with Matt Keating and shared his interest in trade union and political matters, as well as an occasional drink and, in later life, game of bowls, remembers him as a good tradesman and worker who was active in the boilermakers' union. Marsh, too, was an officer in the union and was secretary of the New South Wales Labor Council from 1968 to 1975. Matt Keating was elected assistant secretary of the Chullora branch of the boilermakers' union in the early 1950s, and later was secretary for three years. His subsequent promotion to the position of welding inspector put him into a salaried staff position and out of the union. His interest and involvement in politics, though, never flagged, and he was a member and later president of the Central Bankstown branch of the Labor Party and then of the Condell Park branch.

A staff reshuffle in the mid-1950s, and the phasing-out of steam trains in favour of diesel engines, with a consequent fall-off in demand for boilermakers, brought another turning point. Matt Keating decided to set up his own business with two other boilermakers, Col Blake and Frank Martin. The three men formed Marlak Engineering Pty Ltd, a general engineering company at Regents Park which specialised in manufacturing batching plants, transition mixers and conveying equipment for the ready-mixed concrete industry. Running his own company did not change Matt Keating's views—he retained the mentality of the working man. The three worked well together, bringing complementary skills to what became a thriving business. Marlak was able to capitalise on the building boom of the time and grew into a leading concrete equipment manufacturer in the late 1950s and 1960s.

But life was tough then for small business, even for those which seemed to be thriving. Bank credit was not easy to come by in an era when Australia's capital markets were relatively unsophisticated and consumer finance had not become the part of life it is today. This left a lasting impression on Paul Keating, who says: 'One of the things I always noticed was that small business would never get supported by the banks. They would only take collateral on plant—companies could get good overseas contracts but banks wouldn't bankroll the contracts.' Marlak would have needed to borrow to expand and finance was hard to get. Like many similarly placed small companies, it was swallowed up by a larger operator. Australian National Industries (ANI) bought Marlak in July 1973, paying $376 000 which was split equally among the three founders in a mix of cash and shares in ANI.

John Leard, who, as managing director of ANI from 1967 to 1984 presided over seventeen years of sustained growth and profits, says Marlak was a well-run company and the takeover part of the development and expansion path of ANI. Matt Keating, Col Blake and Frank Martin he describes as 'a good team'. 'They were cautious men who, like most who began with very little and built up a company, were careful not to overexpand. And they would have had to borrow heavily to expand.' Leard remembers Matt Keating: 'A very pleasant fellow—a polite, gracious, type of man, very competent in his work. And very proud of Paul's involvement in parliament.'

His drive and capacity for hard work were the chief legacies left by Matt Keating to the son he trained and encouraged into politics. He also instilled in the young Paul a deep and lasting admiration for Jack Lang, which Paul followed through to the extent of having weekly discussions with Lang. Ralph Marsh describes Matt Keating as someone who was 'not driving for himself but for someone else, and that's a great influence on a young fellow'. Marsh says of his old friend and colleague: 'He was a fine man, a good family man, a good tradesman and businessman. And he was charitable. He had everything.'

Matt Keating was not to live to see most of Paul's achievements. He died suddenly of a heart attack in 1978, while Labor was still in opposition and several years before his son took centre-stage with the treasurer's portfolio. Whether he would have agreed with all that Paul Keating has done is questionable. No doubt both men would have revelled in arguments, as they had in the past. In a rare interview, Min Keating told the *Sun-Herald* in 1986 that the happiest times of her life were spent around the dining-room table listening to her husband and son arguing politics. 'They often clashed and could get quite heated. I'm sure those days helped Paul's debating skills. He's very like his father but I like to think there's a bit of me there.'

Min Keating was a strong influence on all members of the family but a special relationship grew with Paul. Matt's long working hours meant he was often absent from the house and Min came to depend on her eldest son. And he was very much the affectionate older brother figure to the others. The family was certainly close, with most of the children choosing to live at home until marrying. Father McCarthy puts that down to Min's running 'a good club'. 'She was a great mother, ran a welcoming home.' Anne Keating says they were 'a great family for talkers. The family would sit around and talk and if Paul had been to a meeting and came home late we'd sit around and talk till after midnight.'

After leaving school the young Keating quickly found a job—but one which suggested a life ahead of stolid, secure ordinariness. In January 1959 he started work as a junior clerk with the Sydney County Council. He stayed in that job until October 1965. During those years, though, he learned much that was to shape the budding politician.

2 The first ballot box

Preselection ballots, even in safe Labor seats, are not a tea party.

JOHN DUCKER

AT HIS first job, which he started two days after his fifteenth birthday, Keating had a taste of how a bureaucracy works. He was working as a clerk with the Sydney County Council. His first year was spent in the Queen Victoria Building, in Sydney's George Street, then he moved to Pyrmont. He worked a 7.30am to 4.15 pm shift in the transformer handling department. It was from the engineers he mixed with there that he picked up many of the vivid expressions which he was later to use in parliament to such effect. While with the Sydney County Council he studied for his leaving certificate in the evenings at Belmore Technical College, and went on to study mathematics and electrical engineering part-time at Sydney Technical College. That fitted well with the work he did in the engineering section at the SCC. Keating looks back on those years as a time when he was trying to work out what to do with himself. 'I was thinking during those years,' says Keating, a self-confessed intellectual gadfly, who soon realised that he did not like the tedium of studying.

The years between fifteen and twenty were his most carefree, when life encompassed a job, study and plenty of teenage fun. Keating was still mixing with former schoolmates in Bankstown, and the local Catholic youth organisation was a focal point in their lives. That organisation, he says, had 'a lot of guts, was a great thing for boys and girls'. The young Keating was in demand as a partner to squire young debutantes to the annual CYO ball. At weekends he and his friends would take off for the beach, perhaps driving to Austinmer, 60 kilometres south of Sydney (Keating had a Morris Minor by then), or take the ferry to Clark Island in Sydney Harbour for a barbecue. Conventional pursuits of Australian teenagers in the early 1960s.

In those years the young Keating indulged a number of pursuits as he felt for his way in the world. He and some friends dabbled in farming, becoming sharecroppers in the Riverina, at Urana, north of Rutherglen. Keating spent only short periods on the land, working part-time or during holidays, but he talks enthusiastically about the 'beguiling' bush lifestyle. The introduction of farm quotas ended a pastime that he describes as having given him 'a peephole into the psyche of the bush'.

Cars were an early and consuming interest. Keating graduated from the Morris Minor to an Austin Healey, and a Fiat 1500 which was then known as the 'poor man's Alfa Romeo'. 'That car could take a lot of punishment, and it had to,' says John Grayson, who later worked with Keating at the Municipal Employees' Union. 'Paul Keating drove hard and fast. He never did anything by halves.'

The interest in cars has always remained, although it has competed subsequently with a passion for silver, a preoccupation with an aviary, a fierce enthusiasm for photography, a love of music (rock 'n' roll and classical), a fondness for fob watches and, later and most enduringly, an intense interest in the art, architecture and history of the French Empire.

By the time Keating was eighteen he had put his foot in the door of the Labor Youth Council (later renamed Young Labor). Membership of the Youth Council was voluntary but would have been a natural move for a young enthusiast such as Keating, and his local branch would have encouraged him to participate in what was regarded as a good forum for developing skills. The Youth Council had evolved in the 1930s, when it went under the quaint name of The Younger Set. Members can attend NSW state annual conferences, and their resolutions at these conferences carry the same status as resolutions from the party branches. At the time Keating joined the Youth Council it was bitterly split between the Left and the Right. The Left tended to attract university students, which branded it as 'middle-class' in the eyes of the Right, who were more indentified with the right-wing unions.

It was through the council that he met Laurie Brereton, a

young man from a background very similar to his own, from a working-class family in which politics was a consuming interest. Brereton, who was training as an electrician, shared the young Keating's passion for fast cars. Greg Keating remembers Laurie Brereton driving a 'beat-up ute' and helping Paul with the wiring and the lights in the new house in Condell Park when the family moved there in the mid-1960s. The tastes of Brereton and Keating were to grow more sophisticated as their means improved, but both showed early signs of an appreciation of the good things in life. Later, Laurie Brereton, with his chiselled features, neat hair and impeccable clothes, was regarded as the one person who could out-do the faultlessly-dressed Keating for cut and style. Keating has always dressed neatly. Even as a young clerk in his early jobs he left home looking as dapper as a chairman of the board, shoes polished, trousers with a knife-edge crease. He is careful about making a good impression: in later years he was to arrive for his first television interview with a selection of suits, shirts and ties to ensure he went before the cameras wearing the most flattering combination of colours.

The Youth Council introduced Keating to many people who would become long-time political allies. It also introduced him to the tactics of 'machine' politics. In the mid-1960s Keating was already an active member and, with Brereton, was putting together a ticket for the Youth Council elections—Keating for president and Brereton for secretary. Keating and Brereton and their group put together what Brereton calls a 'centre-unity-style operation' (although that name was not used then) which had the backing of the NSW Right machine, the dominant faction in NSW. The Right had controlled the Youth Council for as long as anyone could remember. The new group's aim was to put the Youth Council under 'moderate and sensible control'. Their organisation and effort paid off, the ticket was successful and they had their chance to revitalise what had become a fairly moribund organisation. The Keating–Brereton team was in office from 1967 to 1969. Ron Dyer, later a NSW member of parliament, was vice-president during those years.

The Youth Council was put on the map in the 1950s and early 1960s by John Ducker (later the president of NSW Labor Party and chairman of the Public Service Board) and John Johnson (later president of the NSW Legislative Council). Ducker, who was president of the Youth Council until 1961, calls it a 'good training ground'. He played something of a link role, through the Youth Council, between the older and younger generations. He says:

> Younger people who wanted to make their mark in terms of policies and personality found the Labor Youth organisation to be exhilarating, to provide opportunities to develop skills in the cut and thrust of debate, to hone parliamentary tactics. And Labor Youth has had a long history of throwing up a range of people who have gone on to be active in commonwealth and state parliament—people like Laurie Brereton, Graham Richardson, Johnno Johnson, Dierdre Grusovin, Paul Keating. That's not a bad crop.

In those years the Labor Party hierarchy perceived the Youth Council as having an important role in grooming young politicians. It was a combative arena, a forum where young people could learn the skills of politics, develop their ability to analyse people and issues, hold a debate and work out a solution. As Keating says, to stand up and speak in front of an audience that could be hostile, if the numbers are not with you, is a big deal for a twenty-year-old.

Young Labor in those days met monthly in the Labor Party offices in Elizabeth Street in Sydney, next to the Hyde Park Hotel. Headquarters later shifted to Sussex Street. Those who attended the regular meetings remember them as earnest times, coloured by passionate arguments over issues such as state aid for Catholic schools, abortion, or the level of foreign investment in Australia. Some who attended described the meetings as a 'bear pit'; others dismiss the wrangling as a bunch of kids at play. As the 1960s progressed, Vietnam became more and more a central topic of debate—as did the possibility of Gough Whitlam's leading Labor to power. There were no wild teenage dances, no frivolous social life. Says Laurie Brereton: 'It was all politics—a far cry from the young Libs with their socials.'

The aim of the serious young souls in the Youth Council was to rejuvenate Labor. And they were a well-organised, power-hungry group, out to reform and save Australia. In the late 1960s the Labor Party had been in opposition for nearly two decades. It was seen as a losing affair; it looked decrepit. In New South Wales and Tasmania the Right were in control but in all other states the Left dominated—and was seen as old-fashioned by the new wave of energetic and youthful Labor supporters. Gough Whitlam, who succeeded Arthur Calwell as leader of the Labor opposition in 1967, became the bright hope for young Labor supporters on the Right. Bob Carr, who joined Keating and Brereton among the ranks of Young Labor in 1968, relates how they would sit over coffee after a Young Labor meeting and talk about how the party could revive itself under Whitlam's leadership.

> We used to meet in a Cahill's restaurant in one of the arcades before a Young Labor meeting and then stroll up to Elizabeth Street, and go to one of the greasy spoon coffee shops afterwards. Then we'd talk about what we'd do to beat the Left, rebuild a popular Labor Party. We'd gossip about politics and about how Whitlam had to 'crash through' in his attempt to reform the party, how he had to do something about the Left in Victoria, how John Ducker had to take over the state ALP leadership because he was the only one who could rejuvenate the right-wing machine, how the Left were wrong in their analysis of macro-economic or foreign policy. These were the things we'd talk about.

This was the coffee-shop generation, sharing the 1960s with the hippies and the flower children, inclined to sit over one cup of coffee for hours and dissect the world. They were less affluent than their yuppie counterparts of the 1980s, but they were a generation with a goal, a cause for which to fight, battles to win along the way.

Every generation has to provide a new impetus, has to fashion a set of ideas and a leadership that is credible, accepted by the party membership, and successful—and the period of Paul Keating and Laurie Brereton was one of those times of renewal. Their aim was to get Labor back on its feet, to get their hands on the holy grail of power. Carr says that on policy matters they went along with what Whitlam was enunciating at the time. 'Whitlam was the shining light,' he says. 'We were Whitlamites.'

Keating's life at that time was not all serious work and no play. Parallel with his early involvement in the Youth Council was his interest in music and his association with a young rock group called The Ramrods, who were playing in the western Sydney pubs. Keating the aspiring entrepreneur wanted to turn The Ramrods into something more, to get them away from the pubs and into the big time, out of their lurex trousers and luminous socks and into the ranks of spruced-up, professional performers. The five Ramrods—bassist Brian Hall, guitarist Barry Brady, vocalist Barry Connors, keyboardist Gary Moberley and drummer Quentin Chadwick—met in 1961 when they were working in the art department of the *Sydney Morning Herald*. It was not long afterwards that their path crossed Keating's. He had come to listen to them play at the Ashfield Hotel, and was impressed by their sound. He asked if they had anyone promoting them, and offered to take on the role, beginning an association that lasted several years. Barry Brady says Keating's presence lent them a bit of moral support, as well as pushing them publicly. 'He was genuine and sincere, very upfront, with a good sales pitch, good at selling himself and The Ramrods,' says Brady.

The Ramrods were playing in the style of a number of English groups of the time who were following the US rhythm and blues material. Keating likens their music to the Beatles' numbers, which were already big hits in the UK. In Australia, though, The Ramrods were 'fish out of water'. 'Australians were still playing Col Joye and surf-and-stomp stuff. No-one was interested in what one might call serious blues music,' Keating says. Former Ramrod Barry Connors agrees that The Ramrods' enthusiastic fans were never into stomp. 'Our followers were the western suburbs bodgies,' he says. 'Most of them would rather have had a fight than a feed.'

The group played several nights a week in a succession of hotels, moving from Ashfield to the Boulevarde at Enfield, where they enjoyed a successful two-and-a-half years, then to Revesby and Blacktown. It was during their time at the Enfield Boulevarde that the Bee Gees appeared as a supporting act—and were booed off the stage. By now Keating had organised TV appearances for his charges. But the high point of the association was his success in stitching up a twelve-month contract in 1966 for The Ramrods with EMI's Parlophone label. Under the contract the group was to cut three records for EMI. They cut two. Both discs were, in Brady's words, 'smash flops'. By mutual consent no third disc was cut. Brady says the lack of hits was no reflection on Keating's management. 'Chart hits meant national tours and full-time commitment. We were happy just to play music,' he says.

Expiry of the contract, though, signalled decision-time. Keating, already interested in politics, wanted to know if the band members were keen to commit themselves to a career as full-time musicians. 'If you do, I'll stay. If not, I'll do politics,' he told them. By then one or two of The Ramrods were contemplating marriage and were conscious of commitments that might not be supported by a career as musicians. The association ended. Keating still believes that in a different environment The Ramrods could have flourished. 'They were unusually good,' he says.

Keating might have been toying with the notion of becoming a rock 'n' roll entrepreneur in the 1960s but he still had enough time in those years for his growing interest in politics. From the time he turned eighteen he had been making regular visits to Jack Lang, who, then in his mid-eighties, was still editing his newspaper, the *Century*, from his office in Nithsdale Street, Sydney.

Lang was anathema to some in the Labor Party and a hero to

others. He is a hugely symbolic and hugely divisive figure in Labor history, a source of bitter disputes that lasted for decades. Many Laborites are either staunchly pro- or anti-Lang; either admiring him for the measures he put through that helped the working-class or viewing him as a Labor Rat, a man whose line contributed to the party's defeat in 1949. At one stage state treasurer, later premier, of New South Wales, Lang is remembered for significant social innovations such as widows' pensions and child endowment. In the 1930s, in his second term in office, Lang had to cope with the problems of the depression and his solution—the Lang Plan, not to pay interest due on loans from Britain—almost bankrupted NSW and certainly alienated federal Labor. Lang's government was dismissed in 1932 and in 1943 Lang was expelled from the Labor party. In 1946 he won election to a federal seat and served for three years in federal parliament, where he was a bitter critic of the Chifley government. He was readmitted to the Labor party in 1971, four years before he died. Labor does not usually re-embrace those it deems to have ratted on the party. Keating was at the forefront of a group pushing for Lang's readmission. He told delegates at the 1971 NSW state annual conference that if the ALP did not accept him 'it brands itself as a party of great and unyielding spite'.

To the young Keating Lang was a living Labor legend, the 'Big Fella' in Labor circles, a strong man who had made tough and unpopular decisions and been ostracised from the party. Born the son of a watchmaker, and forced to supplement the family income as a child by selling newspapers, Lang was determined to shake free of working-class poverty. He became a successful accountant and a wealthy real estate agent, and later a newspaper publisher. His entrepreneurial streak and profitable business interests would have appealed to Keating, the son of a successful small businessman and already taking more than a passing interest in commerce and investment. Lang retained some sympathy for the less well-off and maintained a lifelong hatred of the business establishment. Bede Nairn, in his biography of Lang, *The 'Big Fella'*, wrote that Lang had a 'consuming ambition to be rich and well known, and a copious ability to hate and to envy anyone whom he thought was financially, socially or intellectually superior, especially if that individual appeared to be a rival: among these were three of the most outstanding leaders of the ALP—W.A. (Bill) Holman, E.G. (Ted) Theodore and J.B. (Ben) Chifley'. A man with more followers than friends, Lang remained an outsider all his life, his theories on economics and finance fitting nowhere in the Left–Right factions. He was fervently nationalistic and fiercely anti-communist. His searingly vicious tongue earned him a reputation as master of the invective.

For Keating, Lang was a living link with the past and a man who talked passionately about the future. Lang made history come alive—he had attended the Henry Parkes rallies during the campaign for federation, he had personally known (and fought) Labor heroes such as Chifley, Curtin and Theodore. Keating learned much from Lang, who in the 1960s was still writing editorials for the paper, in longhand, commenting on issues such as Britain's entry to the Common Market and whether the gold standard should ever have been abandoned.

In the 1960s Keating was visiting Jack Lang every week, on Tuesdays and sometimes on Fridays as well, for hour-long lunchtime sessions during which he took notes as this living encyclopaedia of Labor history talked. And he encouraged others to come along, urging Laurie Brereton, among others, to meet the man he described as 'the greatest living Australian'. John Grayson, who worked with Keating at the Municipal Employees' Union, often accompanied him to the Tuesday meetings with Lang. Grayson says that Lang was fastidious about punctuality. 'We would go to see him from twelve noon to one o'clock—not one minute before or after. Lang's fob watch would go on the desk and he'd signal the end of the hour by closing the watch and standing up.' The Nithsdale Street office was austere: bare boards, chairs and a desk. 'It looked like it hadn't changed in 60 years,' says Grayson. Lang by then was 'deaf as a post' and Keating would write down the topics he wanted to discuss. The image of Lang is still sharp in Grayson's mind:

> He was old but still gave the appearance of a big man, with piercing eyes. He wore an old-fashioned detachable collar and studs, and braces, and his trousers came up to his second or third rib. His collar would be off when we arrived, but at the end of the hour he'd stand up, pull up his braces, put his collar on, and his coat and hat, and go down the steps to the nearby barber to get a haircut and a shave, even though he hardly had a hair on his head.

Lang's tutoring, over a period of several years, added to Keating's store of knowledge and helped hone the political drive and ideals that he had learned from his father. Matt Keating had been a staunch Lang supporter and Keating grew up in a household where both the history and mythology of Lang were frequently aired. The visits to Lang's office were a rare opportunity for a young man to sit at the feet of a figure about whom he had heard so much. Keating picked up valuable lessons in the art of vitriolic rhetoric and a great deal about Labor myths, as well as useful insights about government and its administration and finance from the old political warhorse. Keating continued to talk regularly with Lang until the 'Big Fella' died in 1975 at the age of 98, although the visits became less frequent after 1969 when Keating won election to federal parliament.

In 1965 Keating left his first job with the Sydney County Council. He worked for eighteen months with a Hong Kong trading company, Wheelock Marden, and spent a year with the Electricity Commission of NSW, before joining the Federated Municipal Employees' Union as a research officer in 1968. By then not only his jobs but the pattern of his life had changed. From the time he turned 21, in January 1965, he was intent on winning preselection and getting into federal parliament. It was to take him four years. Evening classes, The Ramrods, social life—all went by the board as he became consumed by what his contemporaries describe as an iron determination to win. His commitment to politics was firm by the time he joined the Municipal Employees' Union, which was close to the Right and part of his faction. Keating says working there suited his preselection aspirations. His colleague, John Grayson, says that Keating's boss, the general secretary of the union, Reginald Arthur Triggs, was not sympathetic to the outside interests of any staff. Triggs thought that preselection ambitions were pie-in-the-sky, Grayson recalls.

Keating would gather with his friends Brereton, Carr and Leo McLeay either at his parents' house in Condell Park or the Brereton home in Kensington. His younger brother Greg remembers the group, sitting on the front lawn talking and planning, all of them firmly wedded to the idea of politics. They were single-minded about getting elected to parliament. Dierdre Grusovin, who also entered state politics and is a sister of Laurie Brereton, recalls Sunday morning meetings on the back patio of her parents' home, the serious discussions enlivened by Bob Carr's impersonations of the luminaries of the day.

> Their whole life, their social life, revolved around politics—what was going to happen, where they were going. Every ounce of energy went into what they were doing. They were a new breed of young people and their age did not make the path easier. There was considerable prejudice against them because of their youth.

Keating was busy building up his base, door-knocking, drumming up support for the coming preselection contest in the seat of Banks. The timing of the preselection ballot was determined by the state central executive (now the ALP administrative committee) about one year ahead of the federal election expected in 1969. Within the NSW

ALP, preselection ballots are designated 'rank-and-file' which means that every member of standing votes. Several candidates might stand for preselection and the winner is the endorsed candidate for that electorate, eligible to stand for federal parliament.

Keating knew that the only way to get into politics in the Labor Party was to get the numbers in the local area to win the rank-and-file preselection ballot. He also understood that the only way to get the numbers in the area was to go out and get people to join the branches of the Labor party in that area. And the way to do that was to spend every evening knocking on doors, persuading friends of friends, families of existing branch members, people who were suggested by acquaintances as potential party members, getting them to join, to get there within the next two months and take out their ticket, and then getting them back to subsequent meetings within the ensuing twelve months. Party rules meant members had to get to two meetings to take up their party ticket, and attend a total of three meetings within twelve months and sign the attendance book before being entitled to vote in a preselection ballot.

Bob Carr points out that a further challenge is to see that the branch secretary records all this properly because one mistaken entry, or failure to get one of the new members to sign at a meeting, means their names are not recorded and they do not get a vote. 'That means mastery of minute detail,' says Carr. 'It's quite remarkable for someone that young to appreciate that that's the only way to do it. Keating's appreciation of all that would have grown from his father's knowledge of the ALP. His father's background in the party would have helped. And pretty hard ambition on Keating's part.'

But Keating's plans were tripped up early in 1968 when the electoral commission announced a redistribution of the boundaries in a way that effectively divided his supporters between two electorates. The ensuing preselection ballot, which was held in October 1968 and which Keating won, has gone down in history as one of the most controversial held in New South Wales. It was the subject of an investigation by the federal executive of the ALP and is still a subject of heated contention between Left and Right. It is also an illustration of the effort Keating is able to put into winning. Controversy or not, Paul Keating was going to make it into federal parliament.

Laurie Brereton, who played an active role in Keating's preselection campaign and on the night of the ballot, says:

> There would have been some controversy about Paul Keating getting into parliament no matter which seat he had gone for,

> because he set about it with enormous purpose, the way he sets about everything that he has in mind. He knew that to get into parliament he needed to get the numbers in the preselection ballot—only New South Wales had rank-and-file preselection ballots—and the only way he could do that was to recruit a substantial number of supporters. And he did, with great success.

When Keating started his preselection campaign he was preparing for the seat of Banks, in the expectation of succeeding Eric Costa, an old-style right-wing Catholic who had announced he intended to retire. But the redistribution of the electoral boundaries changed that probability. Keating and Brereton collected the maps showing the new boundaries and retreated to study them and to plan a course of action. The boundaries, which had broadly run east–west, now ran roughly north–south.

Keating had to choose between an easy preselection in the altered seat of Banks, which was now considered less safe electorally, or a tougher preselection in Blaxland, which was considered an easier electoral win. He decided to go for Blaxland, which included his power-base among the party branches, Central Bankstown (which previously had been in Banks). The switch meant that he would have to confront hostile territory that included only a part of the support he had been building, and to deal with branches which were new to him, where he had not been cultivating allies. He faced a tough preselection in an area that was regarded as a Left stronghold. Keating planned his campaign with military precision. On his bedroom wall was a cardboard placard recording his preselection voters' names in alphabetical order.

The sitting member for Blaxland was Eli James Harrison, who had held the seat since 1949 and had indicated that he did not intend to stand again. Paul Keating's rivals as Labor candidates for Blaxland in the 1968 preselection included Doug Sutherland (later Lord Mayor of Sydney), Jack Stewart (a cousin of Kevin Stewart, later in NSW parliament) and Bill Junor, an academic economist. Junor, the Left's candidate, was to prove the most serious competition for Keating. The two shared a disadvantage in being younger than the other candidates, but there the common ground ended. And Junor had a good story to tell—a childhood in straitened financial circumstances, undoubtedly tougher than Keating's, leaving school at fourteen, studying at night, winning a scholarship to university, studying economics. Junor was a highly credible candidate who presented well as he door-knocked around the area.

But while Paul Keating's electioneering patter might have

been less compelling in those days, before his rhetoric achieved its later flair, political determination was already in his blood. Moreover, Junor and his supporters were up against the full strength of the Keating team: a father with an influence and a respected name in local Labor circles—though more so in the former seat of Banks than the new Blaxland—determined to see his son succeed, a forthright and equally committed mother, a united family throwing its weight behind its son. Matt Keating's former colleague, Ralph Marsh, was secretary of the NSW Labor Council, which would have added to Keating's credentials with the right-wing machine, including the unions. And Keating was determined that the three years of effort he had invested in building support in his branches was not going to be undermined in the final round by a change in the boundaries. All the ingredients were there for a fierce contest.

The challenge was already brewing by the time voting closed at 6 pm on Saturday 26 October 1968. The controversy involved two issues: the challenge by the Left to the bona fides of a number of preselection voters who had joined the party to support Keating, and the Right's challenge to the Bass Hill branch (assumed to be in favour of Junor) on the basis that a previous secretary had not properly kept the books and that the branch was not eligible to vote. At the core of the dispute were 49 challenged votes: 30 from Condell Park, two from Central Bankstown, fourteen from Bass Hill and three others.

The ballot boxes, which had been held in safe keeping once voting had finished, were carried to a scout hall in Weigand Avenue, Bankstown, where counting was to take place that evening. Excluding the 49 challenged votes, Keating polled 81 votes, Junor 88, with the balance among the other candidates. With preferences Keating secured 108 votes to Junor's 124, while the challenged votes were still uncounted.

Tension mounted. The Right wanted the challenged votes counted, the Left did not. The only way out of the impasse that had developed was to call the general returning officer, Lindsay North, who had the power to intervene in any preselection ballot.

There was no telephone in the scout hall. Laurie Brereton roared off into the night on his motor cycle, to call North. The returning officer had just got to bed after counting a preselection ballot in another seat, and refused to come out again. Brereton decided to go straight to the top and rang Gough Whitlam, then leader of the ALP, at his home in Cabramatta. Whitlam remembers the call. He was unwilling to become involved in a preselection dispute, having always distanced himself from 'machine' business, but he rang North and ordered him out of bed and to go and seize the ballot box.

Time dragged among those waiting in the scout hall. Abuse flew between the opposing sides. Around 1am North arrived in the hall, his pyjamas visible under his clothes, and, declaring the votes to be in dispute, confiscated the boxes. This meant the matter was to be referred to the disputes committee of the federal executive. It was almost 4am by the time the long night ended.

The disputes committee debated the issue for about a week and then dismissed the complaints of the Left and accepted the challenge of the Right. The final ballot figures announced on 1 November were 146 for Paul Keating, 125 for Bill Junor. The disputed votes gave Keating the seat.

Brereton says:

> Keating had recruited supporters who had attended the requisite number of meetings. Forty had joined in one meeting, which was quite an influence, and it was suggested that that amounted to branch-stacking, shovelling them. But they were members who had been recruited quite properly by Paul Keating who had been developing and organising support at the appropriate time. The Left complained, challenged the preselection, but the challenge was dismissed and Paul Keating's preselection was confirmed.

The ballot and the Left's allegations of dirtier-than-usual tactics stirred enough of a furore to provoke a federal inquiry, conducted by Tom Burns, then federal president of the ALP. Writing in their biography of the former New South Wales premier Neville Wran, authors Milton Cockburn and Mike Steketee comment:

> . . . his [Burns] secret report gave a detailed account of the practices adopted by the ruling right-wing faction: the stacking of annual conferences, blatant bias shown by the Conference chairman, a 'contempt for proper procedures' on the Finance Committee, 'rorted' preselections for Federal electorates and the Senate, use of the Party journal for factional advantage and expulsion of opponents.

Burns reported that 'complete restructuring in NSW is the only way to overcome this very disturbing situation'. Commenting on the Blaxland preselection, which was one of the several areas examined by the inquiry, he wrote:

> The action of the NSW Executive secured the result by allowing supporters who had joined the Party outside of the expressed Party rules to participate. Twenty-seven supporters of Mr Keating who

> were allowed to vote were admitted into Central Bankstown Branch, yet they not only lived in the Condell Park area but in joining Central Bankstown Branch were outside their State Electorate and their Federal Electorate subdivision.

Discussing the challenge to Bass Hill, Burns wrote:

> Twelve long-standing members were denied a vote because it was alleged the branch had lost its charter . . . because the branch secretary failed to carry out his duties, yet whilst the branch did not have a charter, three members who were supporters of Mr Keating, and who incorrectly joined the Central Bankstown Branch, were transferred to the Bass Hill Branch and ruled by the executive . . . to be the only ones eligible to vote. So we have three members of a branch without a charter . . . a non-existent branch, voting, whilst the members of that branch are unable to vote.

Burns went to say that he believed the 'decisions made by the Executive were slanted to support Mr Keating and were inconsistent with decisions made in respect of the Chifley preselection [which had involved similar arguments over the eligibility of voters but which had been examined by a different group]'. John Ducker says that Tom Burns made it clear to him in a letter, written to Ducker as president of the NSW branch of the ALP that he (Burns) had only collated allegations and he had formed no value judgment as to the substance of the allegations. And just because he had reported on those matters it was by no means to be construed that the allegations had any substance. Ducker says: 'The matter was debated at the NSW Labor conference in 1970–71 and the view of the NSW branch was endorsed by the conference and that was the last time that Paul Keating has been a subject of conflict and argument in regard to his standing as a member of the House of Representatives.' Ducker is dismissive of the whole episode, saying Paul Keating would have won the contest because of his ability and determination. He adds: 'Preselection ballots, even in safe Labor seats, are not a tea-party.'

In those early days the Left often reminded Keating about the controversial circumstances. And they have kept up mild attempts to undermine him. 'But he would have got in anyway—he always had the single-mindedness,' says Brereton. The Left still believe the episode reflects badly on Keating; they say it is not something about which he should feel proud. They feel it should haunt him more than it does. The Right remains equally critical of the practices of the Left. The preselection process would have been smoother had it not been for the resdistribution. But the electoral commission does not take into account the aspirations of preselection candidates. 'Fucking awful things, redistributions,' Keating was later to remark to Bob Carr. His years of intensive effort had paid off—he had won nomination for what was then the sixth-safest Labor seat, and he was merely 24 years old. As he said to the *Age* political correspondent Michelle Grattan in 1979: 'You've got to get out of bed very bloody early to do that.'

With the preselection behind him, Keating threw all his energy and ingenuity into the federal election campaign in 1969. The Kennedy style of campaigning in the US had captured his imagination. Friends remember Keating quoting passages from *The Making of the President* by Theodore White, which documents the clever campaign the Kennedys organised to defeat Richard Nixon. He acquired bundles of election material from the US and had silkscreen portraits of himself mounted on big placards. 'We take those for granted but it was new stuff then,' says John Grayson, who remembers shinnying up street poles with Greg Keating, tearing down Liberal posters and putting up Keating's picture.

Even though Keating was campaigning in a safe Labor seat, he was determined to leave nothing to chance. Labor, under the leadership of Gough Whitlam, did not carry off victory federally that year, but its fortunes were improving. Graham Freudenberg, writing in *A Certain Grandeur*, his biographical tribute to Whitlam, says that the 1969 election was the most significant Australian election since 1949. 'As a genuine political watershed it is more important than 1972, and may yet prove more important than 1975.' For the first time in years the Labor Party had sparked the interest of Australia.

Out in Bankstown, Keating was breaking new ground. He bought a twenty-year-old bus for $1800, painted it white and put his name on the side and 'Next stop Canberra' on the back. The whole family pitched in, taking turns on a loud-hailer as the bus cruised the streets of Bankstown, a sight never seen before in the suburb. It was a direct steal from the Kennedy campaign. 'John Kennedy's supporters used a white bus in one of the southern states,' Keating said. 'It sure stops the crowds.' Keating was giving Bankstown a taste of a new style of political pageantry. In an article in the *Sydney Morning Herald* of 9 October 1969, headlined 'Joe Glascott finds a young Labor lion', reporter Glascott wrote:

> Bankstown has been hung with 300 three-feet by two-feet placards; yellow lettering on a blue background and featuring a circular photograph of candidate Keating. The poster is straight from John Kennedy's presidential campaign, he [Keating] said, only the party name and the photo have been changed.

Keating drew up pamphlets and sent them out to 27 000 electors, urging them to 'put Paul Keating to work for Blaxland'—another line from a Kennedy campaign, this time Robert Kennedy's electioneering in New York. Even then, Keating was smartly turned out. According to the *Herald* he wore a $300 gold fob watch in the vest pocket of his slim-line, navy blue suit. 'Both in his dress and his views he's a mixture of the old and the new,' said the paper. 'And he has the world of politics at his feet.'

Keating's views were remarkably conservative and in some instances starkly different from those he espoused in later years. In his concern for preserving family life, and for the traditional role of women as mothers, he is unchanged, but in 1969 he was concerned about the growing overseas ownership of Australian industry, was strong on the social ownership of key industries (both Lang inheritances) and was a firm supporter of price controls. And the man who was later to liberalise the Australian financial system and restructure other key areas such as taxation and superannuation, was writing in the Labor periodical *Radical* in 1969: 'There can be little doubt that the Australian electorate possesses a very deep rooted conservatism, in the sense of an aversion to rapid change . . . The ALP has never behaved in any way other than as a moderate socialist party.' He was dismissive of 'irresponsible university "Labor" clubs' which, he wrote, 'no matter how explicit our repudiation of them, damage our prestige as a major political party and alternative government.'

His electioneering efforts paid off. The Keating family celebrated on the night of Saturday 25 October 1969. Matt and Min Keating threw open their Condell Park home to some 200 well-wishers. Sam, the family's black kelpie, ate so many sausage rolls he was ill. Paul Keating had made it to parliament.

The 25-year-old Keating had become NSW's youngest member of parliament when he won the election for the federal seat of Blaxland. He polled 61 per cent of the votes in an electorate that covered 55 400 voters in an unpretentious, hard-working area of Sydney's western sprawl. By that time he had been a member of the ALP for eleven years and had been absorbing Jack Lang's advice for four. *Sydney Morning Herald* writer Margaret Jones reported that he saw 'nothing incongruous about adopting many of the ideas of a radical now approaching his ninety-third birthday'. Jones wrote: 'He regards the apparent changed image of the Labor Party as a matter of presentation, not motivation, and feels there is no gap between his own attitudes and those of the stalwarts of the past.' Jones described the new, young MP as 'a sharp dresser, within a completely orthodox framework, and his hairstyle is standard Bankstown'. Keating told Jones that his only relaxation was flying and that he was on the verge of getting his pilot's licence. He got as far as clocking up the requisite 40 hours for a restricted pilot's licence. Politics left little time for flying, or any other relaxation. By October 1969, for Paul Keating, it finally was a case of 'Next stop Canberra'.

3 In—and out of—power

He was an old young man—he was always an old head.

KIM BEAZLEY JNR ON PAUL KEATING

KEATING DESCRIBES his first few years in parliament as a time of finding his feet, learning things, working out how the system works. 'You have to find out who's who in the zoo at Parliament House—where you are in the pecking order.' As a young backbencher in a Labor opposition, Keating was a long way down in the pecking order but he was mindful of the advice of his mentor, Jack Lang. That battle-scarred political warhorse had told the teenage Keating: 'Don't think you've got a lot of time, young man. When you get into parliament you haven't got a minute to waste.' Fred Daly, a veteran of 26 years in political life when Keating arrived in parliament, endorses that view. 'I didn't have much time for Lang but that's not bad advice,' he says. To old hands like Daly, who had been on the receiving end of Lang's abuse of the Chifley government and endured his bitter attacks on Labor in the 1940s, Keating's view of Lang was a starry-eyed adulation that fed more on folklore than fact.

The young MP had arrived in the world of Parliament House, where life is governed by bells and lights—green for the House of Representatives, red for the Senate, with carpets in matching colours—and bears a striking similarity to that of a boarding school. The members sit together, eat together, have to be punctual and obey the house rules. Greater space and comfort make life easier in

Canberra's grandiose new Parliament House, opened by Queen Elizabeth in May 1988, but Keating's introduction to federal parliament was in the cramped conditions of the old 'temporary' building, opened in 1927. Politicians and journalists talk about *living* (not working) in Parliament House—a reflection of how all-consuming the crowded atmosphere can be. Writing a requiem to the old House in the *Sydney Morning Herald* in January 1988, the seasoned press galley correspondent Peter Bowers likened the place to a boarding house where 'the landlady was crazy, the food was terrible but [people] could not leave because they were having too much fun and the board was cheap.' And Keating is not alone in using the analogy of a zoo when describing the life. In the same article Bowers recalled the advice he was given by another journalist, Alan Reid, who was an experienced hand when Bowers was a trainee and felt moved to advise on how close a journalist should get to a politician. 'When you work in a zoo,' the older man cautioned,'the keeper does not get in the cage with the animals.'

In the new building greater space and increased security puts a wider distance between members, and between members and the press, whom Keating had described as 'living above us' [in the press gallery]. Politicians and the reporters will no longer be living in each other's pockets; the doorstop interview, where a journalist can collar a politician at the threshold, will be a feature of the past. But in the late 1960s politicians and journalists jostled along together. And Keating was busy putting Lang's words into action. Daly recalls:

> He was different from my generation—in my days if you bobbed up for any job in the party under eight or ten years you were crushed, but Paul gave effect to Lang's theory straight off. He was an active campaigner from the minute he got in and at that stage was particularly interested in Rex Connor's portfolio, mining and energy. And he applied himself with a thoroughness and determination.

From the time Keating arrived in Canberra he was recognised as a politician who assiduously worked the press gallery—who cultivated journalists of his own age, rather than the elders of the pack, on the grounds they would be around to grow older with him. He wanted to make sure his views, rather than his public image, got through. His colleagues saw him as being fairly raw, but quite brash and pushy, a small fish in a big pond that was determined to make a notable splash. A later *National Times* article by Alan Ramsey described the newly-arrived Keating as having 'a hide as thick as an elephant':

> . . . he wasn't in the place five minutes before he was running in caucus ballots, twisting arms, organising numbers and generally operating like a political Sammy Glick who'd pick your pockets while he wheedled your vote. In those days there was none of the gloss and very little of the urbanity Keating [later] acquired . . . He had some style but it was the style of the confident hustler from the rough end of town.

Fred Daly says it was obvious that he was going to be a force to be reckoned with—hard-working and with a great amount of commonsense. 'In my book he exemplified even at that early stage all the attributes of the Chifley generation, of men without any academic talents who had great commonsense and a fund of ability.'

And Daly remembers Keating as already being 'a thorn in the side of the enemy':

> When you're speaking in the House it's not what you say but how you say it. You could go to sleep in the parliament with four speeches out of five, but the minute Keating got up, you knew not only was he talking with a knowledge of his subject, well-prepared, but in his voice there was something that made you listen—and if you butted in you were liable to be sunk.

In Daly's view Keating has proved to be the most destructive speaker in the House since the days of Eddie Ward, the Labor member for Paddington in the days of the Menzies Liberal government. The talent for getting under the opposition's skin was there from the beginning. He had learned from Jack Lang how to hate. Daly says:

> His choice of words, and the fierceness with which he spits them out, puts him head and shoulders over the most devastating debater in parliament, puts him in the Ward class. And he's the most feared. He mixes a cruel kind of humour with it, and ridicule. He's a masterful parliamentary performer. And he does it cheerfully, enthusiastically and with immense capacity.

At the time Keating first arrived in Canberra it was the custom for backbenchers to share offices. For about three years Keating shared with Lionel Bowen, who had been elected in the same 1969 federal poll to the seat of Kingsford Smith. Bowen and Rex Connor followed Matt Keating and Jack Lang as guiding and influential figures for the young politician.

Keating remembers those early years of his parliamentary career as still part of the era of post-war growth. At that stage, he says, no-one knew the growth was finished. Governments were concerned with the distribution, rather than the creation, of wealth. Paul Keating, the newcomer, was still developing his political views. But he was learning—quickly—the skills of survival.

In those days Keating read his speeches, unlike today when what he has to say is in his head and he can cruise through with a few notes. But the young, determined member carefully constructed the addresses he gave. On one occasion Gough Whitlam approached Keating after a particularly good performance and said: 'That was a good speech. You should go back, comrade, and get yourself an honours degree.' Keating was deeply offended at what he read as a patronising comment. 'What for? Then I'd be like you,' he retorted to a startled Whitlam. It was not to be the only occasion when Keating's response surprised the Labor leader. On a later occasion, when Whitlam was urging Keating for his support on a caucus vote, Keating was unmoved. The clear-eyed young politician told Whitlam: 'You need me more than I'll ever need you.'

Keating's ambitions were not hidden, and they were high. He scorned Daly's suggestion of running for Whip, believing it would be a waste of his time. 'His ambitions were always higher than Whip, which to poor mundane thinkers like me was a stepping-stone to great honours,' says Daly.

During those early years Keating spoke on a number of major policy issues. He had a fascination for defence equipment, as distinct from defence policy, and his interest was developing in minerals and energy. He brought a young man's views to politics—broader conceptions were yet to develop—but he always did his homework. The Hansard records of those years show Keating already taking an interest in the financial world, and in the media. He had been in parliament only a matter of months when he raised a question, in April 1970, about media ownership:

> Is the Prime Minister aware that the US Federal Communications Commission announced recently that in future in the US a newspaper will not be able to acquire a radio or TV station? . . . will the Prime Minister introduce similar legislation prohibiting a newspaper from acquiring a broadcasting licence and will he further break up existing multi-media combinations in Australia?

Keating was to come back to this theme during the 1970s. In May 1972 he pointed out that in the US the Federal Communications Commission 'busted the newspaper and TV monopolies but this government has done nothing in that direction'. And in November 1976 he presented the Broadcasting and TV Amendment Bill. He was to revive these arguments in 1986, when the Hawke Labor government came to implement changes to the legislation governing media ownership.

Labor was in opposition during Keating's first three years in parliament. Then, in December 1972, Whitlam led the Labor Party to its first federal victory in more than twenty years. The Whitlam campaign slogan 'It's time' signified a fresh, new era in Australian politics. The Labor government of the early 1970s presided over a time of idealism, affluence and enthusiasm in Australia. When Gough Whitlam came to power the post-war 'baby boomers' were going to university—and among them were the first generation of working-class Australians who could afford to do so.

On the back benches of parliament, Keating was spending the years between 1972 and 1975 cultivating the numbers that would get him into the ministry. He tested a ministerial ballot in 1972, but was unsuccessful, losing by a narrow margin to Bill Morrison. In 1974 the ministry was unchanged, so that it was not until October 1975 that he became a minister, filling the vacancy left by Rex Connor. He was already becoming known as something of a power-broker, a good numbers man who could cajole, persuade, organise and use whatever methods were required to muster support in caucus. Getting the numbers behind him in caucus was important. Caucus, especially under the Whitlam government, was the principal policy decision-making body. Every Labor member of parliament is a member of caucus. Ministers in the Whitlam government had to pay attention to the weekly caucus meetings, held every Tuesday morning during parliamentary sitting sessions. Whitlam believed in an all-powerful caucus, so much weight was attached to the discussions that took place before any legislation went before cabinet, whose decisions are subsequently endorsed by caucus. It is in the interests of the different factions—Left, Right and, under the Hawke government, Centre Left—to line up their support ahead of a caucus meeting, to 'get the numbers' that will help push their preferred measures and decisions through. Often positions have been resolved and agreement reached before a matter goes to caucus. Under the Hawke government caucus became known as registering more complaints than changes.

Keating's interest in finance was developing through the 1970s though he is remembered at that time as being no more financially or economically literate than anyone else in the Whitlam government. 'He was as ignorant [about economics] as the rest of us, and that was pretty bloody ignorant,' says Jim McClelland, a minister in the Whitlam government. But Keating was dedicated to self-improvement—at home he was reading the economic texts of Adam Smith and Paul Samuelson, in Canberra he would haunt the office of the *Australian Financial Review*, absorbing information on how the economy ticked from Max Walsh. He chased news. He chased angles.

Keating's questions about interest rates were interspersed with those on coal and gas and minerals. In May 1973 the future federal treasurer and deregulator posed a question about the introduction of unsecured notes, an innovation introduced by Australian Guarantee Corporation, the finance company subsidiary of the Bank of New South Wales (later Westpac Banking Corporation). He demanded of treasurer Frank Crean:

> Is the Treasurer aware that AGC . . . is seeking to attract finance at the rate of 6 per cent by offering what are termed unsecured notes repayable on demand, a practice never previously carried out by fringe bank organisations in Australia? Will this device move huge amounts of funds on a scale comparable with that of funds moving into the building societies area and away from the trading banks where . . . deposits . . . are a source of low-interest-rate funds for housing and other desirable priorities? Is the government to tolerate the private trading banks' circumventing the banking system?

Less than a year later, in March 1974, Keating was querying the wisdom of introducing Bankcard and the instant credit it would make available. A few months later, in July 1974—a time of record high interest rates in Australia—Keating was demanding an explanation of the high levels of certificates of deposits issued by the trading banks.

> Why did the Government permit the Reserve Bank to allow the certificates of deposit issued by the trading banks to reach such absurd levels in the last six months? Why, in the latter part of the year, did the Government permit the Reserve Bank to allow the trading banks to move into speculative investment loans whereby a liquidity crisis arose only to be covered by certificates of deposit at high rates of interest? Why was the bond rate moved to 11 per cent to reinforce the general level of interest rates that was created by the absurd level that was being paid for certificates of deposit?

Crean replied:

> The certificate of deposit is a relatively new form of transaction in Australia. I believe it has enabled the trading banks to become more competitive in the total credit field than previously. I think that in some respects the medicine was a little bit heady to begin with but that things have now settled down somewhat. I hope that there will be greater stability in the use of those instruments in the future than perhaps there was in the first six months of their operation.

Although he began to be noticed within the parliament, Keating spent most of Labor's three governing years in relative obscurity. There was considerable competition for the media's attention and young backbenchers did not stand much chance of developing a big public profile. Meanwhile he looked to Lionel Bowen and, particularly, to Rex Connor as his political mentors. His friend and colleague Kim Beazley jnr says: 'Keating had a romantic view of aged Labor figures, especially Lang, whom he found fascinating and whom few others liked. And he was an old young man—he always was an old head.' Connor looked the part. He looked like a leftover from the Chifley government, although he had entered federal parliament only six years before Keating and had not entered state parliament until 1950. But, with Lang, he became part of the package of Labor heroes to whom Keating looked for inspiration.

Reginald Francis Xavier Connor was born on Australia Day, 26 January 1907, a fitting birthday for a man whose opposition to foreign ownership in Australia was raised to the level of a lifelong crusade. Lang and Connor had several points in common, apart from their shared xenophobia. Like Lang, Connor had business interests; born the son of a labourer in Wollongong, he later completed law articles, became a garage proprietor and the owner of a 32-acre property. Like Lang, Connor was a small suburban businessman who detested the business establishment, whose theories on economics and finance ran counter to accepted ideas and branded him an outsider. But Connor had some good ideas, and Keating has always liked people with ideas. He admires strong men with simple solutions.

Both Kim Beazley and Bob Carr read an advantage into Keating's not having gone to university, which might have insulated him from the realities which shaped his political ambition. Carr says: 'Most people at the age of 22 are just emerging from their university cocoons, looking at getting a job, and have only the vaguest ideas of advancement. Keating was unusually strong-willed and smart for his age.' Keating had been out in the workforce since he was fifteen, mixing and working with adults. Says Carr: 'I think it was a positive advantage for Keating that he hadn't been at university. And little things helped too—even at that age he was very smartly dressed. It was quite noticeable. I can remember in Young Labor days he said to me: "I can never resist a good piece of tweed, young Robbie." '

Keating was picking up, in the 1960s, bits and pieces of what was going to be important in the 1980s. He was already developing a multi-faceted character that defies political stereotype. He was a young man with impeccable Labor credentials, in some ways a throwback to the radical 1940s yet with none of the inhibiting preoccupations of the party traditionalists. He had tutored himself to become one of the best Labor historians in parliament, with a strong sense of the continuity of the past. Yet he was very much a man of the future. He was beginning to use what he had seen as Jack Lang's great strength—a knowledge gained from being steeped in the past while harnessed to a view of the future.

He liked Connor's vision of a minerals-backed future for Australia, and was supportive of development, already talking in terms of 'making the cake bigger rather than fiddling around arguing about who gets what piece of the same-size cake'. Keating admired what Connor was trying to do. He admired Connor's guts. Connor believed that the mining and petroleum industries were big and should be made big for Australia. And he was determined to see Australia recover, process and distribute its own resources, without involving foreign ownership. Keating continued to learn from Connor and he became an expert on the subject. Daly comments: 'There again he was wise because in the party no-one knew anything about it and that's why Connor got away with so much.'

Connor's vision of the development of Australia's resources excluded the big multinational companies. He was a passionate nationalist who was convinced that the large resources companies in Australia were opposed to him and his government—so he took great pleasure in treating senior businessmen contemptuously, leaving them waiting. Connor saw the minerals companies in Australia as agents of international firms whom he wanted replaced with Australian companies. To him the foreign companies and their representatives saw Australia merely as a quarry, not as a processor, and this irritated him. He wanted to develop Australian minerals, not sit on them, but he would rather they stayed in the ground than fall into the hands of foreign companies. He wanted Australia to process minerals, build refineries and finishing plants—hence the search to borrow $4 billion to finance this.

To business, Connor was a left-wing lunatic, though he was in fact on Labor's Right. The distrust was on both sides. Connor's wariness of big business extended to the banks, and to Treasury. This led to the plan to borrow funds in a way that bypassed Treasury, the Reserve Bank and the big international banks that traditionally raise funds on behalf of government. The plan involved using a money-broker who could raise funds in the Arab world and culminated in the ill-fated 'loans affair' that ended Connor's political career and contributed to the demise of the Whitlam government in November 1975.

Connor's idiosyncratic vision of Australia has to be seen in the context of a period when the whole world was going through very difficult energy problems. The price of oil had quadrupled, the Arabs were imposing embargoes on certain countries and the Australian government was determined to ensure that the country had adequate supplies of oil. Sir Leslie Froggatt, then chairman of Shell, says that the Australian government 'wanted to make sure that not only did the country have everything it needed but that it wasn't lightly giving away its own resources to somebody else'. Froggatt talks of the 'formidable pressures of the times' saying:

> The government got a bit nervous. They needed calming down at times, if they thought one oil company was favouring another country and not giving them all the supplies they needed. They never went short—but then it was such chaos in the Middle East and Europe and countries were boycotted and somehow people were trying to get round that and maybe a shortage occurred, and people would say, 'Oh, maybe we haven't got a cargo for Australia this week,' but in fact we had stocks, we had everything we needed. But they wanted to make sure they had everything, they'd rather buy it from overseas and hang on to it, make sure they had their full ration. But they didn't want to start a project and export it. They were so immediately alarmed by the situation that they didn't want to be held to ransom in the future. 'We'll hang on to it all ourselves,' they said.

The oil industry, though, was concerned about exploration, development and export; the industry believed that merely leaving resources in the ground would kill off the incentive to explore. 'That was the battle we had,' says Froggatt. 'To try to convince Connor that not developing resources could ruin, destroy the exploration effort in this country.' In his words:

> Rex Connor's idea was to conserve Australia's reserves and buy other people's oil and gas. Our argument was firstly that if you didn't develop your resources no-one would look for them in the future—and secondly that by the time they did come to be developed they might have become obsolete or maybe other supplies in great quantities might be found elsewhere and your market would no longer exist. The argument we tried to mount, and which I think is a sound economic argument, is that you develop the resource and with the export value you get you'll be able to buy your requirements from somebody else. It's all a matter of trade and barter. The fact that you've got it [oil] in your own country I don't think is a long-term prospect when it comes to an asset such as oil—there will be something else, an alternative.

Many associated with the mining industry of the time remember Connor as 'the biggest thing bugging the industry'. A decade-and-a-half later they still recoil at the notion of Connor as 'the man of vision', trying to rescue Australia from being sucked dry by international capitalists. They would not see him as he is described by Manning Clarke, in *A Short History of Australia:* the man who 'wanted to stop foreigners from grabbing the mineral resources of Australia . . . with a vision of the greatness of Australia and Australians'. Manning Clarke says Connor believed in these words:

> *Give me men to match my mountains*
> *Give me men to watch my plains*
> *Men with freedom in their vision*
> *And creation in their brains.*

Connor read out what he described as 'an old Australian poem' at a special one-day session of parliament called by Gough Whitlam on 9 July 1975 to discuss the loans affair. In fact, the nationalistic Connor was reciting lines from a patriotic American ballad, *The Coming American* by S.W. Foss.

Connor was, and will always be remembered as, a *bête noire* of the mining and oil industries, the implacable enemy who stood in their way. Charles Copeman, formerly chief executive of Peko-Wallsend Ltd, says: 'Rex Connor based his antipathy on good old-fashioned grassroots Labor bias against big business.' Copeman recalls Connor being blunt and gruff to senior people who had only known the cossetting embrace of the Menzies Liberal government. They were not prepared for a government that was hostile to them, for Connor's criticism that they were not selling Australia's resources at the best prices, that they were not paying adequate taxes and were involved in the 'conspiracy of transfer pricing'. Connor saw the difference between an industry lobby group and the companies and he insisted on dealing with the individual companies, on the smart tactical ground that that was the best way to divide the opposition. He was remarkably dismissive of the Australian Mining Industry Council, saying he'd talk to the individual companies–'to the butcher, not the butcher's block'.

The oil and mining men remember Keating as more pragmatic, not bound by outdated ideology. Keating would admit that he 'had to make noises to satisfy the Left'. However much Keating absorbed in those early years of Connor's view of big business, he was soon to realise the value of flattery in getting points across. He carried on some of the prejudices of Labor—including an assumption that anyone who was a business executive was affiliated with the 'born-to-rule brigade' and unlikely to vote Labor—but he had fewer chips on the shoulder about business than most Labor politicians of the time.

Paul Phillips, who was chief executive officer of the Australian Mining Industry Council in the 1970s, says: 'What I admired about Paul Keating, apart from his capacity for hard work, was his realism.' But during the early 1970s Paul Keating walked very much in Connor's shadow. He was not a controversial figure; he was busy soaking up information, travelling the length and breadth of the industry. He showed tremendous application but was associated with the limelight and controversy only as Connor's pupil. He was not seen publicly as anyone who called the shots. It was Connor who first gave resources a higher profile, who made the area controversial.

Keating's private status changed in 1975. The man billed as one of federal parliament's most eligible bachelors became a married man in January that year when he wed Dutch-born Anna Johanna Maria von Iersel (known as Anita). Keating had met Anita—an air hostess with Alitalia, living in an apartment in Rome—about eighteen months earlier, during an overseas trip. According to friends, he was 'besotted' from the beginning. After their first meeting he pursued her round the world, meeting in Europe and Latin America (in Rio, it is said, he challenged a rival suitor to a swimming race, and won). The newly-weds spent their honeymoon in the Austrian ski resort of Kitzbuhl where Keating's prowess on skis was put in the shade by that of his new wife. Ski-ing is not one of his strengths.

Keating was 31 years old when he married. He and Anita moved into the Bankstown house which he had already bought, and which bordered on his parents' home. During the week, he returned to Canberra and to the government benches of Parliament House—until that stopped on 11 November 1975.

Keating had achieved his goal of a ministerial portfolio on 21 October 1975, three weeks before his government fell. In a twist of chance, he had won the vacant ministry post left by the resignation a week earlier of his old friend and mentor, Rex Connor. He beat eight other candidates for the vacancy. At 31, he had become the youngest minister in Labor's history. He was appointed minister for Northern Australia, a role he saw at the time as not merely overseeing the reconstruction of Darwin (after the damage caused by cyclone Tracy in December 1974) but 'impinging on minerals and energy more heavily than anyone understood'. He told the *Australian*: 'I was very close to Rex Connor. The only sadness I have about today's election is the fact that I had to replace him . . . His name will be synonymous with the cry of "Who owns Australia?"' The newspaper commented that it was a cry which Keating obviously intended to keep alive. 'His main interest is the economy (he suggested a form of tax indexation before the Budget), manufacturing, defence and mining industries,' the article said. At that time he was also interested in primary industry, and had played a key role in the establishment of the royal commission into the public service. He supported a scheme to make the interest on home mortgages tax-deductible.

Keating had made it into the ministry after only six years in parliament. Fred Daly remembers him complaining about how long it had taken. Daly retorted: 'My, they *have* kept you waiting!' Ebullient after his success, Keating remarked to a colleague: 'It's easier to get elected than to be picked for the ministry.' He did not let the grass grow under his feet. He issued a press statement on 23 October discussing the outlook for the Northern Territory, which was under reconstruction after floods. On 31 October he introduced his first bill into the House of Representatives—the Queensland Grant (Proserpine Flood Mitigation) Bill. He was to enjoy his new-found prestige for a mere three weeks. Legend has it that Keating was the first to encounter an enraged Whitlam, returning to Parliament House after the dismissal at Yarralumla on 11 November. 'You're sacked!' Whitlam growled at a shocked Keating. 'What for?' Keating called back, unaware that the entire government had been deposed.

The events of 11 November 1975 smashed Labor hopes throughout Australia. When the then governor-general, Sir John Kerr, sacked prime minister Whitlam and installed Malcolm Fraser at the head of a 'caretaker' government, many thought Labor was finished. The Liberal-Country Party coalition, led by Malcolm Fraser, had won office by engineering the dismissal of the Whitlam government. It was often said later that the Liberals ripped up the Australian constitution to get into office. And it seemed that the achievements of the Whitlam government—a new national pride, increased justice in social areas, an increased awareness in and encouragement of arts and culture, a general lifting of Australia's intellectual tone—had rapidly been forgotten. Little tribute was paid to the trail-blazing reform; rather, the imprint that endured was one of inept economic management, although that judgment was made of a government trying to steer Australia through one of its toughest post-war crises. Labor's image with business, the banks and the mining industry was seriously tarnished.

The events of November 1975 wrenched political success out of Paul Keating's grasp before he had time to savour it.

4 Making friends with Labor's enemies

Labor had its guts ripped out in 1975, and again in 1977. Many of the survivors were too old and disillusioned for the fight. Keating was one of the few with any fight left.

KIM BEAZLEY JNR

KEATING HAD not come to Canberra to wither on the vine. But he was back in opposition after three years in government, and a mere few weeks in the ministry. He was mindful of Jack Lang's advice. He had no time to waste. He had to keep learning, pushing forward, making his mark. Returned to opposition after three years in power, the Labor Party was disillusioned, disappointed and demoralised. But it was to take only seven years to claw its way back to federal power. The last interval had been almost a quarter of a century.

Keating's first shadow portfolio was agriculture. Whitlam, ever the intellectual snob, considered this low-priority area a fitting one for someone who lacked the tertiary qualifications he believed to be so important. Keating described the task as 'a damn good challenge'. He retained an interest in the portfolio, which he held only briefly in February 1976, after he ceased to be shadow spokesman and the portfolio shifted into the hands of Arthur Gietzelt in the Senate. The bills, though, were presented in the House of Representatives, so Keating had to keep himself in tune with Labor's policies and attitudes.

March 1976 brought Keating a promotion: a shadow cabinet reshuffle resulted in his becoming Labor spokesman on minerals and energy. In his enthusiastic approach to that portfolio, which he held from March 1976 until January 1983, Keating took himself into what was indisputably foreign territory for a Labor politician. When Labor won federal power in 1972 the mining industry had received a shock: it realised it knew no-one in the incoming government. It had never bothered to woo Labor in opposition; almost a quarter of a century of benign Liberal government in Canberra had lulled business into a belief in its permanence. Suddenly there were alien faces round the negotiating table. The game had changed. By the time a new government came to office in 1975, business had learned that it could not afford to ignore a Labor opposition. Keating made sure business did not forget that lesson.

Whitlam knew that Keating would deal effectively with the portfolio in the House of Representatives. Says Keating: 'It was a period of great development and I was intensely interested. I've been in every mine in the country.' And he rattles off names—the old gold mines at Kalgoorlie, the nickel operation at Kambalda, Mount Isa, through the coalfields of the Bowen Basin, through the Pilbara. 'You name it and I've been there,' he says. 'That's how you get to know the economics of a mine, and you get to know its structure.' He also went offshore, to the Bass Strait and the North-West Shelf oil and gas fields, and on related trips to Japan. Keating says of that time: 'It was the nearest you could get to an executive role, or a quasi-executive role in those days, in opposition. They [the mining industry] knew who I was and they'd come and see me.' Keating made sure he got to know the prime movers in the mining and energy area. The concept of active shadow ministers was fairly new, and reflected the growing complexities of politics. He milked every advantage he could out of that role. Susan Ryan says:

> During that period in opposition—slightly more than seven years—a number of us really ran with the fact that as shadow ministers we could get access to all kinds of groups. We could, in lots of ways, behave like an alternative government. Keating was very energetic. It was quite a remarkable period of concentrated activity for him and I suppose what made it even more remarkable was that he was working in alien territory. He was operating in an extremely unsympathetic context for a Labor person, so it was extremely good training. The fact that he did so successfully demonstrates his extraordinary talents. It also demonstrates his radical and creative approach to policy. Although he's a Labor traditionalist . . . he'll try new things. He won't say, well, Labor people have never done it that way—or that these have been traditional enemies of Labor so I won't approach them. He will go into the lion's den.

Barbara Ward, who worked as Keating's assistant from early 1979 until April 1985, believes he took a conscious decision fairly early in his minerals and energy career to get to know the people in the industry. In her view:

> It may have been partly a reaction to the Connor–Whitlam days—yet there's a real contrast because Paul was a staunch supporter of Connor and Connor was one of his great mentors. But at the same time I think deep down he did recognise what Connor did to relations between the Labor government and the industry. So I think Paul consciously went out of his way to try to improve those relations.

Keating's willingness to challenge conventional Labor wisdom made an impression when he spoke at the Australian Petroleum Exploration Association conference at the Lakeside Hotel in Canberra in September 1976. The *Sydney Morning Herald*, talking of 'Connorism in retreat', reported that Paul Keating was a Connor protege but 'very much his own man . . . he showed his paces . . . announced his petrol policy in a way that indicated the 32-year-old former industrial advocate had done his homework. He had been out talking with industry and lobbying bodies, exploring and learning.' Keating's policy on petroleum was regarded as a shift from the Connor stance, a policy more conciliatory towards the industry.

One of the first challenges Keating had to deal with was to smooth feathers that had been ruffled by the Fitzgerald report, a study commissioned by Rex Connor and carried out by the respected financial journalist Tom Fitzgerald. The report was to examine the broad questions of what Australia was getting out of the minerals industry and whether the tax concessions enjoyed by the industry were appropriate. The concessions had been given to the minerals industry by the Chifley government in the 1940s and had the effect of permitting deferral, even non-payment, of taxes. And much of the tax relief was going to foreign owners. The industry was angered by what it perceived to be selective examples in the report, such as highlighting the companies that were eligible for certain exemptions and overlooking those that paid full tax. It felt the report was prejudiced, and a dangerous document in Connor's hands. John McLeod, chief economist with CRA, says: 'Fitzgerald didn't seem to realise the damage the report created. It added to the industry's distrust and did a lot of harm in terms of industry hating Labor. And it made Keating's job that much more difficult. But he sat and listened, and the industry had never had that before, from either side. And he's a fixer, he's always been a fixer.'

Keating did not fit the prevailing mythology (in the eyes of business) that Labor believed only a traitor would walk in the front door of a company such as BHP or Shell or CRA. He wanted to build bridges with an industry that he recognised as battle-scarred and therefore receptive. Says Sir Leslie Froggatt of Shell:

> Paul Keating turned it all around without appearing disloyal. He took a little at a time, and was operating against a background of easing international problems. We were getting our own house in order, not misusing oil supplies. You could see there would be great benefits, Bass Strait was coming on strong and Australia was taking care of its own supplies. It all reflected the move from times of crisis to a more reasoned evaluation of the world situation.

By October 1976 Keating was calling for a profits-related tax on high-earning resource projects, and was prodding the ALP into updating its energy policy. In November 1976 the ALP sponsored a national debate on the future of uranium mining. Keating was in favour of continuing to mine and export uranium; Tom Uren, deputy leader of the party, was opposed to this. Keating attacked Uren's stance, declaring that he had the backing of a caucus decision which said that overseas contracts should be met. The upshot was a statement that Australia should meet existing uranium export commitments but that Labor wanted a moratorium on all other mining of uranium until the final report of the Fox Committee, which had been established to examine the consequences for the environment of the Ranger uranium project. This decision was regarded as a victory for Keating.

Keating's approach to the mining industry and business in general in the 1970s helped to lift Labor's profile with these sectors. Having decided to talk to business, Keating had experienced the mutual benefits of communication. He impressed the mining industry as diligent and genuinely interested in resources—an interest which the industry felt it deserved.

An important issue confronting the resources sector in the second half of the 1970s was the North-West Shelf oil and gas project. The Liberal–NCP coalition endorsed the proposal for an export permit for most of the gas but the project was expensive and was expected to extend over twenty years, so the operators pushed for support from both the major political parties. Froggatt says that unless exports could be guaranteed there was no justification for the development of the billion-dollar project. 'That really was where Paul Keating came in,' he says. 'There was no way the consortium would have embarked on such a major investment if we hadn't been able to obtain a bipartisan agreement to it . . . he quickly seized the importance of getting approval from his party. How he did it I don't know.'

Russ Fynmore, an executive with BHP, remembers Keating as someone who 'set about understanding the industry by talking to its people—not just the chiefs but by identifying with people down the line. You felt he understood the industry. By the time Keating got into government in 1983 he understood mining and energy better than any politician. And the more he learned about the industry, the more he knew that Connor had been wrong.' In the late 1970s Keating had successfully lifted the status of Labor with the resources industries—without being disloyal to Connor. Although he had developed reservations about his predecessor's policies, he continued to admire Connor as an individual and a man with good ideas. At the same time, Keating was spreading the message that there was now a new generation of Labor politicians who had not grown up in the trade union movement and who were not bound by dogma. He was openly scathing about the party's Left wing, whose members he referred to as 'troglodytes' with outdated attitudes.

By and large, the mining industry held Keating in high regard. Some business leaders tempered their praise with the qualification that by the late 1970s resources were provoking far less controversy, with the exception of uranium mining—and it was the Fraser government which was fielding the criticism on that score. According to Charles Copeman, by the time Keating got his shoe into the area, after 1975, much of the conflict surrounding the mining industry was over. The Whitlam government was out of office, Rex Connor had died. Paul Keating represented a different kind of Labor figure, operating with a clean sheet. Says Copeman: 'From 1975 there was nothing controversial or bloody-minded to do and that gave Paul Keating a smoother ride. He could come in and be Mr Nice Guy, a willing learner on a steep learning curve—and people responded to that. He didn't need to put his head up too far. He could be everybody's friend—and he can be most engaging when he wants to learn something. And he was young, and willing to learn.' Sir Leslie Froggatt remembers Keating as an unusually energetic shadow minister. He says: 'It's one thing to have a good mind, which he has; it's another matter to work so hard, to cover all the ground, and he really does. And he does not see the world in terms of "them and us". He never treated me as an enemy—he realised that whatever he felt about my company or my industry, we had a role to play and if he felt that the ideas that I was postulating were in the interests of the country, he'd go ahead.' Learning by talking to others, to expert and more knowledgeable people than himself, has long been a Keating trait. Barbara Ward says:

> He's always been one of these people with an uncanny ability to pick other people's brains rather than sit down and read a whole book or a whole paper. He'd much prefer to sit in a room with someone for fifteen or twenty minutes and just *extract* information out of them. He's almost like a sponge, just soaking it up. He *loves* talking to people, and getting information that way.

Keating's capacity to listen, though, can be selective. He is good at listening to learn, but less willing to listen to the opposing side of an argument. Mild dissenters are dismissed as idiots, so much so that a colleague was provoked into saying he was 'all mouth and no ears'.

Keating kept up a relentless criticism of the Fraser government's energy policy. He made speeches at industry conferences and seminars, travelled the country and overseas and became a familiar figure at boardroom lunches where industry executives were impressed by his knowledge of the subject. The man who was later, as federal treasurer, to forge an unusually strong and mutually amicable relationship with Treasury was scornful of the department's contribution in 1979.

> No department in the Western world has had such a rein on economic policy, with a more compliant cabinet, than the Treasury in this country has had for four years . . . it has doubled the unemployment level in Australia, has failed to contain inflation and has dragged Australia deeper into recession. Now it is running an energy policy for Australia . . . The gurus of everything else in the bureaucracy—the Treasury officials—are now the energy gurus of Australia.

There was little then to foreshadow the market-oriented approach that Keating was later to adopt as treasurer. He accused Treasury of 'suffocating every alternative area of advice to the government' and of an 'unimpeded, uninhibited market-place philosophy'. Fraser later moved the energy portfolio away from Kevin Newman and the House of Representatives and into the Senate, to John Carrick, to get it away from Keating's tongue. Keating spat back in a press release dated 7 December 1979 and headed 'Mr Newman's incompetence':

> The removal of Mr Newman . . . is an admission by the Fraser Government that the important area of energy has been entrusted to an incompetent for two years. The Prime Minister's choice of Senator Carrick for the energy portfolio is a blatant act to remove this difficult portfolio from the House of Representatives—I have

> nailed Mr Newman in the House and I will nail Senator Carrick if he demonstrates a similar level of incompetence . . . The appointment of an energy minister in the Senate, the unrepresentative chamber of the Parliament, is itself a cynical and devious act by the Prime Minister.

And at the same time he took a swipe at the press gallery, accusing it of failing to chronicle the split between the Liberal and National Country parties. In characteristic Keating style he thundered: 'At one time we saw some sensible and decent investigative reporting of these matters in weekly columns by members of the press gallery. Now we see nothing . . . There have been massive splits in the government and they have not seen the light of day.'

Although throwing himself wholeheartedly into the politics of minerals and energy, Keating had not abandoned his interest in the media. In November 1976 he introduced a bill to prohibit investment by newspaper publishers in radio and TV. The bill was to end what he saw as an 'undesirable concentration of ownership of the Australian electronic media in the hands of newspaper monopolies'. It was defeated by 81 votes to 31. Even at that time, say his colleagues, he had an intense interest in economics and a liking for defence and foreign affairs, in the areas themselves rather than in the portfolios. Barbara Ward says one of the reasons he employed her was her background in general economics. 'The idea was that I'd get him up to speed on economics. The problem was that I never did: we didn't have the time. Once I got there we spent the whole time on minerals and energy.'

Keating is credited, along with Mick Young and other 'younger' members such as Susan Ryan, with keeping Labor alive in those dismal years of opposition. Kim Beazley jnr says: 'Labor had its guts ripped out in 1975, and again in 1977. Many of the survivors were too old and disillusioned for the fight. Keating was one of the few with any fight left. By 1980 the load was more widely spread and there were younger faces on the backbenches, but up till then Keating and Young kept things going.' Susan Ryan agrees, saying of that time:

> All of us who went through those opposition years really paid our dues. We really did drag the party up from a quite abysmal result in 1975 and an equally abysmal one in 1977 to a very successful and apparently long-lived government. And that doesn't happen without a helluva lot of effort of all kinds.

For someone keen to be seen to be in the front-line politically, life continues to be hectic even in opposition. Opposition ministers do not have the staff and resources that go with government. Barbara Ward remembers the opposition years as

> enormously busy . . . we were fighting on several fronts. There was the policy development area and that can be slow in the Labor Party because you've got committee phases and committee structures to go through and that takes time. Then there was the sheer politics of Question Time every day. Even though Paul's area wasn't front-line he'd ask a couple of questions every day and handle MPIs [matters of public importance, debated after Question Time each day].

The big issue at that stage was petrol prices. This was particularly significant for the Labor Party because Keating's market-oriented attitude towards pricing policy conflicted with the Connor inheritance that favoured government intervention. Keating and Ward had to come to grips with what the market approach should be and what the policy approach should be—they had to find a policy that did not differ substantially from what market forces dictated but which also did not impose a huge economic burden on Australian consumers. The Fraser government's policy of import parity pricing was economically efficient but not politically popular as it had resulted in huge increases in petrol prices. Keating was trying to tread a fine line between economic forces and social pressures. It was good training for the future treasurer. Ward says: 'Policy for the Labor Party was still the old Connor policy which was pretty much interventionist—buy back the farm—whereas Keating took very much the opposite approach, the market approach, so there was an enormous selling job within the party in terms of policy.'

Keating gave keynote speeches to many conferences and seminars as part of his aim to establish Labor Party philosophy in the resources area. His aggressive, anti-goverment line was not always well received. Addressing a conference held by the Australian Petroleum Exploration Association (APEA) at Surfers Paradise in March 1980, he drew boos from the audience when he recited a series of figures showing how much exploration had fallen since the Fraser government came to power in 1975. The industry representatives in the audience, mindful of the lagged effect of the heavy hand of the Whitlam government on their sector, were stung into retort. There were cries of 'Who is he trying to fool?' The answer was that Keating was out to give the press a good story.

And he worked the parliamentary press hard and well. He would disappear for an hour or so after Question Time, only to be found up in the press gallery, going from office to office, making sure his points were understood. Says Ward: 'There was no worry about ego with Paul. He'd go off and tell the press how brilliant he was in Question Time, and got a fair bit of press as a result. If they didn't necessarily understand the angle he was coming from he made sure they did . . . in those days he needed the press to build himself up as much as possible.' Unlike many opposition ministers, though, Keating avoided churning out press releases every day. He and Ward made a conscious decision not to inundate the journalists with paper that simply found its way into the garbage bin.

Life was crowded with committee work, shadow cabinet and caucus meetings in Canberra, sessions in the electorate in Bankstown or with the NSW branch of the party. With the administration, the correspondence, the visitors and the meetings, it was not hard to fill a fifteen-hour working day—which was usual when parliament was sitting until 11pm. 'There was a lot of shit-work, to put it mildly,' says Ward, referring to the endless letters and calls, the cutting and pasting and filing. These were also the days of numerous political sensations, the resignations and sackings of more than a dozen ministers in the Fraser government. Keating's verbal skills meant he often became involved in these matters in the House, which meant homework had to be done and files kept on members of the government. And Keating, being a numbers man, always had a finger in internal politics, talking with backbenchers, particularly if there were votes coming up in the party.

Success in Keating's professional life was marred in 1978 by the sudden death of his father. Matt Keating had been dogged by heart trouble for years, but had recovered after each attack. His death was a shock for the whole family. Paul Keating was the last to see his father alive. Matt Keating had gone for a walk to the local shops on a Saturday afternoon—he liked the exercise—and paused by his son's garden to chat. A few minutes later he had collapsed and died. Paul Keating was the first to hear. Matt and Min had planned a visit to their daughter, Anne, who was living in London at the time. Her brother rang her with the news and she flew home. 'Paul bore the brunt of it all,' says Anne. The man who had first kindled the interest in politics in the young Keating, and steered him through his initial campaigns, was only 60 when he died.

The following year Keating was faced with a new challenge. In September 1979 he was persuaded to fill the vacuum left in the NSW ALP by the early retirement of its president, John Ducker. Ducker had been a dominant figure in NSW Labor politics for a decade, holding the two key positions of president of NSW Labor and secretary of the Labor Council, as well as being a member of the Legislative Council and sitting on the boards of several radio stations. It was early in Ducker's reign that the NSW ALP headquarters had relocated to the ninth floor of the Labor Council's building in Sussex Street, taking much of Ducker's empire under one roof. By 1979, though, the man who had been at the forefront of the Labor party action was feeling the weight of his responsibilities and pressures. A few months earlier, in June that year, a bitter state annual conference had topped off a difficult period for Ducker. He decided he had had enough.

Keating was the one person the party officers felt was of sufficient stature to fill Ducker's shoes as president. But Keating's time and attention were firmly vested in Canberra and the federal ALP. He was conscious of the demands of his shadow portfolio and of the effort needed to stay on top. The state presidency offered the prestige of a war-lord position but there was little in it that appealed personally to Keating. The pressure of the party overcame his hesitancy. The party needed him; the Right needed him to fend off the Left which was gathering strength and could make inroads. Keating reluctantly agreed. He would take on the job, but on strict terms: the structure of the NSW ALP was to be opened up to young people, to win back youth that had become disaffected with the party, and he would not 'mess around in Macquarie Street' or become involved in state political power struggles. Keating was elected by the administrative committee (the state executive of the ALP), to be president for the balance of Ducker's term, which was to end in June 1980. At that year's state conference he was overwhelmingly voted in as president in his own right.

Despite the early reluctance Keating took to the presidency 'like a hand fits into a glove', according to Stephen Loosely, secretary of the NSW ALP. Keating enjoyed the scrapping and lobbying, up to a point. As NSW president he was in demand, on the phone, in factional disputes and policy decisions. He was deeply involved in party organisations, attending state electoral councils, branch meetings and informal party activities as well as regular administrative committee meetings and annual conferences. He cooled much of the factional heat and is credited with lifting the image and rebuilding the strength of the NSW Right. Working closely with Graham Richardson, then secretary of the NSW branch, he took a detailed interest in organising the 'machine' and formed the Centre Unity group, a move designed to soften the image of the right-wing faction. By 1982 the Right had reasserted its dominance in NSW.

Keating's ability to feel the tone and flow of a meeting, to sense when and how to defuse an issue and to preserve some humour, made him a respected chairman. He is remembered as an approachable president and a first-rate chairman of the state annual conference, described as a more gladiatorial forum than the national ALP conferences. NSW state conferences have been likened to medieval warfare, where the barons turned up with their private armies, went into battle and then everyone retired intact. Delegates enthuse about the sense of theatre and drama.

As NSW Labor president, Keating was also chairman of the Newcastle radio station 2HD, owned 60 per cent by the ALP and 40 per cent by the Labor Council. He took an active interest in improving the station's efficiency, a role that brought him a deeper understanding of the benefits of management and of facilities such as company credit cards. That information was to prove useful when later, as federal treasurer, he launched his assault on such tax-free fringe benefits.

Keating shared his week between parliament in Canberra, his electorate in Bankstown and the demands of the NSW headquarters. He and Anita were then living in their Sydney house at Condell Park, so the NSW duties brought him home. During those years Keating would travel back to Sydney on Friday mornings, after the last session of the House on Thursday nights, head straight for the Labor Party office in Sussex Street and stay there until about 8pm. Meetings were generally held every second Friday. He says:

> We'd have a meeting of our factional group. I'd have the routine duties of an office bearer and have to attend some of the committees of the party, as well as formal meetings of my fellow officers and a meeting of what's called the officers' group—that's the president and secretary and two assistant secretaries, of whom one was a member of the Left. And that would set up the agenda for the administrative committee meeting, which generally began around 3pm or 4pm and would continue till around 7pm.

In non-sitting weeks he would spend time in his electoral office in Bankstown and have a lunch once or twice a week with leading businessmen. In those days he frequently chatted with John Leard, the politically ultra-conservative head of Australian National Industries. As Keating agrees, that might seem strange now, given Leard's strident criticism of the Hawke government. 'But as a bloke in the manufacturing industry I'd go and get his views. And I'd talk to the developers, the money movers, the people who were making the city tick over.' Keating says that wages would crop up in every conversation he had in the 1970s. 'It was a central topic. There was no co-ordinated policy.' He went out of his way to keep in touch with a wide range of business, talking with stockbrokers, bankers, mining industry executives and property developers. 'I tried to keep as alert as possible and digest as much as possible. And I was always interested in what was happening in the economy,' Keating says.

His term as president is remembered as one that broke new ground in a number of areas, particularly in his efforts to make the system more professional. Before Keating became party president the decision-making process was vested in a relative handful of individuals and much power had been concentrated in John Ducker's hands. Keating changed the system by creating an inner group executive of six or seven people who were consulted on major decisions and who met frequently, and by establishing what became known as the political committee of the Centre Unity group. This is about 180-strong, made up of rank-and-file trade unionists, parliamentarians, constituency party members, Young Labor people and so on. According to Loosely, Keating also emphasised the need for the party at federal level to improve the calibre of people being endorsed for federal seats and to ensure there was a continuing process of regeneration at state level.

Keating was determined to run a highly professional, modern political office and, working with Graham Richardson, he introduced a system of computers to the Sydney headquarters. The Left was unconvinced of the advantages of computers but Keating saw them as an essential tool in party administration and organisation.

It was during his years as NSW president that Keating stepped up his already familiar invective against the inner-city Left, whom he castigated for their anti-enterprise attitudes and lack of policies. Keating the pragmatist was very much the child of the NSW Right—no dreamer of dreams. The Left he saw as ideologists who were not interested in increasing the size of the economic cake: rather, they wanted to go back and change the ingredients. In selling his brand of pragmatism, he helped Labor shed its image of being hostile to business. Ironically, a decade later Labor was being accused of being overly friendly with big business, supporting its 'rich mates'.

Keating's complaint about the Left, then and later, was its opposition to so many moves that he sees as necessary to 'stop the joint going backwards'. His famous remark about 'Balmain basket-weavers' was part of a diatribe against the Left's anti-growth stance, which he derided as an attitude that boiled down to 'wider nature strips, more trees and making wicker baskets in Balmain'—

another version is 'wider nature strips, more trees and eat your own shit'. Keating identified Balmain as the home of left-wing trendies—the former working-class Labor stronghold in inner Sydney had been gentrified in the late 1960s by an influx of academics and young professionals.

Keating accused the Left of claiming to favour growth but opposing uranium mining, coal mining and minerals booms—in fact, finding a reason to be opposed to all forms of enterprise. He says: 'They were anti-resources. They actually wanted to stop smelter development. I said to them, "You've got to take these chances when they come because they won't keep coming. It's a phase that'll pass, a window of opportunity that'll shut."' In Keating's view the Left represents a class of people who believe that individuals are virtuous and harmonious when living on the land, running small plots, growing their own potatoes, concentrating on cottage industries. 'Then we'll all live in renovated terraces in Balmain, and we'll have the arts and crafts shops, and everything else is bad,' he says. 'Technology is evil, financial services are out.' Whitlam and the post-Whitlam years, he says, brought out the 'Balmain trendies and lefties', products of years when growth just happened, when governments did not have to focus on creating growth. 'Growth' had become an unfashionable word with Labor, whereas to Keating it was the engine of everything. Growth had to be put back into the lexicon of the ALP. Conversations with Keating have always been studded with references to 'making the pie bigger' not squabbling about who was getting what size slice. He recalls:

> I remember saying to Hayden around 1980 that growth was one word he was not using. Because after 1975 there were people running around saying: 'What do you want growth for? Why growth for growth's sake? What's wrong with a static economy?' That was all right for them, they were all on good incomes. The people who took the buck at the end of the queue were all out in Blacktown, Green Valley; they didn't know them because the Balmain lefties were OK, they were all in good restaurants quaffing wine till 3.30 in the afternoon. That's what always galled me. That's why the NSW Right of the party was always working class, it always had the working class, trade unions, trades hall—that was my show. And still is my show.

Keating was adept at using the media in NSW, putting his point across effectively, just as he had worked the press gallery in Canberra. And if he threw himself into a debate, that debate was won. 'His tongue could draw blood,' recalls Loosely. 'He was a formidable asset to have on the platform at a party conference.'

At the state level, Labor entered the 1980s well entrenched in New South Wales, into the fourth year of the Wran government. The history of NSW Labor is different from that of the other state branches: NSW was not affected by the ideological split in the 1950s to the same extent as Victoria and Queensland or Western Australia. NSW prided itself on a healthy sense of political realities, with its idealism tempered by pragmatism. And NSW Labor has a history of being in government, whereas in many other states Labor's history has been one of opposition. Federally, Labor was in less healthy shape at the start of the new decade. The shattering events of 1975 had been followed by a savage electoral defeat in 1977. After the dismal results in 1977 Gough Whitlam stepped down and Bill Hayden became leader of the ALP. Fraser's government won federal office again in 1980, but with a decreased majority, and Labor's hopes began to rise.

In 1980 Keating was still chiding the federal government over its approach to uranium mining, criticising it for pressing ahead with uranium developments which was contrary to the recommendations of the Ranger inquiry. The government, he said in parliament in March 1980, was

> undeterred by the need to find solutions to the problems associated with the nuclear fuel cycle . . . the Australian Labor Party on the other hand has taken a responsible approach to those matters and recognises the need to find adequate solutions. Since 1977 we have a clearly defined policy with respect to the mining and export of uranium—a policy which has been articulated often. Briefly, it states that a future Labor government will not permit uranium mining or export until the problems evident in the nuclear industry have been resolved to the satisfaction of the party.

Within the federal Labor Party rumblings were heard in late 1980 that heralded a new drama—the resolution of who would lead the party into the next federal election. Bob Hawke had resigned as president of the ACTU and entered parliament as the member for Wills. His move unnerved both the prime minister, Malcolm Fraser, and Bill Hayden, who was leader of the ALP. Hawke's popularity was a threat to both. If the year 1980 marked the opening of a new chapter for Labor, it also brought the beginnings of the end for the Fraser government. Writing in *The Hawke Ascendancy*, Paul Kelly says: 'Assessed both in retrospect and at the time the 1980 election was the watershed which broke the Fraser regime into its two periods—the opening five years of dominance and the final two-and-half years of decline.'

Kelly cites a number of factors that contributed to the decline of the Fraser government. Fraser's own power was waning and the economy went into a recession in the early 1980s instead of the predicted boom. Last, but far from least, was the arrival of Bob Hawke in Canberra. Hawke's entry to parliament threw down the gauntlet to Bill Hayden, then Labor leader, and also changed the outlook for Paul Keating—by delaying his own prospects of becoming party leader. And Keating was to be faced with a difficult choice: to support Hawke, in the interests of Labor winning the next election, or to remain loyal to Hayden. The latter course carried with it the chance that Keating could soon follow Hayden as leader; the former was more and more favoured as being in the best interests of the party.

By November 1981 another topic had come to light that was to provide significant interest and activity for Paul Keating in later years—financial deregulation. That month saw the release and tabling in parliament of the final report of the Campbell Committee's inquiry into the Australian financial system. The committee had been established in January 1979 by the then federal treasurer, John Howard, to carry out the first far-reaching examination of the country's financial system since the Royal Commission into Money and Banking of 1936–37. Australia was far from alone in reviewing its financial system. The topic had been widely examined overseas, and several countries had chosen to deregulate their financial markets—to remove out-dated government controls and to allow a greater role to market forces to achieve a fair and efficient financial system. The Campbell Committee carried a far wider brief than the earlier royal commission. The committee's investigations covered all aspects of the Australian financial system: the banking sector, foreign exchange and the appropriate method of setting the exchange rate, the best methods for raising government funds, stock exchange regulations and the tax system.

The Campbell Committee was chaired by the late Sir Keith Campbell, then chairman and general manager of the property company Hooker Corporation Ltd. Other committee members were Alan Coates, then general manager of the AMP Society, Keith Halkerston, a financial adviser, the late R.G. (Dick) McCrossin, general manager of the Australian Resources Development Bank, Jim Mallyon from the Reserve Bank of Australia and Fred Argy from Treasury. The committee, supported by a team of economic advisers, conducted a wide-ranging investigation of the financial markets. They sought opinions from a wide range of sources and encouraged written submissions from different market sectors. Public hearings were organised throughout Australia, giving those interested a chance to have their say. The written and verbal opinions provided much of the groundwork for a debate that aired issues that had escaped discussion and scrutiny for years. Controls and regulations that had existed for decades were examined in a process that aimed to end distortions and produce the recipe for a fairer and more efficient financial system.

The very existence of the Campbell Committee stirred up debate and was itself a catalyst for change. Important deregulatory steps were taken while the committee was deliberating. In December 1980 the then federal treasurer, John Howard, freed the banks from government controls on the interest rates they could pay on deposits. That move, small as it seemed at the time, set in motion a process that would see the unravelling of a whole range of regulations and controls on the financial system.

The final report of the six-man committee broadly recommended that the banking and financial markets be freed of government controls so that interest rates and the exchange rate would be determined by the markets and not by authorities such as the Reserve Bank, the Treasury and government. Banks would be free to set their own rates and charges and to determine the maturity of the deposits they accepted from customers. The Australian banking system, which, apart from the Australian Bank's arrival early in 1981, had not increased in numbers since the 1940s, should be expanded to include new, and foreign, banks.

The report was praised as a blueprint for the future. It was recognised at the time that the report stopped short of telling government how to implement its recommendations—the 838 pages were devoted to vigorous argument and explanation of *why* the changes should be made and the benefits that would ensue. The Labor opposition was not in favour of the general thrust of the report, particularly where its recommendations could affect, possibly increase, interest rates for home-buyers. Overall, Labor was hostile to the market-oriented bias of the report. If there were supporters of the Campbell report's arguments within Labor ranks at that time, they were not vocal.

By the end of 1981, then, the seeds of several dramas had been sown. In the political arena Hawke had entered parliament, adding an important figure to the stage on which would unfold the final scenes of the Fraser government and the steady progress of Labor towards federal power. In the financial area deregulatory progress was being made but hard decisions lay ahead. Though he did not know it at the time, the agenda had already been set for Paul Keating as treasurer.

5 The reluctant treasurer

I've been given the poisoned chalice, mate.
PAUL KEATING WHEN FIRST MADE SHADOW TREASURER

WHEN 1982 opened Paul Keating was clearly the spokesman for what was tagged the 'new' Right in ALP politics, a group personified by, besides Keating, figures such as Neville Wran and John Cain who were challenging the ideas and claims of the 'new' Left. This 'new' Right in Labor was less ideologically hidebound than its counterpart on the Left and was commonly identified as bent on making Labor as relevant federally as it had been at state level, particularly in New South Wales. Keating had risen through the ranks of the NSW Right, sharing its militant opposition to what it saw as an ideology-ridden Left. Keating has little time for what he perceives as the UK 'lefty socialists' who have become irrelevant. He reads the British political theorist Anthony Crosland in preference to Stuart Holland, who is regarded as the Left's intellectual fountainhead.

In the 2 February 1982 issue of the *Bulletin*, Max Walsh summed up Keating's stance in an article headed 'How Paul Keating is taking on the Left'. Walsh's article was largely inspired by an earlier speech in which Keating had used the colourful 'Balmain basket-weavers' analogy to express his contempt for the trendy, inner-city Left. Walsh was writing shortly after the NSW Right had won a preselection contest in the seat of Lowe. He described NSW as 'more than the jewel in Labor's crown—it is where the New Right and the New Left of the party are engaged in a fight for what amounts to ultimate control of the ALP's destiny'. Each side claimed to be the true representative of the party. Walsh used two quotes to illustrate the point, one from Keating and one from Jan Burswoods, a leading New Left figure who had been defeated in the Lowe preselection. Keating's words:

> The continuity (through the governments of Lang and McKell) is as clear as day. The powers are handed down from one generation to the next. These people (the Left) are trying to make my party into something other than it is. I'm in the mainstream of my party, a lot of others are not. They're appendages. That's why I'll never abandon ship, and never let those people capture it.

Burswoods said:

> Too often the Right wing tends to be so cautious that the ALP, which is supposed to be offering the radical alternative, starts coming over as a pale imitation of what it is supposed to be.

Walsh went on to comment that attempts to pigeon-hole Labor people into Left and Right camps reflected images of a

> stereotype which has only limited relevance to contemporary politics and even less to what will be the shape of the future . . . .The conventional view is that the Left of Labor has been the keeper of the party's conscience . . . aided in this by its constant reiteration of party doctrine and by cowing the Right in this area of doctrine. The Right or conservative side of Labor politics, has rarely been prepared or able to articulate an alternative doctrine . . . That sketch of past Labor stereotypes was never totally valid. It is much less so today.

In Walsh's view the Right, under Keating's leadership, was undergoing a profound change. Keating, he wrote, had a coherent view of where the party should be going and what it had been. 'He [Keating] is a rare creature of the Right, being prepared to passionately argue his case for party legitimacy in terms of the party's tradition, performance and beliefs. He is not the slightest bit intimidated by the claims of the Left to be custodians of party ideology.'

Walsh talks of Keating's 'unique education' at the hands of Lang and Connor—'walking encyclopaedias . . . and rather in the way that the tribal witch doctor passes the totems, myths and incantations on to his acolyte, Keating was the legatee of Lang and Connor'. This inheritance provided Keating with an armour of self-righteousness and conviction that was generally lacking in the Right, 'where pragmatism is treated not as part of the party tradition but the means of every-day survival'. Walsh likened Keating's philosophy to 'corporate socialism', a term coined by the British political analyst H.M. Drucker, in his study of the UK Labour Party entitled *Doctrine and Ethos in the Labour Party*. Drucker's corporate socialism would be in the form of extreme pragmatism: 'It has no goal but possesses an astute and sensitive awareness of what it wants to protect: the economic standards of employed working-class men.' Keating considered many of the Left's convictions to be a liability for Labor, while the Left believed that Keating was guilty of a sell-out of the Labor platform. Susan Ryan says:

> Keating's a traditionalist in ways that many people in the party are not now—he *knows* the history of the Australian Labor Party in his lifetime better than any academic Labor historian I've ever encountered; and he learned it from Jack Lang's knee, from Rex Connor's knee, so he does have a very detailed and personal sense of Labor history. But in his working methods and his approach to getting a policy together and then getting it implemented he is really quite new.

Keating insists that his views have not changed since he first walked into the party. He inherited from his father what he calls a 'capacity to reason things out' and says: 'You don't have to be a genius—if the private economy is rooted then we haven't much of a chance. There's nothing the government is going to be able to do bar short-term employment stimulation. But the government can do a lot to get things flowing. In other words I do believe in the big machinery of growth—I'm a growth person.' And Keating quotes a line from Jack Lang, who said: 'All our aim is to lift everyone up, not push others down.' 'And that's exactly right,' says Keating. 'You lift them up by making the system work . . . the system accommodates the shifts . . . if the incentives are there, if the sums make sense, it'll work for you. Make it work for the Labor government and you sit in the box seat—you've got the social side, you've got the business side, you're on top.'

Keating differs from most in the Labor Party, he says, in that he has always believed in the private economy of Australia because it is the generator of wealth. And he has recognised that the machine producing the wealth has fallen badly into disrepair; his view is that taking steps to fix it will benefit everyone in Australia. He adds:

> The economy needs a decent social security system, not a stupid one. It should have a decent education. But the private economy ought to be able to function properly. I always thought it's the job of

> the commonwealth government to run the private economy well. And if you're going to do that you've got to sit down and work out where all the impediments are. The you tick them off, clear the decks. And a lot of this comes from my family background, from basic tolerance. I've got no envy in me and there are a lot of people driven by envy. A lot of the Labor party is about the politics of envy. Well I don't have any of that shit in me. I can look at things pretty dispassionately and say, right, these blokes are doing well, that's good. They can do better. Whereas others might say: they're doing well, let's cut them down.

And he is contemptuous of those who wear what he calls the uniform of the Left, who arrive at conferences in cardigans, sleeves rolled up, but who become highly elitist once they become ministers. Keating believes it is hypocritical to arrive at a party conference in a flashy car but to park it around the corner, as he claims Tom Uren did. Keating parked his E-type Jaguar outside Sydney's town hall and came out to find it daubed with a corrosive fluid. He blamed the Left of his own party.

Keating's political fortunes in 1982 were inextricably caught in the mounting drama between Bill Hayden, the existing ALP leader, and Bob Hawke, seen by many as pretender to the throne. Each was seeking to tighten his claim on leadership of the ALP. Keating, still loyal to Hayden, had little involvement in the early manoeuvrings though he was well aware of the developments in the power struggle between the two men. Keating's role encompassed a number of strands—his own ambitions, his wish to see the party in power, the weight of the numbers he represented.

Both Hayden and Hawke entered 1982 full of confidence. Hayden was into his fifth year as Labor leader and felt comfortably on top of the job. Hawke had recovered from a disappointing performance at the previous year's special ALP national conference and was working towards challenging Hayden. Hawke firmly believed he would lead Labor into government. His confidence was boosted when, in May 1982, the Australian National Opinion Polls (ANOP) produced the results of a poll that reflected badly on Hayden. The poll was followed by strategic press leaks contrasting a buoyant Hawke with a faltering Hayden. Hayden did not help his own cause with his clumsy handling of the question of nuclear warships' access to Australia under a Labor government.

By the middle of 1982 Hawke was ready to move against Hayden. As Paul Kelly recounts in *The Hawke Ascendancy*, he went to visit Graham Richardson, then NSW state secretary and a long-time friend, in Sydney in June 1982 and told him of his plan to challenge. Kelly wrote: 'He [Hawke] was irritated by Richardson's hesitation. The NSW secretary felt the timing was wrong; the parliament was not sitting and the 1982 ALP national conference was about to begin. Richardson knew that while some NSW right-wing members wanted Hawke, enthusiasm among the majority was barely luke-warm.' The NSW Right felt that Hawke was running ahead of sentiment and trying to pull the party in behind him.

Keating held loyal to Hayden. At the NSW Labor conference in June 1982 he spoke warmly of Hayden's 'courage and determination ... integrity and principle'. He admired Hayden's tactics on the uranium issue. And Hayden handled himself well at the July ALP national conference, where he, Keating, Hawke and Richardson all spoke in favour of toning down Labor's anti-uranium stance. The push to reverse the ALP pledge to repudiate existing uranium contracts was based on Hayden's and Keating's belief that prevailing ALP policy undermined the credibility of a Labor government. Hayden was worried about prejudicing mines already operating with investments based on overseas loans financed by international banks. Hayden spoke of a 'moral, political responsibility to compensate these people' and used the 'banana republic' analogy—later, in 1986, put to effective use by Keating—saying: 'We would almost become a banana republic in the standards of the condition of the economy ... people who have got money here are going to start hauling their money out.'

Hayden emerged from the July ALP national conference triumphant and confident. Hawke was equally convinced that it was now his time to strike. Keating disagreed:

> The run at that time in 1982 was such an ill-conceived, ill-timed, ill-thought-through, ill-advised operation. We were just finishing a national conference, where Bill emerged as a winner and a bloke who defended the things we wanted defended, such as US bases. Capital gains tax we didn't want on the agenda—oppositions can't mount tax changes. The case had merit but we had to put the merit to one side. It was not politically meritorious. Bill had a very strong conference. We had to say after all that that it was no good, we wanted someone else? That didn't fit. The conditions were wrong even though Bob was doing much better in the polls. And the Left were going to get square—uranium was a big issue ... Bob was sort of running without talking to us, he was running without us for a while. Everything has a natural timing in politics and that was out of sync.

By the end of the national conference Hayden concluded that the situation could not continue. He felt obliged to call a leadership challenge to retest his position. Keating faced a dilemma that involved his own leadership ambitions, loyalty to Hayden, factional considerations and the ALP's chances of federal power.

The ALP might have seen Keating as a Hawke supporter but until that time Keating was still very much in the Hayden camp and, in fact, was one of the last to switch allegiance to Hawke. At that time, in mid-1982, Hawke was widely regarded as a newcomer making a tilt for the top job before finishing his apprenticeship. Keating had doubts about Hawke. Keating, the NSW state president, talked about the NSW Right supporting Hayden, a position that opposed the views of Graham Richardson who, with Keating, was a key figure in the NSW Right and state secretary of the party. Richardson had already shifted behind Hawke and was pushing to get the NSW Right firmly committed to that position. Keating, accused of sitting on the fence, was finally persuaded, two days before the ballot was to be held, to go with Hawke. He set aside personal ambitions and loyalty to Hayden to throw his weight behind the man he now believed was mostly likely to win federal power for the party. On Wednesday 14 July he announced:

> The centre-unity group [of NSW Labor] respects Bill Hayden's capacity and contribution to the Labor movement and will support him absolutely, without reservations, in the event that he wins Friday's ballot. I believe, however, that the NSW members will take the view that the best interests of the Labor Party, and the millions of Australians who deserve and need a Labor victory and the end of Fraserism, will be best served by Bob Hawke now becoming leader.

Barbara Ward says Keating had taken about four days to come to that decision in July 1982. 'And he did go through hell for those days,' she says. 'Paul is a bit of a softie in his own way and the reason he went through hell was not a political thing, it was a personal thing. Bill had supported him and he'd been a supporter of Bill's and he'd worked with Bill for ten years and Hawke had only been around for a year or two and wasn't overly impressive at that stage. It wasn't an easy decision. He really did agonise for quite a while.' Once Keating had made the decision and was publicly aligned with Hawke, he threw himself behind the move. He was hardly off the telephone, persuading others and drumming up support for Hawke.

Hayden won the challenge—but Hawke had come within five votes of overthrowing the leader. Keating was initially distraught, but recovered to deal with the depressing prospect of working with a leader who knew he had backed Hawke. It was another episode in what has been described as the 'on-again, off-again' relationship between Hayden and Keating. Paul Kelly accurately summed up the feelings between the two men: 'Hayden was suspicious of Keating and Keating was finally disappointed in Hayden.'

Hayden did not understand 'numbers men' and Keating was acknowledged as a numbers man *par excellence*, able to drum up a block of votes when needed. It was a characteristically NSW tactic, quite foreign to Hayden, who knew that just as those votes could be delivered, they could also be taken away. Hayden would not have felt directly threatened by Keating but he knew that the younger man was there, queueing up for the leadership. Keating's place in the queue was another factor in his early reluctance to desert Hayden—he knew that once he threw his support behind Hawke he would have to shelve his own leadership aspirations for some time. Ward says: 'Paul does normally go for Number One first, but in the end he decided that the future of the party was more important than his own political ambitions. They could have been out for a long time if they lost—and he believed Hawke had a better chance of winning government than Hayden.'

The whiff of change was undeniably in the wind. But it is unlikely that anyone, in the closing months of 1982, foresaw the speed with which the fortunes of the Fraser government, the Labor Party, Hayden, Hawke and Keating would be changed by the next few months.

By this stage the suggestion of being shadow treasurer had been made to Keating more than once. Hayden had drifted the idea past him after the 1980 elections but nothing was done and Keating's interest in the role waned. Ralph Willis was looking good in the job. Hayden tried to tempt Keating again in 1982, but Keating was ambivalent about the switch. Hayden kept the pressure on. But while the influence of treasurer was appealing—particularly for someone who was expected, one day, to claim the prime ministership—Keating was inclined to see it as a bad-news portfolio, a graveyard post that could be used to defuse a bright rival. A treasurer is rarely a popular figure. John Martin, a long-time friend and vocal supporter of Keating, remembers his indifference to the prospect of being shadow treasurer. 'We were lunching at Russets, in North Sydney. Keating was talking about Hayden being leader but Hawke looming on the horizon. He said that Hayden wanted him [Keating] to be shadow treasurer. He was not enthusiastic about the prospect, which would involve new areas for him.' In November 1982 Hayden was giving assurances that there would be no reshuffle of the shadow cabinet.

By early January 1983 Hayden had changed his mind. An election was clearly looming. The bad result for Labor at the Flinders by-election had encouraged Fraser and added to forces pushing Hayden towards changes that would strengthen his position. Late on Thursday 13 January, Hayden rang Willis and Keating and told them of their changed roles. Hayden had been trying to reach Keating earlier in the evening; Keating was out and it was after 11pm when the two men spoke. Keating was taken aback at being told he was to be shadow treasurer. It seemed late in the piece for a switch of portfolios. Barbara Ward, who was holidaying in Brisbane at the time, says: 'The phone rang late, after 11pm—typical Paul style—and I remember answering and there was this very shaky voice on the end of the line saying, "He's made me shadow treasurer." It was a bit of a shock. He really didn't expect it at that stage. I think once the suggestion had died down people had really given up the idea of a reshuffle, or if they hadn't, he had given up the idea of being treasurer.' Keating and Ward 'talked and talked and talked about what being treasurer would entail'. Tax was a major question. In *The Hawke Ascendancy*, Paul Kelly says:

> Keating was caught amid swirling emotions. The job which he had secretly feared, yet always assumed to be his fate, had now been thrust upon him. It was the worst possible time. Keating said later that if Hayden wanted him, then the change should have been made the previous July. Of course he was right, but that was Hayden's failure. Keating saw that Hayden was trying to hitch Keating's star to his own leadership and drive a wedge between Keating and Hawke. This was fine politics; but it was too late . . . Hawke was worried and resentful, and fearful that Hayden may have outmanoeuvred him. Hawke told Keating: 'He's fucked us all. He's fucked you by giving you the job. He's fucked Ralph [Willis] and he's fucked me.' Keating saw both himself and Willis as victims of Hayden's personal war but . . . he needed Willis badly. Willis had all the expertise but no wham. Keating had wham but little expertise . . . He was particularly worried about the technical grasp needed to handle taxation legislation.

That problem was resolved immediately by dividing the treasurer's role and leaving Ralph Willis, who had been shattered by the loss of the portfolio, with responsibility for taxation and commonwealth–state relations. A restrained Willis told the *Sydney Morning Herald* that he was 'most disappointed at losing most of the Treasury portfolio'.

Keating had been made shadow treasurer on 14 January, five weeks before parliament was due to resume sitting and, as it happened, less than five weeks before a federal election would be called on 3 February. He had inherited the mantle of shadow treasurer from a trained economist who had handled the role for four years. It was Keating who convinced Hayden of the wisdom of dividing the portfolio between himself and Willis, so that Willis maintained responsibility for tax, commonwealth–state financial relations and the prices-incomes policy. Keating felt he had enough to worry about, mastering the Treasury portfolio, without shouldering these areas as well. In fact, after the election tax was given to John Dawkins, as minister for finance, a development that proved unsatisfactory to both the new treasurer and Treasury. After several months tax was brought back under the treasurer's wing.

But in early 1983 the normally dauntless Keating was for once unnerved by what lay ahead. He had been chosen for the role not because of expertise in economics but because of his forcefulness and political skills. Keating, the salesman of Labor policy, had won out over Willis, the economist. Willis had been a good shadow treasurer; although he displayed little flair, he had a clear set of ideas and a reputation as a logical thinker. But, in government, Labor would need someone like Keating who could match Treasury and its secretary John Stone—an iron-willed conservative for whom the ALP had little love. 'You're the only bastard tough enough to handle Stone,' Hayden had told him during that unwelcome phone call on 13 January. And Hayden was keen to make sure he had the NSW Right on his side; there was no better way of locking in its support than to put its leading luminary, Paul Keating, into a key role.

The outlook for Keating was indeed formidable. The Liberal treasurer, John Howard, had been in the job for five years and had the advantages of that experience. All that Keating appeared to have was his reputation as a political killer. Friends say he was deeply unhappy at getting the shadow treasurer's job. He suspected it was a move to be rid of him, to reduce his power because Hayden saw him as a Hawke supporter. 'I've been given the poisoned chalice, mate,' Keating said to his industrialist acquaintance John Leard. But he was determined to master the brief. Jim McClelland remembers coming across Keating at that time, at the corner of Sydney's Elizabeth and King Streets, with a sheaf of papers under his arm. 'How will you cope with that?' McClelland asked his former colleague. 'Like any other problem, I'll get it up,' Keating replied. 'By Christ, so you will,' thought McClelland. (Years later McClelland, who still admires

Keating's abilities, was being openly critical of Keating in his newspaper columns, criticising his style and accusing him of superficiality.)

By February 1983 Malcolm Fraser's political nose was telling him that a Labor leadership crisis was imminent. He knew he should beat Labor to the punch and get an election out of the way before Labor resolved its problems. Fraser was also irritated by his lack of majority in the Senate, and, on 3 February 1983, he used this as the excuse to ask the governor-general for a double dissolution. The Senate's rejection of certain legislation was the formal reason given by Fraser to the governor-general, but the real reason for calling an election was to get that over before the ALP changed leaders from Hayden to Hawke. Fraser took a calculated risk that the ALP crisis would be a prolonged and bloody battle that would allow him time to keep the lead.

Fraser miscalculated. Hayden's political antennae were also hard at work; he was alert to the urgency of the occasion. While Fraser waited, on 3 February 1983, for approval to his election request from the governor-general, Hayden outsmarted him by announcing his resignation to the press. His loyalty to the party had won out over his own ambition. By the time Fraser held his press conference at 5pm, Hawke was holding the reins of the ALP. Fraser's election request had set in motion a train of events that culminated in his party's defeat and established a Labor government in Canberra, under its new leader, Bob Hawke. In one move Fraser had secured a double dissolution and toughened the odds against himself.

Keating was quite shaky during the 1983 election campaign. At that stage he did not believe in an incomes policy and had little faith in the Prices and Incomes Accord which had been struck between the ALP and the ACTU and now formed a key plank in the ALP platform. He was unsure if it would work. He even said so publicly, letting his uncertainty slip through during a lengthy interview with the radio commentator John Laws on 24 February. The opposition seized on the shadow treasurer's doubts. Hawke defended Keating for being honest but both were unsettled by this evidence that Keating was not yet convincing in the role of treasurer.

Keating's ego had already taken a beating at the launch of the ALP economic program at the Wentworth Hotel in Sydney on 10 February. The program, devised by Ralph Willis and his economics adviser, John Langmore, was destined to be scrapped, but at that time it was the official policy. Keating, travelling from Bankstown to the Wentworth Hotel, was nervous about the coming test. Usually, once under the spotlight and behind the microphone, he stages a confident, compelling performance. For once, this did not happen. Hawke dominated the launch. Keating was shattered. For the first time in as long as he could remember he felt failure. Later that day he turned in a polished television interview on the *Carleton-Walsh Report*. But he was still smarting from the earlier disappointment.

Keating may have faltered during the 1983 election campaign, but Hawke flourished. The historian Manning Clarke has contrasted Hawke's rousing rhetoric with Fraser's defensive style: '[Hawke] talked of his hope of creating a better Australia, a country in which there was genuine equality of opportunity. Women wept when they heard him, old men began again to dream dreams, and the young, if not to see visions, then at least to entertain hope again. By contrast Malcolm Fraser played on fears . . .'

A striking example of Fraser's tactics of playing on fears was his deliberate attempt to undermine Labor's profile with the financial community and to feed uncertainty about its investment policies. To its discredit, the Fraser government's election propaganda fostered nervousness that a Labor government might introduce regulations that would hamper investment, or that it might even prevent funds from leaving the country. Much of the fuel for this fire came from Malcolm Fraser himself. In a hysterical and widely-reported outburst on 22 February he told an audience in Melbourne that their savings would be safer under the bed than in banks under a Labor government. The banks were furious, depositors were concerned and several senior Liberal politicians began to have doubts about their leader.

Fraser had damaged his own image with the silly outburst but had succeeded in planting doubts about Labor's intentions. In the five weeks ahead of the March election some $3 billion was shifted out of Australia; about $2 billion of this left in the first week of March. This loss of funds coincided with an outflow of money from the banking sector as companies paid their quarterly tax instalments. The combination sent interest rates soaring and increased speculation about the appropriate level the government would choose for the Australian dollar. Speculation was rife that a Labor government might implement part IV of the Financial Corporations Act—a piece of legislation passed in 1974 which, if fully activated, would give the government wide powers over the interest rates and lending policies of non-bank financial institutions. Nervousness about the possible composition of this legislation added to capital markets' and investors' concern. The heavy outflow of funds was evidence of their apprehension.

In late February the Fraser government blundered in another area. During that month the then federal treasurer, John Howard, had received a warning from Treasury that the projected budget deficit for 1983/84 could be as high as $8 billion, about double that of the previous year. Nothing was said or done about this. Howard was jolted into action, though, on Monday 28 February when he received word from Treasury secretary John Stone that, if no changes were made to policy, the projected budget deficit for 1983/84 would be in the order of $9 billion. Howard's attempts to persuade prime minister Fraser to reveal the true figure fell on deaf ears. Paul Kelly relates:

> Hawke appeared at the National Press Club . . . and positioned himself perfectly to exploit the blown-out deficit projections. They were still secret but the Hawke camp had received an excellent tip-off. Hawke specifically warned that if the Fraser government's budget deficit proved bigger than expected he reserved the right for an incoming ALP government to modify its policy.

In remaining silent about the changed deficit outlook the Fraser government did a service to Hawke and a disservice to itself. Hawke had an excuse to change policy and the Fraser government was vulnerable to accusations of hiding the truth. Fraser's electioneering efforts to cut the ground from under Labor were in vain. After more than seven years of Fraserism, the Australian public had decided to pin its hopes on Bob Hawke. Labor won government in March 1983 in a triumph that gave it a majority of 25 in the House of Representatives and a stronger position, although not control, in the Senate, where the Australian Democrats held the balance of power.

This new government was determined to prove itself responsible: what it lacked in the idealism of the Whitlam years it would compensate for by implementing sound social change that would improve lives for all Australians. The Labor Party might still dream dreams but these were the visions of pragmatic reformers with few illusions about the task they were embracing. In fact, the new Labor government had little time in which to savour the fruits of its success on Saturday 5 March 1983. On the following day it was to discover the true extent of the problems it had inherited. Hawke and Keating and their team would be buckling down to business straight away.

6 Accord at the summit

Reform needs targeting—you don't throw dollars out of the window in a benevolent way and hope the poor catch some.

BILL KELTY

FOR THE newly-elected Labor government, getting down to business in March 1983 meant confronting a range of economic problems and challenges. Keating faced a torturous first six months as he mastered his new role. Not least among the issues he had to face as new federal treasurer was the task of coming to grips with the ACTU and the workings of the Accord.

Keating and the Accord have both developed in government. Both were still largely untested when the Hawke government came to power in March 1983. Keating had been catapulted into the shadow treasurer's role only weeks before electoral victory turned him into federal treasurer. The Accord had been only recently endorsed by the unions at a special conference held on 21-22 February, when the election campaign was already under way. It was the national economic summit, held in April 1983, that brought the Accord formally into government policy.

Keating was initially cool about the Accord. He was far from hostile to it and hoped it would work. But he had not been involved in its earlier development and drafting and had had little contact with the ACTU. He was sceptical that the trade union movement could be turned to an economic plus. And the Accord was untried. Hence he had doubts. However, his early doubts turned to a strong commitment as he came to realise the Accord could give him a third limb of policy, enabling a balance to be struck between fiscal, monetary and wages policies. He says:

> What we had was a basic document that said wages shifted too much. But what had come together was the willingness to comply with restraint. And of course what happened was that the Accord really developed in government, in the relationship between the government and the ACTU, with Ralph [Willis] and myself and the principal officers of the ACTU and their wages committee. We have developed a close working relationship, and after a time you build up a fair bit of trust so that people have more of a mental framework than a document. So the Accord really developed during the government's period in office.

The Prices and Incomes Accord is a vital component of the Hawke government's economic as well as financial strategy. The seeds of the 'Statement of Accord by the ALP and the ACTU Regarding Economic Policy', as it was formally titled, were sown in the 1970s when the ACTU and the Labor Party were examining the interaction of wages and the economy. A key figure in the group which devised the Accord was Ralph Willis, Labor's shadow treasurer until January 1983 and later minister for employment and industrial relations. Willis recognised that Labor's economic credibility would be hugely boosted if it could forge a policy that counteracted inflation and avoided the blow-out in wages that occurred whenever the economy showed signs of improvement. This had been identified as a constant problem for Australia. Labor wanted to learn from its earlier mistakes; relations between the Whitlam government and the unions had been unproductive. Bill Kelty, secretary of the ACTU, says:

> It was clear to unions and some in the Labor Party that we really had squandered an opportunity with the Whitlam Labor government. Despite the fact that there were international pressures, we had really let it get away from us. The result was that in economic management the Labor government did not have a good record and unions appeared unco-operative. A number of unions were determined not to squander an opportunity again.

Willis had explored wage systems in the UK and Europe in the late 1970s. He felt that the Labor Party was well-positioned to reach an agreement with the unions, and discussions began with ACTU officers Bill Kelty, Simon Crean and Jan Marsh. Willis, with input from his economics adviser, John Langmore, worked with the ACTU to draft the original Accord document. The concept had the enthusiastic support of Bill Hayden, the then ALP leader, and was a topic of discussion at the 1979 biennial ALP conference. By the time the agreement was finalised, late in 1982, the former ACTU president, Bob Hawke, had entered parliament and was shadow minister for industrial relations.

The Accord was created as a new attempt to answer an old problem. Since the 1920s successive Australian governments had been dogged by the difficulties of establishing a viable wages policy. Wage indexation, which tied wage rises to increases in the cost of living, had prevailed in one form or another since 1907, but was abandoned in 1953 on the grounds that it was not effective in restraining inflation. Various alternatives were tried, from fixing the basic wage according to a range of economic indicators to collective bargaining between unions and employer groups. The explosion in wages in 1973–74 produced a 28 per cent jump in average weekly earnings, mostly against a background of collective bargaining. This reawakened interest in wage indexation, which was reintroduced in April 1975. Indexation survived until July 1981, when the Fraser government drew back to partial indexation in an attempt to restrain inflation. Then followed a period of individual bargaining between unions and employers. But a minor economic recovery in the early 1980s was followed in 1981–82 by the second disastrous experience, in terms of wages growth and soaring unemployment, in little more than a decade. There had to be a better approach. Bernie Fraser, secretary of the Treasury, says:

> Things really got out of hand in the mid-70s with wages—the real wages overhang put Australia at an enormous disadvantage competitively. We paid ourselves more than we could afford. That took a long time to work off. There was no justification for huge wage increases. But the economy was strong, there was talk of a resources boom, oil prices had been good and people were anticipating an improvement. And the same thing happened in the early 1980s—then the unions got in and anticipated higher gains, as did business. There is a more sober view on both sides now.

Bill Kelty recalls that the concept of the Accord was put to prime minister Malcolm Fraser in May 1982 but he rejected it. 'The government had lost its way,' Kelty says. The Liberal-Country Party government could not see itself winning votes by co-operating with the unions. It followed a policy of confrontation, trying to curb unions however it could, making no real attempt to use persuasion or compromise to achieve agreements that would be more rational from a national point of view.

By the end of 1982, however, substantial wage rises had been secured across a broad range of industries through case-by-case bargaining. Unemployment and inflation had also risen. The government's response was to introduce a 'wages pause' which came into effect on 23 December 1982 and was to last for six months. The Fraser government had created the wages pause but had not devised a policy for coming out of it. And the ACTU had accepted the concept of a wages *pause*, not a wages *freeze*, and wanted a guarantee that there would be a 'catch-up' or adjustment at the end of the six-month period.

Meanwhile, the Hawke Labor government was elected to office. The new government had made a commitment to the ACTU that it would foster the Accord. Keating had become involved in the last series of discussions on the agreement just before the election. In those early days of the Accord, before it had a chance to prove itself, its supporters had to contend with stiff opposition from John Stone, then secretary of the Treasury. Stone never believed in the Accord. He was at the vanguard of the traditional Treasury view that an incomes policy was an interference and bound to fail. Governments should rely on a combination of economic, fiscal and monetary measures, he asserted. Unions should be beaten into submission. Treasury has not entirely shaken off its image of being hostile to an incomes policy and preferring a free labour market. But this has been toned down since John Stone's departure. Treasury now sees the Accord as workable. Stone dismissed the Accord as a process that lent respectability to wage-bargaining and regarded it as unhelpful in the long run. Keating's response to Stone's attitude was that the government had made a commitment to the Accord, and that Stone had better get that into his thinking. Keating says: 'We would not have got to where we have if we had just relied on monetary policy. We would have got slow growth and high unemployment. We said we'd do unemployment and inflation simultaneously—we said we'd have growth without inflation. Stone said that was nonsense.' In Bernie Fraser's view, the Accord had to be made to work. He says:

> The alternative was the confrontationalist approach and that had been tried earlier on, to kick unions into submission by imposing short, sharp shocks or long, sharp shocks, using tight fiscal or monetary policy measures to achieve wage restraint. The conclusion was that that does not work. It might appear to work but the moment things pick up then the legacy of that approach would be a wages break-out. And that really has been the story of Australia's performance over the past twenty years. Things build up steam, wages blow out, which is inflationary. You get this cycle through a combination of a strong union movement, weak

> management, closeted arrangements so that unions could make wage claims and employers grant wage rises because in many cases they operate in protected industries where they can pass on the costs. The costs spilled on to exporters, who are exposed.

The economic summit held in April 1983 cemented the Accord into government policy, giving Labor the tools with which to fight both inflation and unemployment. The agreement with the unions to work out those two problems at the same time was one of the chief achievements of the summit. Simon Crean, president of the ACTU, says the summit scored two strong points: it got significant agreement on the problems to be faced and the direction to be pursued to solve them, and it established the mechanisms on a tripartite basis for solving the issues. It was at the summit that the tripartite nature of the Accord was established. Crean says: 'The Accord was struck between two partners [the ALP and the ACTU] but its implementation envisaged tripartism [to include employers]'.

The four-day economic summit, held in the House of Representatives and attended by 330 delegates representing government, industry and the trade unions, provided a platform for Keating to demonstrate how rapidly he had recovered his former nerve. In his first major speech as federal treasurer he rejected the strategy of tolerating high unemployment in order to control inflation and said the Hawke government would fight inflation and unemployment simultaneously, using firm monetary policy and a prices and incomes policy. In outlining the problems that lay ahead, such as the high budget deficit and the need to fight inflation, he helped pave the way for wage restraint.

Keating's stance was endorsed by the late Sir Keith Campbell, whose short, forceful speech was heard in respectful silence. Campbell told his audience that it was unthinkable for Australia to tolerate higher unemployment in order to fight inflation. He said: 'For an intrinsically rich country we are, indeed, in a sick and sorry economic state. One of the worst manifestations of that state is unemployment of more than 700 000 people with more to come . . . Both the treasurer and the ACTU reject any strategy that suggests one could temporarily tolerate higher unemployment in order to fight inflation first.' Campbell supported John Leard's call for a freeze on the salaries of higher income groups and a freeze on dividend increases.

The Accord has provided a framework which links industrial relations and economic strategy. It is not a formula simply of dollar increases. Elements of the Accord embrace industrial relations, occupational health and safety, industry policy, training and price surveillance, as well as wages. Tax is also taken into account. The summit broadened support for the Accord and gave recognition to the need for a wages policy to buttress economic policy. The challenge for the rest of 1983 was to translate the Accord into effective action.

Responsibility for getting the Accord up and running lay with Ralph Willis, backed by a strong team, including Keating and Hawke, which worked in a consultative process involving government, Treasury and the ACTU. The Accord is reinforced by an extraordinary synergy among five key figures—Hawke, Keating and Willis from the government and Crean and Kelty from the ACTU. Crean and Kelty represent a new intellectual generation at the ACTU. Professionally educated, white collar, they come from strong union backgrounds but are of a different calibre from their predecessors. Kelty and Keating focus mainly on wages policy. Crean is less of a wages strategist and more the presenter of overall policy—the ACTU figurehead, diplomat and public spokesman whose finger is very much on the pulse. Kelty and Keating, mutual admirers and good friends, are the two who talk regularly about wages, who hatch the shape, direction and dynamics of wages policy and the trade-offs to be made.

The first issue to be decided in 1983 was when and how to unlock the wage pause and return to a centralised system of determining pay and related issues. The pressure-cooker atmosphere which had built up during the wages pause was dissipated by the broader approach to incomes policy provided by the Accord. The 9.1 per cent catch-up claim of early 1983 was lost during the pause and replaced by a commitment 'over time' to maintain living standards. The new system began in October 1983, with half-yearly indexation of wages to the consumer price index (CPI), using the March and June quarters, and was to remain in place until October 1985.

The year 1984 was hugely successful for the Hawke government, not least in the area of wages. Hopes for agricultural prosperity were restored by the breaking of a long drought, the world economy had improved, inflation was dropping in Australia and the country had recorded buoyant economic growth of 5 per cent. The Accord was credited with facilitating the combination of the 'kick-start' or fiscal stimulus delivered to the economy in the 1983/84 budget, and a reduction in the inflation rate. The wage adjustment scheduled for August 1984 did not occur, as changes to health insurance charges had produced a fall in the consumer price index for the previous two quarters. The government had revamped the earlier Medibank (which was scrapped by the Fraser government) into Medicare, a move that took private health insurance out of the CPI. This substantially lowered the measured CPI, as private health insurance had been a big component. It was a statistical quirk rather than a fudge, and meant that the change in the CPI for the previous two quarters was -0.2 per cent. The unions accepted the measured CPI figure, effectively instituting a twelve-months wage pause. The pay increase of 4.1 per cent granted in April 1984, in line with movements in the CPI, held until April 1985 when a further CPI-related increase of 2.6 per cent was awarded. The one wage increase of 1983 was followed by only one wage increase in 1984. This gave the economy a useful breathing space.

The prospect of no wage rises over a twelve-month period was facilitated by the tax cuts announced in the August 1984 budget. These were the product of extensive negotiations between government and the ACTU, to secure a wage/tax trade-off. The ACTU was particularly influential in the design of the cuts, which were blatantly tailored to favour the ACTU's constituency. The $7.60 cut, effective from October 1984, had the most impact on lower incomes and provided a real improvement to living standards. The government was keen on the cuts for political reasons. It was planning an election before the end of 1984, ostensibly to get the House and the Senate into line after the double dissolution of March 1983 but also because the time seemed right, economically and politically.

The outlook was savagely altered early in 1985 when the Australian dollar tumbled and it became clear that the balance of payments was deteriorating. Big problems were on the horizon; adjustments would have to be made and clearly wage rises would have to be held to less than full indexation. A way had to be found to ensure that the inflationary effects of the depreciated $A were contained.

The result was the September 1985 agreement, tagged Accord Mark II, which was the product of a series of meetings between Keating and Willis and the ACTU wages negotiating committee. In reaching Accord Mark II, the government had overcome ACTU opposition to discounting of the CPI in fixing wages. The new version did not involve any re-writing of the original Accord, but was an agreement between government and the unions on compromises that would help to offset the inflationary impact of the devalued $A. Keating was anxious to maintain the international competitiveness of the lower $A and to show domestic and overseas financial markets that the government was taking a tough line on wages policy. The compromises are a good example of how Keating and Kelty, two lateral thinkers, can dream up gimmicks and deals as answers to problems, and sell them well. The measures included partial discounting of wages and a superannuation trade-off. Indexation of wages would continue, except that the March–April wage adjustment would be discounted by 2 per cent. The *quid pro quo* for discounting was the prospect of personal income tax cuts later in 1985. Productivity claims would be put off until July 1986 and then benefits would be taken in the form of new superannuation arrangements which would cost employers the equivalent of 3 per cent of wages and would be spread over the following two years.

Willis says the September 1985 agreement was important as it broke away from the wording of the Accord which referred to 'indexation and maintenance of real wages'. 'Accord Mark II deliberately said the CPI less 2 per cent,' Willis says. 'From then on it was a new ballgame. The Accord became a document adhered to in spirit though not by the letter.' The Accord had shown itself to be a flexible framework rather than a narrow system for indexing wages; rigid indexation of wages would have been a disaster under the discipline of a floating dollar.

But problems associated with a falling currency were far from over in 1985. The following year brought a downturn in Australia's terms of trade. A worldwide collapse in commodity prices slashed export income and the weaker $A increased the cost of imports. This put further pressure on the Accord and forced it to respond to a set of problems that had never been envisaged. Kelty, who likes to plan years ahead, found his schemes shattered by the collapse in the $A. Keating's predictions and plans were also thrown out of line by the extent of the fall. By 1986 the government was faced with having to admit to the unions that they had a wage indexation system that could not produce indexation. Real wages could not be maintained, given the downturn in the economy. In his budget speech of August 1986 Keating said that the government was committed to further rounds of discounting that would go beyond the tax trade-off of Accord Mark II. This created more problems for Kelty because of union hostility to discounting. Kelty's way around the problem was to devise a new system which related pay increases to improved productivity. That was the birth of the two-tier system, which came into effect in March 1987. Under this system a first round of partial wage increases takes place, related to the CPI, and a second round of a specific proportion is negotiated on the basis of productivity. Willis says:

> It met the needs of the time. The new system was to give more emphasis to skills formation, opening up career paths, giving blue-collar workers a ladder to climb. And it provided more flexibility in wages outcome. Previously we had people getting the same increases, regardless of their industry, conditions or industrial pressures. We needed more variability. And the last few years have brought tremendous pluses. Through the Accord, the concept of the co-operative approach to industry, to the workplace and workplace issues and to wages policy, has developed to a degree that was unthinkable a few years ago. Unions and employers are talking about training and so on, and are 90 per cent in agreement. There are many companies with consultative arrangements as a result of the second tier. We have a co-operative approach that historically has not been the case in Australia.

The two-tier structure has had a dramatic effect on labour management, forcing firms and unions to communicate effectively and increasing each side's awareness of the other's problems. It carries a stronger emphasis than Accord Mark II on genuine consultation with employers, who had felt left out of the earlier negotiations and who saw Accord Mark II as a deal concocted by the government and the ACTU. Accord Mark III, or the two-tier system, got a warmer reception. And employers are recognising the benefits of co-operation. Crean points out that this awareness has taken time to develop. 'It's what the Accord envisaged,' he says. 'But you can't legislate for co-operation. You need a change in attitudes.'

It is Willis who, as minister for employment and industrial relations, is constantly talking and working with the ACTU. Willis is the chief mechanic who maintains the day-to-day workings of the Accord. As treasurer, Keating is involved in every area of expenditure and in setting, though not implementing, wages policy. He becomes involved at times of crisis or turning points in policy. He has spent more time than previous treasurers with the ACTU, and has forged a close and effective working relationship with its secretary, Bill Kelty. The two men have a high regard for each other's abilities which underpins the teamwork involved in implementing the Accord. Kelty likes Keating because he likes creative thinkers. Keating likes Kelty because he is a quick learner who does not have be told anything twice. They both like to find quick solutions.

In Kelty's view the government's achievements have not been sufficiently highlighted. 'It has not sold itself as a government of reform,' he says. 'It has sold itself as a government of economic responsibility. But reform has to be targeted—you don't throw dollars out of the window in a benevolent way and hope the poor catch some.'

It had taken five years to shape a wage structure compatible with the economic vagaries that accompanied the deregulation of the financial system. The Accord has attracted criticism—at times the unions have felt uncomfortable with what they see as the ACTU's closeness to government; at other times employers have felt left out of behind-the-scenes discussions between government and the unions. But the Accord has shown itself to be resilient and elastic enough to cope with unforeseen circumstances, and to provide a flexible link between the political and industrial arms of the ALP. It is a dynamic, rather than static instrument that has to change with the needs of the time.

Keating, at first barely involved in the question of wage determination, had come to recognise how inextricable it was from the larger questions of economic and social management that preoccupied the government—questions that included trade balances, taxation reform and frightening budget deficits. As the Accord grew towards legitimacy, Keating was coming to terms with these challenges.

7 Hands on the levers

Paul Keating has blossomed in government. There are some people who were very good in opposition and didn't blossom in government quite as much as expected, and there are some who do better than expected. In Paul's case power really suits him; he has performed in government even better than expected.

SUSAN RYAN

FROM 1983 onward, Paul Keating's story is also the story of the Hawke Labor government. As federal treasurer and a key figure in cabinet, in parliament and in the expenditure review committee (ERC), Keating made a huge contribution to the government's impact. In this, of course, he shares the spotlight with other senior members of the government and with the prime minister, Bob Hawke. Hawke included in the frontbench of his government some of the brightest and best brains to have entered parliament for years. Fate also smiled on this new generation of Labor politicians by presenting them with a weak, divided and often ineffectual opposition.

History has yet to judge the long-term effects of the substantial reforms that the Hawke government engineered after it gained office in March 1983. What can be said is that the government acted with an enthusiasm and determination born of seven years of pent-up frustration in opposition, of watching and waiting to seize the chance to regain federal power, and of a dedication to pushing through structural changes that would remove anomalies in the social and economic systems to rejuvenate and invigorate the nation. It has been determined to show itself a government of sensible economic management as well as one of reform.

By the time Hawke led Labor to federal victory in March 1983 not only the faces of the Labor politicians had changed; Australia itself was a different nation from the one which had enthusiastically propelled the Whitlam government to power a decade earlier. 'Slaughter of the innocents' is a phrase that has been used to describe the events of November 1975—but in its political re-birth Labor was stronger, more mature and far less innocent. The party had proved itself a more sophisticated organisation than the opposition in 1983; it had capitalised on its electoral improvement in 1980, and used its newfound research strengths to conduct a well-managed and calculated campaign. And by 1983 Australians could see that the comfortable growth of the 1950s and 1960s had been snuffed out by changed circumstances domestically and overseas. High inflation, high interest rates and rising unemployment were the theme in this country which only recently had come to realise that its fate was also shaped by world events.

Bob Hawke and his team had little time to relax. Elation at the victory on Saturday 5 March was dampened on the following day by confirmation that the projected budget deficit for 1983/84, inherited from the Fraser government, was $9.6 billion—not the $6 billion that had been suggested a month earlier by John Howard, federal treasurer under the Fraser regime. On the Sunday after the election Stone gave the $9.6 billion deficit figure to Hawke and Keating. The outgoing Fraser government had presented Hawke with the most defensible of reasons to retract earlier promises and reshape policy to cope with this new situation.

On the same day Stone revealed to the new prime minister and treasurer the extent of the capital outflow that had taken place before the election. The outflow reflected the attitude of investors with holdings in Australian dollars—they were selling their $A assets and taking their money out of the country ahead of an expected devaluation of the currency; borrowers were repaying funds on loan from overseas and replacing them with domestic borrowings.

Stone's two items of news, the deficit and the capital outflow, presented the government with its first major challenges, less than 24 hours after the election. The new government acted swiftly on both counts. Hawke used the huge deficit figure to ditch the campaign package and make a new start. Keating says: 'The intention had been to give the place a bit of a fiscal kick-along and what we found was that it was getting a massive fiscal kick-along. So we cut the budget deficit back from a prospect of about $9.6 billion to $8.3 billion in our first year and even that gave the thing a big bang.'

The new government had not formally taken office when it had to deal with a currency crisis. The former cabinet was technically still in place. These were technicalities but created problems of protocol that could delay urgently-needed action. How best to deal with the situation was the subject of considerable discussion during the weekend of 5-6 March between the Reserve Bank and the government-designate. At that stage the central bank and the new treasurer were virtual strangers. Keating had had little to do with the Reserve Bank in the past; Hawke was more of a known quantity as he had been a member of the Reserve Bank board in the 1970s. Treasury was reluctant to approve a large one-off devaluation on the grounds that it would contradict the existing policy of a managed exchange rate. A large devaluation would also create a precedent which would feed speculation about a future disruptive diversion from policy. Hawke's advice from his department was in favour of a 5–10 per cent devaluation. The Reserve Bank was pushing for a 10 per cent reduction in the dollar.

Hawke and Keating initially agreed with Treasury secretary John Stone, whose advice was to monitor the markets closely to see if the capital outflow had stopped. All seemed quiet during early trading on Monday 7 March, but speculation was building by midday. In an evening phone call to the Reserve Bank governor, Bob Johnston, Keating learned that $200 million had left the country late in the trading day. Johnston repeated his advice to devalue by 10 per cent; Keating and Hawke conferred, and agreed. It was a courageous decision for a new government—but it was early days, and they could lay the blame for the instability on the outgoing regime. Hawke and Keating then enjoyed a post-election celebration dinner with senior staff and advisers, before knuckling down to the task of planning the economic summit.

The decision to devalue successfully reversed the earlier flight of funds. The cut in the value of the Australian dollar, taking it from 94.15 US cents to 85.49 US cents and reducing its trade-weighted index from 81.5 to 73.3, encouraged funds back into the country and allowed conditions in foreign exchange and money markets to settle. Almost $3 billion flowed back into the country in one week.

The Reserve Bank conducted a post-mortem, not just to assess the degree of speculation and profits made, but to examine the effectiveness of the system. The bank was concerned about the volatility that had occurred in interest rates. Hawke and Keating were also interested in an explanation of the swing in rates, of how interest rates and the exchange rate fitted together and of what could be done to prevent a repeat of the volatility. For the disruption to interest rates and to management of the domestic money supply had occurred despite exchange controls and despite a system where the exchange rate was managed. That this could happen was proof that the prevailing system was inadequate. That was the lesson of early March 1983, and it was not lost on treasurer Keating. The events of March, and those later in that year, were to show that a government cannot prevent a disruptive inflow or outflow of funds even while exercising exchange controls and managing the currency. More immediately, the events of March 1983 ensured that John Stone stayed as secretary of the Treasury, a development that was contrary to his expectations and those of the ALP.

Keating needed Stone in those early months. At that stage it was in both their interests to work together. Keating was acutely aware of his deficiencies, having been thrust into the shadow treasurer's, then treasurer's role with minimal warning and therefore little time for preparation. His public gaffe on a John Laws radio program on 24 February, during the election campaign, when he revealed his doubts about incomes policy, and an earlier, disappointingly bad, performance on 10 February at the launch of Labor's economic program, shook this hitherto confident politician. His nervousness in these first few months as treasurer was a rare chink in the armour of a polished professional. He had to learn and perform at the same time.

For this reason, continuity in advice seemed crucial. This could be provided by Stone and, from the opposite end of the political spectrum, by John Langmore, the economics adviser Keating had inherited from Ralph Willis. It was clear from the start that Keating and Langmore did not see eye to eye. Keating the sharp politician was becoming converted to market economics, whereas the thoughtful Langmore did not share Treasury's faith in the efficiency of markets. And the left-wing Langmore and right-wing Stone were like chalk and cheese. Langmore had worked for several years with Willis and had a big hand in drafting the Labor economic policy which was dumped the day after Labor's victory. The unceremonious scrapping of eight years' work left Langmore bitter and frustrated. Keating did not agree with the views of the man who told him he had 'waited all his life to be private secretary to a Labor treasurer'. Keating's reply was characteristically crushing: 'Well, John,' he said, 'you'll have to wait a bit longer.' Keating says at that time the only support system he had in the job was the Treasury and the Reserve Bank. 'I thought it important to have sitting with me as private secretary someone who clearly understood that system and was sympathetic to it, and could work to bring me closer to it and it closer to me.' Langmore left Keating's office in June 1983.

Much mythology has grown up around the Keating–Stone relationship in those first eighteen months of Labor government. The myths were fed by the well-known coolness of the ALP towards Stone, by Stone's opposition to a number of policies which Labor held dear, particularly those relating to wages, and by a media that continually mocked Keating, through articles and cartoons, as Stone's puppet. In fact, as Paul Kelly pointed out in *The Hawke Ascendancy*, the story was that the Treasury was working *for* the Labor party and not against it. Kelly wrote:

> It is true that Treasury remained sceptical about Labor and felt its ministers would probably lose their economic nerve in 1984, but . . . Treasury looked towards its new masters with more enthusiasm than past practice would suggest. There were three reasons for this. Treasury was utterly relieved to be rid of Howard, with whom its relations had collapsed; Stone relished his deliverance from execution; and Keating's direct and forceful personality was the right ingredient to combine with Stone and his senior officers . . .

Keating and Stone were not strangers—they had had time to observe each other in action over the years and while Stone knew full well that Keating was raw in the treasurer's job he was aware of his political skills. The reality is that the two men were good friends on a personal basis and in some ways even similar—they shared a sharpness, a conviction that what each wanted to do was right, and a sense of destiny. Tony Cole, who was on Keating's staff as principal private secretary from May 1983 to October 1985, recalls: 'Stone and Keating got on extremely well personally for a long time, and even after Stone left. Professionally they differed, increasingly so as time went on.' They differed over financial deregulation and wages policy, and these were two fundamental aspects of policy. They had more common ground in fiscal policy and differed only by degree in monetary policy. Keating, once convinced of its effectiveness, wanted to exploit the Accord and support it with firm monetary policy. Stone wanted to pretend the Accord did not exist and to substitute very tight monetary policy. And Stone was not convinced that the government could attack unemployment and inflation at the same time. The Hawke/Keating/ACTU approach was to have the Accord and use that to get inflation down, and at the same time run a policy that would allow the economy to grow more quickly.

In those early months, though, Keating turned to Stone and Treasury for the advice and knowledge that would further his understanding of the job. He was operating in the dark, and with a tiny staff. Barbara Ward says:

> Within the government there was the background that Keating was a bit insecure and not really on top of his portfolio—there's no denying that. So he took a very low profile, certainly publicly, for six months. And he took the attitude, which was a right attitude, I believe, that Treasury did know what was going on and he had to rely on his department. So he went in there with a different attitude to what a a lot of Labor treasurers had in the past. His view was that he had to rely on Treasury, that he had to work with them and he had to get them onside. And at that stage Stone was part and parcel of it. It was a conscious decision not to get rid of Stone. There was pressure [for that] within the Labor Party, but Keating had a big enough problem getting on with being treasurer without having to cope with the politics of getting rid of Stone as well.

In Ward's view Keating did with Stone what he does with everyone—he takes in all the information, although he does not necessarily agree. She says: 'There was no confrontation. Keating listened to what Stone said and then Stone might leave and Keating might say, "Look, I don't believe a word of that," or "What do you think?"—because he relied on his own advisers as well, quite a bit.'

There were, and are, plenty of critics to point to Keating's lack of training for the task, and to deride him for what they perceived to be an over-reliance on Treasury advice. Stone, they say, has always been a clever flatterer, and Keating, eager for encouragement, fell for that. Others dismiss suggestions of a *Yes Minister* scenario. Keating was soaking up information and knowledge wherever he could, and Stone was not the only person he frequently visited in Treasury. Keating was in a learning process and he has always learned by listening. So he listened to Stone, which would have made Stone feel secure. Keating was also building up a good relationship with the Reserve Bank, as an alternative source of advice, and one that was more in sympathy with concepts such as financial deregulation. Stone was antagonistic to much of the thrust of Labor policy. It is questionable how conducive that would be to Keating's learning process, but it would certainly have focused his mind on the search for answers.

Treasury people, whether they admire Keating or not, agree that he has a formidable capacity to soak up a brief. His critics in turn use this as ground to mount the argument that he espouses issues without thinking them through—'intellectually chaotic', said one detractor—and is too willing to seize on what appears a plausible argument without sufficient analysis or reflection. What such criticisms appear to miss is that Keating is first and foremost a politician. He might have been lauded on the world stage as an economist and financial wizard but that confuses his role, which as a politican is to take information, sift through it and make judgments about what technical advice to accept. That he understands what is put before him is an advantage—but his skills are the negotiating skills of a politician, an astute horse-trader who never gives anything away without getting something in return. Significantly, even his critics on the Left are reluctant to undermine him publicly because, politically and in the parliament, he is one of their party's best assets.

Tony Cole says: 'You can't be treasurer by rote, learning it up parrot-fashion. And that's been proved. Treasurers who didn't understand the arguments have failed.' And the argument that Keating had become a 'child of Treasury' does not hold water when it is remembered that he was increasingly running a line significantly different from that of Treasury in areas such as wages and financial deregulation. In other respects, such as tax reform, he has sometimes accepted Treasury's arguments and been put in the position of firing guns that were not properly primed, as occurred with the ill-conceived abolition, then re-instatement, of the exemptions to interest withholding tax, and the removal and reintroduction of negative gearing on property. However, Keating says his relationship with Treasury has been 'tip-top since day one. I think the sense of achievement which the Treasury has had and been able to share with me and this government—the big structural changes which many of them had been looking for for decades, and enormous changes on the tax side—generated huge *esprit de corps*.'

Years later, having had his hands 'on the levers', as he likes to say, Keating would probably prefer to forget it was ever different. But the early insecurity is a humanising streak in a political figure who is normally portrayed as black-and-white and hard. His staff recognised the anxiety. Tony Cole recalls:

> Every day in Question Time was a real challenge. He was always OK once he was into something. But when he was asked to speak for fifteen minutes and take questions for fifteen, he'd have us writing speeches that would last 25 minutes and leave no time for questions. He was so nervous, and it showed initially. It showed at the first Press Club luncheon speech, which was too long, and he anwered a question from the *Age's* political correspondent, Michelle Grattan, giving a reply that was nearly as long as the original speech. So there was only time for two more questions. That showed his lack of confidence.

Keating did not take long to overcome this. A year later, in June

1984, he was confident enough to take the floor and face an audience of the Economic Society, with no set speech but prepared to answer questions, which he did with great dexterity and style for more than an hour. Even in the early days he handled himself competently in discussions in the office and was clearly developing an understanding of the issues. Cole says: 'It got to the point where other than set addresses we didn't write any speeches at all. He'd talk about a theme, maybe three sub-ideas within a theme, he'd write the theme down on a tiny piece of paper, along with the three ideas and away he'd go. And these were definitely the best speeches he ever made.' As Susan Ryan says, Keating has blossomed in government. 'There are some who were very good in opposition and didn't blossom in government quite as much as expected, and there are some who do better than expected. In Paul's case power really suits him, he has performed in government even better than expected.' Jim McClelland takes a different view: 'Power has not done his character any good,' he says.'Keating needs reminding that he is capable of error and improvement. But he is a very gifted man and not many gifted men take politics on in this country.'

The first few months in government were packed with issues and events. In April Labor held its national economic summit conference in Canberra. At that meeting the government set out its aims of fighting both inflation and unemployment—a policy that was facilitated by the Prices and Incomes Accord that had been formed between the government and the trade unions and formally endorsed by the unions in February. The summit also gave birth to the Economic Planning Advisory Council (EPAC) which was to continue the process of consultation. Members of EPAC would be drawn from government, business, unions and community groups and would contribute to the formation of economic policy.

By May 1983 Tony Cole had joined Keating's staff and was handling the economic advisory work while Barbara Ward coped with the political issues and acted as press secretary until Tom Mockridge joined in 1984. Keating is always more comfortable with people he knows and feels he can trust, and is reluctant to forge new working relationships. Ward had handled the press work in opposition, though she was not a journalist or a press officer, but Keating knew that she understood what he thought and knew what to say and what not to say. 'As far as he was concerned it was easier to have me keep doing the job of press secretary,' says Ward.

> There was no ready candidate at that time and Keating really wasn't keen on getting a new person. He knew I'd say the right things, that

I wasn't going to stuff up. He didn't like the idea of getting in a new person who didn't understand him or how he thought, so he just fought it and fought it, and I fought it and fought it too, because it became almost a 22-hour day. He relied on me because he knew me; it wasn't because my economic knowledge was any better than anybody else's. But Keating is reluctant to take on someone new because he has to go through that awful process of getting to know them and it's almost as if that's too hard. I think he would've been happy if I had been his only staff member.'

In May 1983 Keating brought down his first mini-budget—or 'economic statement'. The new government was keen to strike early, make its mark by setting its own policies in train. The May statement rejected the earlier proposals for expansion that had formed much of Labor's election campaign; instead Keating opted to emphasise caution and a firm approach to monetary policy. To underscore this he announced a large commonwealth bond tender of $1.5 billion and forecast that the budget deficit for 1983/84 would be cut to around $8.5 billion. It was clear that the Hawke government was already taking the reaction of financial markets into account. The statement also introduced changes to superannuation payments that led to a new industry in rollover funds, new methods of marshalling savings. Lump-sum superannuation payments were to be taxed at 30 per cent instead of 5 per cent, ending the 'rort' which allowed tax deductions on superannuation contributions, then a lump-sum payout which was lightly taxed and could be converted into assets while the beneficiary drew an age pension.

Keating presented his first economic statement to a packed House of Representatives and crowded press gallery. He was heard in silence at first, but the interjections mounted as he read the tougher parts. Hawke smiled throughout the hour-long presentation of the statement that signalled the birth of Labor's economic rationalists.

In May of that year Keating also announced the formation of a group which would review the Australian financial system and the findings of the Campbell Committee. In opposition the ALP's formal stance had been hostility to the bulk of the Campbell Committee's recommendations, but within the party there were pockets of interest in what the report had to say. Keating was keen on the goal of improving the efficiency of the financial markets, which was a large part of the report's overall objective. Treasury was enthusiastic about the parts of the Campbell report that related to freeing up the domestic market, and had taken note of Keating's interest, over the years, in the financial system.

Establishing its own review group was a way for the Labor government to continue the deregulation process without appearing to adopt a report that had been commissioned by its Liberal predecessors. Keating, and others, had commented that the terms of reference of the Campbell committee, which talked of the government's 'free enterprise objectives', had virtually dictated the conclusions of the report. A fresh look was required, one that would take into account Labor's social and economic objectives—which, it could be argued, also circumscribed the outcome. And the report commissioned by the Hawke government was to be written in a style that was free of the economic jargon which had flavoured much of the Campbell report and which had encouraged animosity to its contents among ALP ranks. Further, the second report was to advise the government *how* to implement change.

The committee that was assembled to examine and assess the earlier report was known as the Martin Group, after its chairman Vic Martin, a man with a career in banking behind him and at that time chairman of the Mutual Life and Citizens Assurance Company Limited. A former chairman of the Australian Bankers' Association, Martin was regarded as someone who could be objective, who was free of political taint. His knowledge of the finance industry and capacity to think clearly appealed to both Keating and Stone. The committee included input from Treasury, the Reserve Bank and the academic world: Richard Beetham, a first assistant secretary from Treasury; the late Des Cleary, deputy chief manager of the Reserve Bank's international department, and professor Keith Hancock, an academic and economist, who was vice-chancellor of Flinders University and had good credentials in the eyes of Labor backbenchers and trade unionists.

At this time there were still nervous fears in financial circles that Labor might extend, rather than abolish, the regulations covering financial institutions. Substantial deregulation had been put in place by the previous government, but tough questions remained, such as the approval of new and foreign banks, whether the currency should float or continue to be managed by the monetary authorities, and whether concessional interest rates should be maintained for home finance and small business. The question of new banks—for which applications had been invited in January by the Liberal treasurer John Howard—was shelved by the Labor government, pending the outcome of the new review of the financial system.

Keating had made clear that the ALP did not accept all of the Campbell Committee's recommendations. Publicly he supported concessions to areas such as home finance and small business; he did not reveal himself as the fully-fledged deregulator he was later to become. His view was that the Campbell Report's suggestions merited further consideration, and he was adamant that the report should not be left to gather dust on a shelf.

There was a perception, in the Labor Party and in the business community, that the Martin Report would provide the tools with which the government could dismantle the Campbell recommendations. An alternative view was that the Martin Report could be used to put a Labor 'stamp' on deregulation—the government would not be seen to be implementing an opposition party's policies. The Campbell Report, with its wholehearted support of market forces, was anathema to Labor orthodoxy and headed in the opposite direction to the prevailing Labor platform. Keating recalls the report being presented to the opposition shadow cabinet: 'Bob Hawke and I were the only people who argued for foreign bank entry. And at the time we didn't carry the day. It became established policy to oppose it all.'

Some of the recommendations of the Campbell Report, such as floating the Australian dollar, had proved too challenging even for the Liberal government, which had spawned the report and fostered a climate for financial deregulation. But the process of deregulation had been set in motion—forces were already at work that were not easily reversed. Keating disagrees that Labor merely followed this momentum.

> You see, there is this line pushed by people from the opposition that the government had to carry on with the thrust of deregulation. When we came to office there was no thrust left. The whole point of the Martin Report was to get the Campbell debate back on the table. I appointed Vic Martin, without a cabinet decision, to freshen up the Campbell debate. Forgetting Campbell would have been the easiest thing we could ever have done.

Keating says he and Hawke took the view after the 10 per cent devaluation in March that the system of managing the exchange rate was finished. Discussions with the Reserve Bank followed, mapping out what Keating calls an inevitable road, a 'war strategy'. The exchange rate issue is a thread that runs through all of 1983, leading to the historic shift to a floating Australian dollar in December. But some water had to flow under the bridge before that eventuated.

By June 1983 the strains of the first six months as treasurer were beginning to show. Keating looked tired. At Hawke's suggestion he accompanied the prime minister on an overseas trip, giving him a chance to test himself on the world stage. And he found he could cope in debates with the giants of international politics and finance. That trip, apart from providing a break from the grind of Canberra, was a considerable boost to his confidence.

Refreshed and invigorated, Keating returned to Canberra to face the next item on the agenda, the annual budget in August. By this time he had abandoned his earlier practice of living in hotels in Canberra and had moved his family to the national capital. This allowed him more time with his wife and three young children. Keating is very much a family man, an attentive husband and doting father who disliked the weekly absences from his Sydney home demanded of a federal treasurer. He took the advice of others in politics—including the previous treasurer, John Howard—who had encouraged Keating to move his family to Canberra. The move made sense but, combined with the pressure of his portfolio, resulted in Keating spending less time in his Blaxland electorate, for which he has been roundly criticised. Keating's view is that he best represents his electorate by being in Canberra.

The budget of 1983 brought in a deficit of $8.3 billion, considerably lower than the $9.6 billion that had confronted the government in March. At the time the cuts to the deficit were much lauded, although not by some in the Left who believed that the economy would benefit more from an expansionary budget. In hindsight the 1983/84 budget has been judged as erring on the side of generosity. But the government did succeed in damage control—things could have been worse. And the budget showed Keating to be firmly on his feet as treasurer. In Barbara Ward's words: 'Once we got through the first six months we felt we knew what we were doing. The first six months were the hard part—the May statement, then the first budget. By the time the first budget was out of the way the Keating office was working pretty well in that we were all fairly confident that we knew what we were doing.'

Hard on the heels of the August budget came Keating's first trip to an annual meeting of the International Monetary Fund and World Bank, held that year in Washington. The 1983 IMF meeting was particularly attractive to Australians, providing a convincing reason to be in the US to coincide with the final races of the America's Cup at Newport. Keating, who enjoys travel, had planned an energetic itinerary which would take him from the US to Europe and London. The trip was to prove particularly demanding, and demonstrated his unusual ability to keep going when the mood takes him. Keating's reputation for endurance is widespread, although he is susceptible to colds and chest complaints. But when the adrenalin is pumping he can maintain a punishing pace. He believes he is lucky in having good resilience, in the sense that he can 'come back OK'. 'One good sleep and I'm very much repaired. But I need seven or eight hours—that's what I call a good sleep.'

Tony Cole observes a similarity between Keating and John Stone: 'They can go overseas, absolutely dead tired when they climb on the plane, fly for 22 hours to London or seventeen to Washington, and be still dead tired when they get off. But they can do a day's work and at the end of the day's work they can then go out, live it up, fresh as a daisy.' The 1983 excursion to the IMF backs up Cole's observation. The Australian delegation heard the news on the flight to the US that the Australian yachtsmen had a chance in the final races of the America's Cup. So from San Francisco they flew on to Newport instead of Washington. Accommodation had been arranged in a furnished apartment for an overnight stay in Newport. The following night, Keating and Cole flew to Washington. They had been at sea off Newport for hours and got to Washington about 8pm that Saturday. The next morning Keating faced a gruelling day that stretched from a 7am pre-meeting briefing to a 3am finish on the Monday, and included the Interim Committee meeting, one of the most important of the IMF session. Keating was representing not only Australia but also his constituency, so he had to study the views of New Zealand, Korea and the Philippines, plus all the agenda items. At the end of the night's business Stone pointed out that the Monday was free. Korea was representing the constituency at the Development Committee meeting so there was no need for the Australians to be in Washington.

'What do we do now, Treasurer?' queried Stone, to which Keating replied: 'Let's go to Newport.'

'That's the best decision you've made since you've had the job,' was Stone's comment.

Cole and one of the Treasury officers arranged an aircraft and they left for Newport after about two hours' sleep. The day that followed was long but exhilarating. Keating remembers it as a funny day. The Australians were scattered among different boats—Peta Furnell, a staffer in Keating's office, and Tony Cole were on one boat, Stone and Bob Johnston (governor of the Reserve Bank of Australia) were on another and the treasurer was on another with Australia's ambassador to the US, Sir Robert Cotton. Stone was a dashing figure in navy blazer and commodore's cap.

At the end of the day Alan Bond's yacht had won and it was Tony Cole's task to round up the party to fly back to Washington. Stone, a beer container full of champagne in his hand, was insisting:

'There's no way we're leaving tonight; we must participate in the celebrations.' Ambassador Cotton and Bob Johnston left, taking Peta Furnell with them, back to the plane and back to Washington. Cole was instructed to 'stay and look after Stone and Keating'. He remembers arranging overnight accommodation in a friend's rented house.

> In the meantime the champagne was flowing. We went on to Bondy's party later. Stone didn't want to leave but we dragged him away. Keating was ready to go. We still had no way of getting back to Washington and we had to be there the next day, for the president's address and the formal opening of the IMF/World Bank meeting, which we'd come halfway round the world to attend.

The group made it back to the house by midnight. For Keating and Stone, it was time for bed. For Tony Cole, it was back to the phone to find a flight to Washington. He secured a booking on a flight that left the nearest airport at 7am—but the nearest airport was an hour's drive, so a hire car was called for 5.30am. Stone snored, deafeningly, until dawn. The trio had no change of clothes and slept in their underwear. Next morning it was back to Washington. Keating worked through that day and slept until the following noon.

The next stop after the IMF meeting was New York, where Keating was to talk to finance houses and make public speeches. Then the Australians headed to Paris, arriving at 9am after an overnight flight. A baggage mix-up meant that Keating reached the hotel with the wrong suitcase. He was slightly irritable—not because he wanted his pyjamas to go to bed, but because he wanted a change of clothing to go out and do the rounds of the antique shops.

Keating is not especially robust, which makes the marathon so impressive. Friends and colleagues agree that, like many Canberra politicians, if he catches a cold it knocks him out, simply because he is constantly living on the edge. 'It's brinkmanship with his health all the time,' says Cole. 'He's always on the brink of exhaustion and that's the way he runs his life. He works hard and enjoys himself hard.'

8 Hero of the markets

We can change the financial system in a way which the so-called businessmen's party never could, or never had the guts to do.

PAUL KEATING

KEATING RETURNED from the IMF and Europe in October 1983 and was plunged into one of the toughest and most controversial decisions the Hawke government was ever to face: whether, or rather when, to float the Australian dollar. The magnitude of this move cannot be underestimated. In one stroke, floating the dollar thrust Australia on to the world economic stage. The float is arguably the boldest but least-understood action taken by the government. It has been misinterpreted, and criticised, as merely a move to woo the business sector, a further embrace in what the Left perceives as the government's 'love-affair with the financial markets'.

Keating scoffs at the notion that the float was introduced to appease business. 'Many in mainstream business were horrified,' he says. 'They would come up to me and say, "Do you know what you've *done*?" ' In his view many people have not thought through the linkages. Bill Kelty, secretary of the ACTU, points out that the contribution is not merely the float in itself but that in floating the dollar Keating forced the nation to face up to the fact that it lives in an international environment. In reality, the float put an end to the easy profits being made by foreign exchange speculators, expanded the role of financial markets and gave the government far greater control over domestic monetary policy. It has been argued that in achieving this control, too much has been lost, that the instability in exchange rates is too high a price to pay for greater domestic control. In a perfect world there would be no instability in any area—but short of that ideal, instability has to show up somewhere and high prices were paid in the past, when the exchange rate was managed, and interest rates had to absorb big swings.

Volatility in exchange rates has been a contentious issue over the past couple of years as central banks have sought to maintain a balance among the key currencies of the world. But what was clear in 1983 was that the exchange rate policy then existing in Australia was not adequate. An alternative had to be found. Keating's interest in the concept of floating the exchange rate had been awakened in March by the speculation on the dollar, the outflow of funds and the subsequent debate about whether, and if so by how much, to devalue the Australian dollar. The Reserve Bank had for several years been studying the implications of a floating exchange rate and had been gradually modifying the system. By 1983 the central bank also had a change of governor. Bob Johnston's predecessor, Sir Harold Knight, had been no devotee of a float, in contrast to the more market-oriented Johnston. The Reserve Bank had come to the view that of the options available, and given the worldwide shift in that direction, a floating exchange rate provided the best solution. Within Treasury, opinions differed. The Fraser government had shied away from as radical a step as floating the dollar, though the move had been recommended by the Campbell Committee.

The background to the float can be traced to the 1970s, and to the quest throughout the world, as well as in Australia, for an appropriate method of managing the exchange rate. During the 1970s several nations had experimented with different methods of exchange-rate management. In some cases they had chosen to allow their currencies to float—that is, to allow the rate to be determined by the market forces of supply and demand, with minimal intervention by central banks and the minimum of exchange controls. Some smaller economies had chosen to tie their currencies to a major world currency, such as the $US. Australia had tried a succession of systems, first tying its currency to sterling, then to the $US, then to a basket of currencies. In 1976 the fixed link to a basket was replaced with a variable link known as a 'flexible peg'. Under this system the $A was valued against a trade-weighted basket of currencies and its daily value was expressed as a mid-rate in terms of the $US.

The exchange rate was a source of trouble during most of 1983. Keating had been confronted by a currency crisis immediately on becoming treasurer. The short-term solution had been the 10 per cent devaluation of the Australian dollar, but it was inevitable that speculative pressure would mount again. The search for the best method of managing the exchange rate—not a new problem, nor one that was unique to Australia—continued throughout 1983.

The rationale behind the move to floating exchange rates was that governments were no better equipped than markets to determine the appropriate level for a currency. The Australian monetary authorities—the Reserve Bank, Treasury and government—were managing the exchange rate but interest rates were determined in the market. And foreign exchange market operators had become skilled at anticipating movements in the exchange rate; successful speculation on the level of the Australian dollar produced fat profit at the expense of the Reserve Bank, that is, the Australian taxpayer.

Throughout the world in the late 1970s and early 1980s the mood was shifting in favour of financial deregulation, rather than government control of interest rates and exchange rates. By the time the Hawke government came to office Australia had moved some way down the path of financial deregulation, the previous government having lifted controls from several key interest rates, such as bank deposits and commonwealth government securities. But the change could not stop there; the combination of market-determined interest rates and a managed exchange rate created an uncomfortable imbalance in monetary management. Added to this was the increased internationalisation of Australia's banks and merchant banks, whose widespread overseas links allow them, and their corporate clients, to move funds fairly easily in and out of the country.

Responsibility for managing the exchange rate rested with a committee of four: the governor of the Reserve Bank, the secretary of the Treasury, the secretary of the Department of Prime Minister and Cabinet, and the secretary of the Department of Finance. Only trading banks were allowed to deal in foreign currencies, at rates indicated by the Reserve Bank, and the banks had to settle any surplus or shortfall with the Reserve Bank at the end of each working day. This latter rule—that foreign currencies had to be converted back into Australian dollars—was a crucial ingredient in the arguments supporting the shift to a float and the removal of exchange controls. At its simplest, it meant that an inflow of foreign funds became an inflow of Australian dollars, added to domestic money supply, and, left to itself, could be inflationary and push interest rates down; conversely, an outflow was a reduction in the supply of domestic dollars, tightening money supply, and possibly causing interest rates to rise. The events of 1983 demonstrated the destabilising effects of inflow and outflow of capital under this system.

Money steadily poured into Australia through the second half of 1983. It had become clear to the new government that the existing system of managing the exchange rate was inadequate. The question was how best to make a switch, and when. The Reserve Bank, which since the late 1970s had been issuing copious discussion papers supporting the move to a floating exchange rate, gave the new federal treasurer its 'war book' or strategy on how to free the exchange rate.

The central bank saw a great deal of Keating during his first year in office. They had got off on the right foot, having been of one mind on the earlier decision to devalue the currency to overcome the crisis in March. In working towards a floating currency, though, the treasurer and the Reserve Bank were working against the advice and convictions of Treasury secretary John Stone. Within Treasury there were conflicting views on the subject, but to its secretary the exchange rate was too important an economic weapon to be left to the market. (He also knew that floating the $A would give more power to the Reserve Bank, which would execute the system, and less to Treasury.) Stone was a free markets man except in the international arena—he did not trust the rest of the world. There was a touch of *Fortress Australia* about Stone. He believed a small country such as Australia could be vulnerable when pitched against the larger players in the world markets. And his preoccupation with fighting the bogey of inflation meant that he rarely supported a downward move in the exchange rate but argued for a high Australian dollar. There were times when Keating's best friends seemed to be in the Reserve Bank.

Exchange rate management was under discussion constantly between April and October 1983 as money continued to flow into the country. Keating was by then seeing the value of a floating currency. Such a system would take the exchange rate off the government's plate in the same way that the earlier relaxation of interest controls had taken the political heat out of that area. It seemed advisable, though, to try for a new system in stages. These intermediate steps came in the form of some 'technical adjustments' to the prevailing system. The changes were announced on Friday 28 October by prime minister Hawke during a speech to the annual dinner of the Australian Merchant Bankers Association, held that year in Melbourne. The prime minister said:

> These changes, though largely technical, should assist in moderating the volatility of day-to-day flows of funds across the foreign exchanges. This volatility has, of course, complicated the task of managing the growth of the monetary aggregates in Australia in line with the objectives announced in the treasurer's budget speech . . . such modifications and adaptations, helpful as they are, should not blind us to the fact that, in the end, the value of the Australian dollar and the flows of funds across the exchanges, will not be determined by the particular system being pursued . . . the final determining factor will be the relative performance of the Australian economy.

The changes were put into effect on Monday 31 October. Under the new system the mid-rate for the $A in terms of the $US was to be announced at the end of the trading day, instead of at 9.30am, and the Reserve Bank's role in the foreign exchange market was reduced. The net effect was to give the trading banks greater scope to negotiate rates with their customers and greater flexibility in managing their foreign exchange positions. The public justification for the changed rules was that they would reduce speculation throughout the Australian and Asian trading day. In reality, the ground was being carefully prepared for the eventual abolition of controls over the exchange rate. Hawke and Keating and the Reserve Bank had made up their minds about floating the dollar. Now they were giving Treasury a chance to catch up. The Reserve Bank was not convinced that the changes would bring better results but felt the testing had to be done. A period of calm did ensue, as tended to happen after a minor change, but this proved short-lived.

The following month provided a turning point. The authorities had freed up the forward (future) market but kept a hold on the spot rate (the rate that prevails each day for a currency). The new system had cooled currency speculation during the Australian day, although it continued overnight. The banks were freer to manage their own positions on currency movements. The Australian dollar began to be traded around the clock, with positions shifted from Australia to Asia then on to Europe and London, then to New York and the US west coast. Trading followed the sun, facilitated as much as by technology and the international banking networks as by the new leeway granted in Australia.

There was a growing expectation that the Australian dollar was headed for a revaluation, a notion that was translated into heavy capital inflow as investors sought an asset that was expected to rise in value. The Australian authorities fiddled with the exchange rate in an attempt to offset this tide but were unsuccessful and the inflow continued. In the week to Friday 9 December 1983 some $300 million flooded into Australia and more was booked for the following week. In that week it became clear that action would have to be taken. The options were to sit out the present situation, shift the exchange rate, introduce capital controls—or to bite the bullet and let the market find its own level. Talks were held through the week by the Reserve Bank, the treasurer and Treasury. The problem was continuing and its dimensions getting bigger. The choice would be either to revalue or float.

On the evening of Thursday 8 December the Reserve Bank had word from its New York office that a substantial amount of money would be arriving in Australia the following day. The Reserve Bank began a round of telephone discussions with the prime minister and treasurer in Canberra. Both were tied up in meetings and hard to find. It was the last night of the parliamentary session, when members and their staff traditionally party on. The prime minister was due at an evening engagement, but Keating talked the matter over with the central bank. By 7pm it seemed they had no choice but to tough it out on Friday. The possibility of closing the market was discussed, but rejected as there would be little point in such a move if the market re-opened with the same system the following Monday. The pent-up demand would be hugely disruptive.

Towards midnight the Reserve Bank governor was contacted by the bank's New York office again—the situation seemed to be worse than earlier thought. It was the reversal of March 1983, but magnified. The amount of money due to flood in would destroy monetary policy, fuelling speculation about the dollar, swamping the system with cash and pushing down interest rates. The system at that time, even with the recent refinements, left the central bank with little opportunity to neutralise the inflow. By now it was not a question of a preferred option. A float had become inevitable. The big question by midnight on Thursday 8 December was whether it would be possible to get a decision. The Reserve Bank was persuaded the float was the right move. Keating and Hawke were also convinced. But Treasury, particularly John Stone, was opposed to the move. And the government had to consider the popularity or otherwise of the float from a political point of view. By midnight it seemed unlikely that any more could be done. The Reserve Bank staff who were still at their posts were told to go home.

They did not rest for long. At 1.30am the governor rang his financial markets adviser, John Phillips, to say that talks had resumed with Canberra and it had been decided, in the light of the latest news from New York, to try for a move the next day. Keating wanted Bob

Johnston and Phillips in Canberra on the first plane. Staff were contacted to make preparations, not least to organise the announcement to the banks that the foreign exchange market was to be closed on Friday, and to tell overseas offices. Thursday's work ended around 3am on Friday. There was little sleep that night for the Reserve Bank officials who were booked on the 6.50am flight to Canberra.

The government, the Reserve Bank and Treasury needed to buy time to review the situation. Hence they had taken the unusual step of suspending the banks' trading in foreign currencies. Foreign exchange operators arriving at their desks on the morning of Friday 9 December found the following message from the Reserve Bank:

> The Reserve Bank has announced that dealing in foreign currencies by Australian banks has been suspended for the time being. Banks' authorities to deal in foreign currencies have been withdrawn except that they may at their discretion meet the needs of *bona fide* travellers for essential travel needs.

The banks could issue travellers cheques but they could not trade on the wholesale foreign exchange market. Operators were stunned. No such step had been taken since the chaotic foreign exchange conditions of the early 1970s; most traders were too young to remember that period and were encountering, for them, an unprecedented situation. The market grapevine buzzed with rumours all day.

While the traders gossiped and speculated about what next might occur, the decision-makers had gathered in Canberra to discuss their strategy. Peter Walsh, as minister of finance, had to fly to Sydney on a few hours' notice and deliver a speech in Keating's place. Senior Reserve Bank officials—governor Bob Johnston, deputy governor Don Sanders, and John Phillips, met first with Keating and treasury officials; a second series of meetings followed, which involved the prime minister and his advisers. Long conferences ensued as strategies evolved. The participants had to decide what to put to cabinet's economic and monetary policy committee; they had to write cabinet submissions and have them circulated. Due process demands that cabinet papers be distributed to members ten days ahead of a cabinet meeting. Stone, who disapproved of the proposal to float the currency only fractionally less than he disapproved of the removal of exchange controls, also frowned on the short-cuts taken to push decisions through. He retreated back to Treasury.

Papers for cabinet were written, largely based on the Reserve Bank's 'war book' on the float, which had spelled out the main arguments. The chief focus was the float of the dollar, but exchange controls had to be covered, too; should they be removed? The bank's view was that a float worked best without exchange controls. To the Reserve Bank it seemed incongrous to free the dollar and leave exchange controls—to constrict the market in one way yet expect it to set the $A rate. With a government willing to achieve as much as possible it seemed best to seize the chance and remove a set of rules which had proved ineffectual when they were most needed. The discussion papers also set out the regulations that would be kept in place to ensure adequate tax-screening of foreign exchange flows.

The decisions were put to cabinet, which having lived through the earlier changes to the exchange rate, was familiar with the problems. There was no time, in the course of that day, to put the complex issues to caucus. A press conference was called for 5pm. Keating asked governor Johnston to accompany him to the press conference; the Reserve Bank was to have a crucial role in the execution of the new system and it seemed appropriate for the governor to be present to answer technical questions. Stone did not sit with his treasurer, a point not missed by the media. Keating announced that the historic decision had been taken to float the Australian dollar and remove most of the existing exchange controls. He said:

> Last night the government decided to ask the Reserve Bank to suspend dealings by trading banks in foreign exchange except for *bona fide* travellers and other small personal transactions. This action became necessary because of the continued high level of speculative capital inflow and advice that the inflow was expected to intensify. On 28 October the prime minister and I announced certain adjustments to the exchange rate management system. These were designed to deal with the problem of intra-day speculation and were generally in the direction of a more market-oriented system, particularly for forward transactions where the rate was allowed to float. The government also had in mind that those changes would give the banks and other market participants useful experience in operating in a less regulated environment.
>
> The government has now decided to take these changes significantly further by allowing the spot market, as well as the forward market, to float. The government has also decided to abolish a major part of the existing exchange controls. This means that the Reserve Bank will no longer announce a trade-weighted index or indicative exchange rates for the $A and the $US. Nor will the banks be required to settle their foreign exchange positions at the end of each day. In future exchange rates will be determined by the market. These reforms of the exchange rate management

> system will also assist the conduct of the government's monetary policy . . . The new exchange rate system should mean that external transactions are no longer a major aberrant factor in determining monetary growth.

Newspaper headlines were effusive: 'Labor's historic switch', said the *Sydney Morning Herald*, and 'A brave new world', trumpeted the *Australian Financial Review*. The new system was to take effect on Monday 12 December. The political process was over but for the Reserve Bank the hard work had just begun. Reserve Bank staff in the exchange control department had been asked to wait back on the Friday evening. The Reserve Bank chiefs flew back to Sydney on the 7pm flight from Canberra and headed for the bank to map out what had to be done next. They had shared the flight with the former Liberal treasurer, John Howard, the man who had commissioned the Campbell Report which had advocated, among other deregulatory moves, a floating dollar. They recall that he was complimentary about the day's achievements.

Work at the bank continued until 3am on Saturday, setting the tone for an unusually active weekend at the central bank's headquarters at 65 Martin Place in Sydney, where senior Reserve Bankers were busy compiling press releases and briefing bankers and foreign exchange operators in the currency hedge market about life with a floating exchange rate. International organisations such as the International Monetary Fund had to be informed of the changes, as did other central banks and overseas branches of the Reserve Bank. Exemptions and amendments to exchange control regulations had to be written. The Reserve Bank had to ensure its own operating systems were ready for business on Monday. The few remaining exchange controls that had been left related to transactions with tax havens and tax-screening, and the central bank had to spell out the traders' responsibilities under these arrangements. It was a big exercise. Some staff slept on the premises.

Operating with a floating exchange rate and without exchange controls imposes a new discipline on government because any deficiencies in its policies—or inherited problems—show up negatively in the exchange rate. With a fixed or managed exchange rate a government can better conceal its warts. As Bob Johnston says:

> Commentators may be wringing their hands but it's a better economy for it. A floating exchange rate can deliver harsh judgments. We're not sweeping the bad bits under the carpet. There is always the possibility of mistaking the messenger for the

> message—blaming the exchange rate for what really are faults in the economy—but the exchange rate will certainly tell you if things are out of kilter. We used to be good at fudging and disguising, hiding and patching. But the market wins in the end.

Johnston recalls defending exchange controls to Milton Friedman, the father of monetarism. Friedman, on a visit to Australia in 1975, was vigorously attacking the use of exchange controls. 'Well, we do use them in a very benign way,' said Johnston defensively, to which Friedman retorted: 'That's the worst thing you can do. You should operate them to the letter. That way their stupidity would be apparent to everybody. People like you make things worse, that gets us in the mess we're in.' There was a lot in what Friedman said, comments Johnston. Keating also talks of the discipline imposed on government by a floating exchange rate:

> One of the things is that the born-to-rule brigade—the coalition—have never lived with the discipline of a floating exchange rate. They think their mere presence will affect how the world markets treat them. It won't matter a tinker's curse. The kind of discipline this government's faced up to would be something I think, certainly in their current state, they'd be totally incapable of facing. The float is the decision where Australia truly made its debut into the world—said, 'OK, we're now an international citizen.'

Keating adds that before the float it was impossible to run a monetary policy.

> We had additions to primary liquidity from the inflow under a managed system and that meant a whole lot of bond sales, friction, higher interest rates. We thought about all that stuff . . . we did know that at one time or another, the $A would fall to find its competitiveness and that would put the pressure on the government and the ACTU and wages, and on fiscal policy and everything else. The only thing we didn't bargain on was the terms of trade collapse at the same time.

The changes introduced in December 1983 initiated an era in which movements in the Australian dollar often become front-page news. The general public now has a barometer with which to measure the government's success or failure; the verdict of international markets and local foreign exchange traders is clearly seen in the exchange rate. This gives a powerful weapon to foreign exchange markets, whom Keating was later to castigate as 'foreign exchange cowboys'. John Phillips, as deputy governor of the Reserve Bank, has described the foreign exchange market as 'a highly strung piece of equipment, prone to react suddenly, sometimes violently, to changes in news, fundamental or otherwise'. It is easy to forget that a fixed or managed exchange rate did not quell uncertainties. And the lesson of 1983 was that it is not possible, in the long run, to hold an exchange rate away from what the market perceives to be its level.

The decision to float the Australian dollar and abandon exchange controls pre-empted the findings of the Martin Review Group, due to deliver its report to the government early in 1984. It also contributed to the widening gap between the policies of the Hawke–Keating government and the beliefs long-cherished by John Stone. And it was contrary to the policies of the Labor Party.

Keating had succeeded in pushing through an economic accomplishment that had eluded his Liberal predecessor, John Howard, in the Fraser cabinet. He had travelled further along the path to internationalisation of the Australian economy than the Fraser government had dared to go. In doing so, he had demonstrated that the Hawke Labor government was ideologically independent, carving its own image and not hamstrung by the past—a stance that was to exacerbate the bitter divisions in the party. He had also demonstrated that he was calling the economic shots. It was less than a year since Keating had been propelled into the treasurer's job, and only a matter of months since he had been taunted as 'Stone's puppet'. He had come a long way.

The Hawke government's first year in office, a year of achievment and euphoria, was garlanded by a Christmas boom in retail sales. For Keating, the momentum of late 1983 was continued into 1984, a year that would see continued economic growth, a further cut in the deficit, his triumph on the question of new banks and further deregulatory moves. The year also won him international status when, in October 1984, the influential magazine *Euromoney* named him Finance Minister of the Year.

At the beginning of 1984, Keating was still defending the float of the dollar and explaining Labor's plans to reduce inflation, lift employment, free up the financial system and get the country on its feet. The question of foreign bank entry to Australia hung in the air. In a radio interview on Melbourne's 3DB in January 1984, the former federal treasurer, John Howard, challenged Keating: 'Paul, it's a plank of Labor to oppose the entry of foreign banks.' Keating replied: 'While it may have been OK for Mr Chifley to oppose foreign banks in the '40s, we are entitled to review that. I don't think we've had a banking system which gave Australian commerce a competitive edge.' He took a similar line in defence of floating the dollar, telling the *National Times* in February 1984: 'Policy can't stay static, because the world doesn't remain static. And the world isn't going to stand still at any given time until the next Labor Party national conference.' And he explained the Hawke government's espousing of financial deregulation:

> For too long there's been a view in the Labor Party that what we've got to do out there in the community is control everything. In fact, all the regulations we've had for years, say, in the banking area, have produced nothing except a great clutch of merchant banks and building societies. People have simply stepped around controls . . . We have to take the broad view. Government control of economic policy and of the financial system has done what, particularly over the past decade? Only given us a miserable growth rate, one which is not creating enough jobs . . . What we have to say is that we have to get the private sector in with the government to have, as far as possible, parallel objectives. It requires a bit of bigness on our part, and I think Bob Hawke has that bigness in him.

Keating went on to assert that the Labor party was poised to change the face of the Australian financial system. 'We can change the financial system in a way which the so-called businessmen's party never could, or never had the guts to do. What is involved is immensely significant for Australia and for our party. There are going to be changes, and I believe they'll be far-reaching changes. And I'm delighted that I'll be presiding over them.'

The Labor government's manifesto for financial reform, the Report of the Martin Review Group, was released on 22 February 1984. The Martin Report endorsed many of the findings of the Campbell Report, including the suggestion of expanding the Australian banking system. Both reports demonstrated how many controls had the effect of limiting competition and efficiency without providing economic or social benefits. As Richard Beetham, Treasury's representative on the review group, later said: 'The difficult task of converting such conclusions into positive action was largely due, however, to the personal and political skills of Paul Keating.'

By May 1984 Keating's reputation as the man at the helm of economic debate and policy was well established. And he was gearing up for what was being touted as the crunch issue at that year's ALP national conference: the question of foreign bank entry. He was drafting and redrafting his proposals. Many watchers claimed he was rewriting the party platform to accommodate government policy. For months he had been arguing in caucus in support of more banks, driving home the view that it was ridiculous that a Labor government should throw its weight behind the monopoly position of the existing handful of trading banks.

The Australian banks, mindful of looming competition, had been preparing their own ground in anticipation of an expanded system. One sign of this had been the mergers in 1981, when the Bank of NSW and the Commercial Bank of Australia merged to form Westpac Banking Corporation, and the National Bank of Australasia teamed with the Commercial Banking Company of Sydney to produce the National Australia Bank. This left Australia with four major nationally-operating trading banks—the two amalgamated groups plus the Commonwealth Bank and the ANZ Banking Group. The state banks at that time operated only in their home states and neither of the two existing foreign banks, the Bank of New Zealand and Banque Nationale de Paris, provided an extensive branch network. Australia's youngest bank, the Australian Bank, established in 1981, likewise operated with only a small number of branches.

Keating argued that the controls on the number and operations of licensed banks had fed the growth of non-bank financial institutions, such as merchant banks, building societies and finance companies, all of which carried out quasi-banking functions and many of which provided 'unofficial' access to Australia for international banks. And he was laying the ground for a more flexible attitude to the number of new banks, and on the level of foreign ownership that might be allowed. Would the government go further than suggested by the Martin Report and allow more than 50 per cent foreign equity in a new bank? Keating's response to this question, as reported in the 20 June 1984 issue of *Australian Business*, contained a hint of increasing flexibility:

> What we'll have to consider is a trade-off between earlier and more robust competition against the control and investment questions that are part and parcel of our foreign investment policy. It'll be a trade between our national economic interest, if you like, and the interests of injecting more competition into the banking system.

Debate about the question of when and how to allow more banks into the country was heating up at the same time as the government was working out its strategy for its second budget. Keating was fending off demands from government ministers who wanted a more expansionary budget than had been planned. In this Keating was again at odds with Ralph Willis, the minister for employment and industrial relations, who had pushed for a more generous budget the previous year and, in company with Tom Uren, minister for the territories, and Brian Howe, the defence support minister, urged an expansionary budget for 1984/85. Willis was concerned that Keating's strategy would lead to the economy contracting. He was not convinced that the private sector recovery on which Keating was relying would be achieved by restraining the public sector. In hindsight, Willis was wrong. The 1984/85 budget, and its predecessor, were judged as being too expansionary. The main achievement in 1983/84 was in preventing a threatening situation—the huge potential deficit they inherited—from becoming a reality.

Keating got his way. Everything seemed on track for a budget deficit of $6.7 billion. Then, on Wednesday 15 August, six days before budget night, a sensation occurred that diverted attention from the annual financial event: Treasury secretary John Stone submitted his resignation. Commentators leapt to speculate about Stone's decision—was he signalling his disapproval of the forthcoming budget? But it was no secret that Stone had disapproved of most of the budgets of the previous decade. More lay behind his move. In fact, the split between Keating and Stone had been growing for some months. Those who had been observing the relationship were not surprised that it had fallen apart. The final clash of two strong personalities had been inevitable, though Keating was reputed to have made more of an attempt to put the past aside, to make an ally of the former adversary. Stone was frustrated. Accustomed to being the dominant force, he had lost on key issues, such as the dollar float and the dismantling of exchange controls. And Keating no longer needed Stone as he had once done. He had grown into his job.

Two specific episodes added fuel to the fire. Stone had objected to Keating's move earlier that year to appoint Dr Barry Hughes, his private economics adviser, to the National Income Forecasting Committee, which Stone saw as the preserve of Treasury, the Department of Finance and the Reserve Bank. But Keating insisted that he would have his own person on the committee. On an earlier occasion his office had successfully challenged a Treasury forecast so there seemed a good case for having some presence on the committee. He and Stone clashed over this. Neither would back down, so in March 1984 Keating abolished the committee. Its role was carried out by the Joint Economic Forecasting Group, which included Hughes. The second episode concerned the budget and comments, critical of wages policy, that Stone wanted included and Keating did not. Stone demanded an 'on-record direction' to clear the matter.

The Treasury secretary was increasingly becoming distracted by non-economic issues, such as the Freedom of Information Act and the public service reforms. Barbara Ward recalls:

> Relations had started to strain not just because of a particular issue but over a general attitude of Stone's. He always had bees in his bonnet but they started to come through really strongly. And he'd ring Paul up about them—it was much broader than the Treasury role. And Paul had started to alienate Stone, a bit, not for any particular reason, just that he found it was better to go to the source of the information in the department and he'd built up quite good relations with the various deputy secretaries and the first assistant secretaries. Once he got to know them he found it was just as easy to ring them—and I think that got under Stone's skin.

By the time of the second budget Keating knew he was not relying on Stone as much as in his earlier days. The new treasurer had won his spurs with his first budget, and had proved with the floating of the dollar that he was his own man. And a change was also becoming apparent within Treasury. First assistant secretaries were daring to disagree with their boss. Stone was encountering opposition from his own ranks for the first time. Ward says: 'You could tell there was a lot of dissension within Treasury. When we first had a meeting with senior Treasury officers no-one ever disagreed with Stone when he spoke, no matter what their views. But it got to the stage where an FAS [first assistant secretary] would directly disagree with Stone.'

Stone had a chance to be vocal about the 1984 budget when he gave the Shann Memorial Lecture at the University of Western Australia on 27 August 1984. He had already resigned as secretary of the Treasury and seized the chance to speak his mind. He warned of Australia's mounting debt, attacked the budget and praised the decision to float the Australian dollar. He strongly criticised the 'over-regulated' labour market and argued for a decentralised wage fixation system and rejected full wage indexation. He delivered a colourful warning to leading companies which supported government policies, reminding them of the fate of 'the good-hearted and well-meaning animals [in George Orwell's *Animal Farm*] which, in a spirit of trust and, one might even say consensus, allowed the pigs under their charismatic leader, Napoleon, to lead them forward through their "advisory councils" and the like to their ultimately bitter end.'

A number of factors clearly contributed to Stone's decision to leave. The budget may well have been the last straw (Stone later described it as Keating's first serious mistake) but disenchantment with his role had been fed by other developments, particularly the Accord, which he viewed as an albatross around Australia's neck.

And Stone had turned 55; he could retire from the public service with full pension entitlements and pursue other interests he enjoyed. He could give rein to the politician, and the frustrated journalist and commentator, that had been imprisoned in the highly disciplined public servant. He and Keating parted amicably; Stone announced his departure to his minister over a bottle of French champagne which they shared in Keating's office.

Keating believes Stone had reached the time of his life when he did not want to serve anybody, any government. 'His own views were becoming more and more strident. And I think he decided to do the only thing he really could do and that was leave.' Stone's departure raised the question of a successor. The deputy secretary, Des Moore, seemed an unlikely candidate to step into Stone's shoes. Relations between Moore and Keating were not warm; their views differed on virtually every aspect of policy. Other choices were Bernie Fraser, who had been persuaded earlier in the year to return to Treasury from the Department of Resources and Energy, and Dr Chris Higgins, a Treasury official who had been in Paris with the OECD.

Keating's choice of Bernie Fraser has been interpreted as another sign that the treasurer prefers the known to the unknown. Keating spent time with both men: Higgins the intellectual and academic, Fraser the self-made man, interested in horses, keen on football, a man of the people who could be a cool performer. Ward says that Keating found Fraser's attitudes more in line with his own. Keating says:

> Bernie Fraser's style, which is a much less formal style than his predecessor's, has allowed Treasury to get out of the intellectual straitjacket that it was in. I'm sure there's a lot more discussion and open-mindedness about the way issues are being confronted. The Treasury is probably seeing its most effective days.

Treasury now feels more relevant, though an old hand like Stone would probably snort that that's not the issue: what is important is the quality of advice Treasury gives the minister. Stone was a firm believer in confronting his minister—he did not dodge an issue just because it would upset someone. He believed it was important to stand up to Keating; he recognised Keating as someone who respects people who fight him vigorously. It takes one to know one.

Treasury officials are working with a minister they recognise as someone quick-minded who puts a great deal of effort into making sure he understands the issues, in his own terms. In their view it is more important for a treasurer to be a good politician than a good economist. They know Keating as someone who will not accept material he does not understand, who will spot something that does not ring true and who, having grasped an issue, holds firmly fixed views. And that, they say, is when he gets into trouble and pushes lines too hard. But they are happy to work with a minister whom they regularly see and talk with—a contrast to the earlier days when treasurers did not dare to set foot in Treasury alone, without a minder.

By mid-1984 more progress had been made in financial deregulation. In June Keating had announced that 40 non-bank financial institutions had been given authority to deal in foreign exchange, a move that was made to counteract criticism that the foreign exchange market, in which only trading banks could deal, suffered from a lack of competition. On 1 August the maturity controls were removed from bank deposits. The so-called 'fourteen-day rule' was lifted, allowing banks to pay interest on funds taken for less than fourteen days, even for funds taken overnight, and to pay interest on cheque accounts. At the same time Keating announced a moratorium on existing foreign investment guidelines that applied to foreign ownership of merchant banks, so that shareholdings could be restructured. Merchant banks seized on the chance to dismantle consortium structures and re-establish as stronger institutions with a single parent shareholder who could provide undisputed backing. The maximum individual shareholding in a trading bank was lifted from 10 per cent to 15 per cent. And the government abolished the 30/20 rule which entitled life offices and pension funds to tax concessions provided they held at least 30 per cent of their assets in public securities, including at least 20 per cent in commonwealth government securities.

In September the Hawke government invited applications for bank licences and outlined the conditions on which they would be granted. Applications were to be lodged by 23 November. The government confirmed that one 'special case' had already been granted a bank licence—the Bank of China, which had operated in Australia from 1942 to 1972, was reinstated as a trading bank.

Keating flew to Washington for the annual IMF/World Bank meeting—and to receive his *Euromoney* award as Finance Minister of the Year. He was also voted one of the world's best finance ministers by the US magazine *Institutional Investor*. Presenting the *Euromoney* award, an engraved silver plate, the magazine's managing director, Sir Patrick Sergeant, was generous in his praise: 'In Australia we find the hour has brought forth the man,' he said, and described Keating as 'the most impressive treasurer since the war . . . his moves have been bold, brilliant and above all, brave.' Keating paid tribute to the Hawke government in his reply: 'I have the privilege of serving with a very enlightened prime minister and a very enlightened cabinet,' he said, adding that financial deregulation was aimed at milking the full potential out of the Australian economy. Buoyed by international endorsement of his government's tactics, Keating moved on to New York and then home, where he was to focus on the year ahead, tax reform and further cuts in the budget deficit. But first there was the challenge of a federal election.

Hawke announced on 8 October that his government would be going to the polls on 1 December for a House of Representatives and half-Senate election. The chief reason given for holding an election when only nineteen months into a three-year term was that it would bring the two houses into line after the double dissolution of March 1983. Other factors influenced the timing of the 1984 election: Hawke's popularity was high, tax cuts would come into effect on 1 November and the ALP was comfortably ahead of the Liberal-National party in the opinion polls. Equally important to the election decision was a forecast that inflation was likely to rise and a growing concern about wages. A half-Senate election had to be held by May 1985. It seemed to make sense to go for both houses.

The Hawke government went into a long campaign. Labor wanted an open position on taxation, which was looming as the next key area of reform. They did not want to close off any tax options but it was obvious that the opposition would make mileage out of such a sensitive issue, particularly in the course of a seven-week election campaign. Governments do not as a rule go into an election campaign with an open position on a topic such as tax—and the Hawke government's stance probably cost it votes in an election that had initially promised to be a landslide. The opposition leader, Andrew Peacock, built his campaign around the possibility of a Labor-introduced assets test, which Labor had not listed as a tax issue but which was identified as one, and he was forecasting a Labor wealth tax and a capital gains tax to follow.

It was during the 1984 election campaign that Hawke revealed his concept of a tax summit. Hawke's advice from his office was that the consumption tax which Keating so vigorously supported would be electoral suicide. The concept of a consumption tax was not new. Treasury had written copious papers on the subject and had advised former federal treasurer John Howard who tried and failed to introduce the tax. Keating had become interested in a consumption tax in the early 1980s. He recognised there were problems in the

Left Three-month-old Paul Keating with his father, Matt, who was to instil in his eldest son a basic Labor-oriented political drive. Matt Keating later became president of his local ALP branch, and the co-founder of a small but successful engineering business. *Right* A one-year-old Keating in 1945 in stylishly embroidered silk smocked suit top, clutching a model car. Cars have always been among Keating's toys. Min Keating made and smocked the outfit.

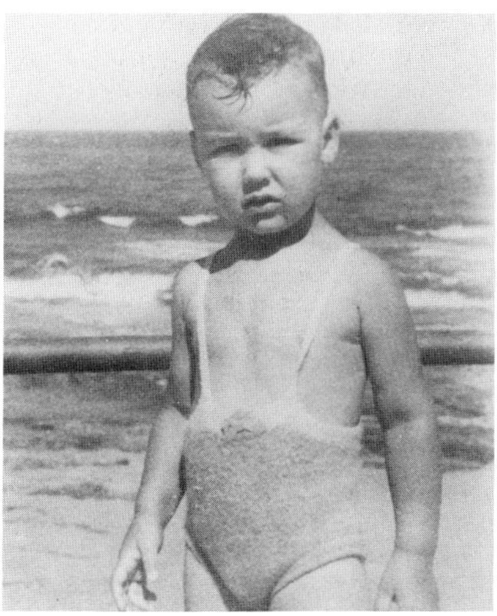

Left On the beach, at the age of two. In 1946 Keating was too young to be aware of events in a national capital that would later absorb him. In Canberra at that time, the prime minister, Ben Chifley, was creating controversy by extending public ownership, establishing the Australian National Airlines Commission and attempting to nationalise the banks. That attempt backfired and helped send federal Labor into the wilderness for 23 years. *Right* In the summer of 1948 the Keating family, Matt and Min Keating, Paul and his younger sister Lyn, spend a weekend in a typical Australian way at Bundeena, one of the nearest ocean beaches to Bankstown.

Left In 1948, the first Holden car came off the production line. In the same year Paul Keating, then four, began his enduring affair with the automobile. Later models included a Morris Minor, an Austin Healey sports and a svelte Mercedes or two. And, of course, the ubiquitous white Ford Fairlane with the Commonwealth Z-plates. *Right* July 1951: seven-year-old Keating, clad in winter coat and shiny shoes, with his mother on a shopping trip in Market Street, Sydney. Min and Paul developed a close bond which always withstood the frictions generated by two strong and often clashing personalities.

Left First communion, August 1951. Keating was brought up in a staunchly Catholic household: the church's influence was woven into the political as well as the social fabric of Keating's upbringing. *Above* Eight-year-old Keating and his five-year-old sister Lyn. The leaning towards sartorial sharpness is already evident — although the adult dresser would no doubt reject the garish floral tie.

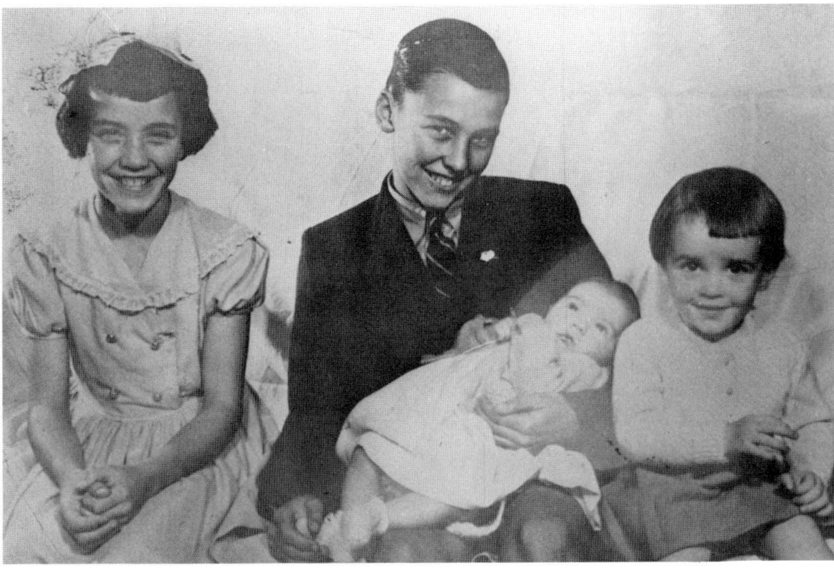

Top Family man: proud brother Paul Keating holds the youngest member of the family, six-week-old Greg, born in 1955, flanked by sisters Lyn (*left*) and 20-month-old Anne. The affectionate older brother later became a doting father of four. *Above* Keating (*left*) grins for the camera at the wedding of his boyhood friend, Mike Gavan (*centre*) in August 1962. Usually Keating, then a keen photographer, was on the other side of the lens, taking shots himself. *Right* Pin-up nineteen-year-old Keating was often in demand to squire debutantes to 'coming-out' balls. Two decades in politics thinned the raven hair and rounded out the face.

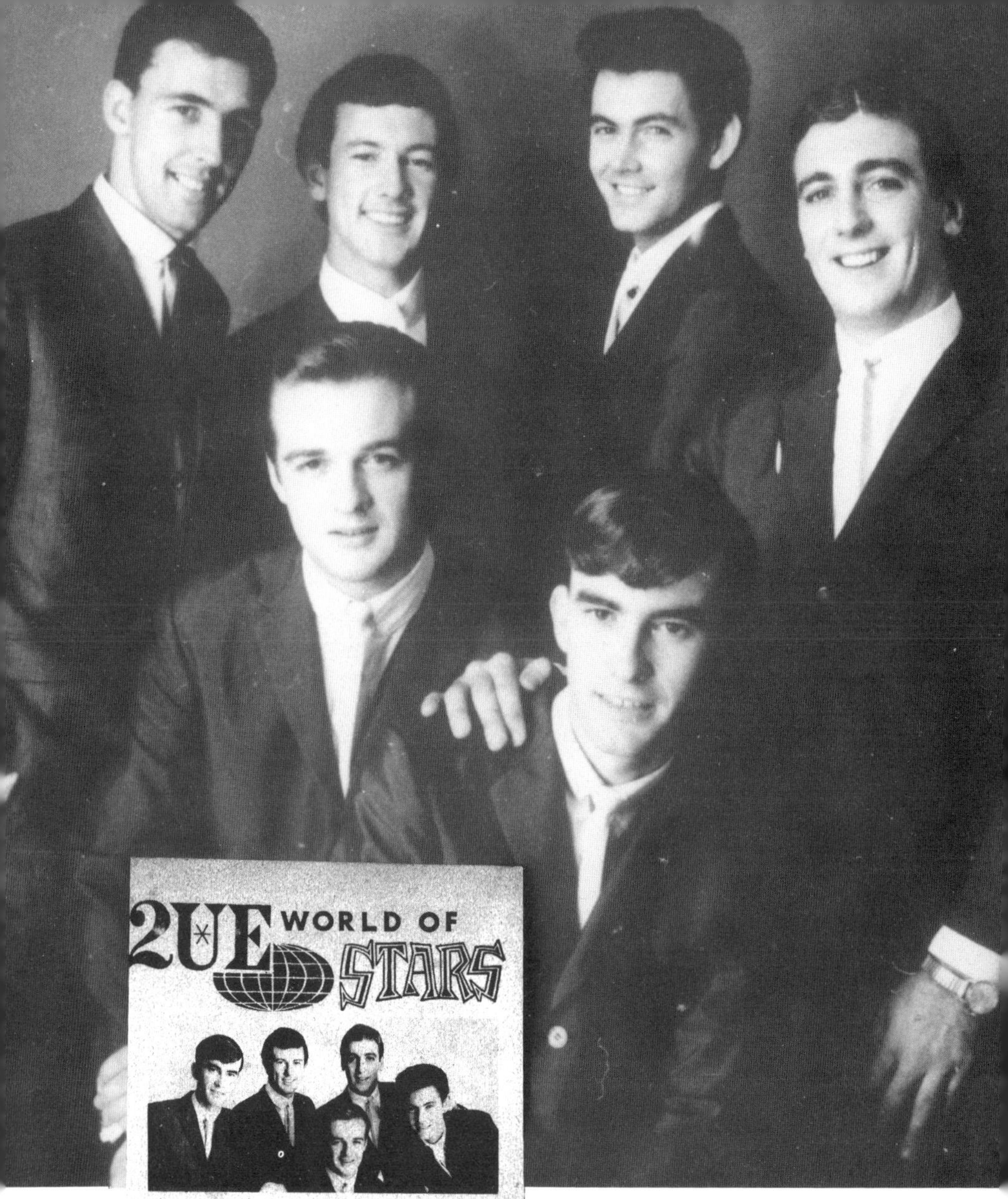

2UE WORLD OF STARS

THE RAMRODS

The group formed as "The Ramrods" in 1959 and displayed then at this early stage an individuality in their style, stemming from a mutual interest in negro music. The original core of the Ramrods — Barry Connors, Gary Maberley and Barry Brady — have been together since the birth of the group in 1959 and together they went through the pains of becoming proficient with their musical instruments, and furthering their knowledge.
In late 1964 the Ramrods' talent was spotted by a young man named Paul Keating who considered Australian audiences should become aware of this dynamic group. He took over management of the group with the result their first recording is released on Parlophone for E.M.I. (Australia) Limited.

NEWS FROM *BRIGHTER* 2UE

TOP FIVE RECORDS IN 2UE HOT LINE AS SELECTED BY OUR LISTENERS THIS WEEK

1. TAR AND CEMENT .... Verdelle Smith
2. PRETTY FLAMINGO .... Manfred Mann
3. BACK STAGE .... Gene Pitney
4. COME AND SEE HER .... Easybeats
5. THE GROOVY KIND OF LOVE .... The Mindbenders

THE THREE NUMBERS MOST DISLIKED

1. JAKE THE PEG .... Rolf Harris
2. ELUSIVE BUTTERFLY .... Bob Lind
3. THE BALLAD OF THE GREEN BERETS .... S/Sgt. Barry Sadler

TRADITION HOUSE Printers 929.8888

Above Keating (*back row, far left*) with the Ramrods, the rock band he managed in the mid-1960s. *Back row, left to right*: bassist Brian Hall, guitarist Barry Brady and drummer Quentin Chadwick. *Front row, from left:* vocalist Barry Connors and keyboardist Gary Moberley. *Left* Keating organised a contract with EMI for the Ramrods. After the release of two unsuccessful singles in 1966 the group had to decide whether or not to pursue a career as professional musicians. They turned their backs on the 'big time', leaving the 22-year-old Keating to concentrate on a career in politics.

The young Keating with Jack Lang. The 'Big Fella' was a man variously admired and detested in the ALP, a one-time NSW premier whose style caused a bitter split in Labor ranks and resulted in his expulsion from the party. Keating, as a teenager, revered Lang and absorbed much of Labor myth and history during his regular visits to the old demagogue. In the late 1960s and early 1970s Keating's name was closely linked with the push to have Lang readmitted to the ALP.

Federal election, October 1969. The intensity shows in the 25-year-old face. Keating is putting into effect his years of training in politics. His all-out election campaign, conducted in a safe Labor seat, borrowed the flamboyance of Jack Kennedy's presidential electioneering and carried him to Canberra.

During the 1969 election campaign Keating, the endorsed Labor candidate for Blaxland, was photographed chatting to young home-builders. Keating missed no opportunity to use family and friends for promotional purposes — in fact, this photograph for his election pamphlet was an elaborately posed shot. The 'young home-builders' were his sister Lyn and his Municipal Employees' Union colleague John Grayson.

The Keating family at Lyn's wedding in February 1970 to Tony King. *From left*, Anne, Matt, Lyn, Min and Paul. The wedding took place in Orange, where Lyn and Tony King ran a property for some years.

The young politician with his prime minister, Gough Whitlam, at a conference in Parliament House, Canberra, in October 1974. A year later Keating won his first ministry, with responsibility for Northern Australia. A further month on, the Labor dream collapsed: Whitlam was out of office and the party went into opposition for seven years.

marginal rates of tax and that the prevailing system of indirect tax was a hotch-potch. He was attracted to a system that would include a broad tax base and low rates that would, in turn, minimise tax avoidance and evasion. His interest was further stirred by a submission to EPAC during 1984, compiled by two leading figures in the business community, Alan Coates and Bryan Kelman, which highlighted the extent to which a consumption tax would allow dramatic cuts in income tax.

The eve of a federal election was not a suitable time to discuss such a contentious issue. The summit idea was a neat way of side-stepping the controversial tax debate during the present campaign, while keeping the issues alive for a later date. Hawke mentioned the proposed summit during a talk-back radio program in Perth. The host, Bob Maumill, later confessed that Hawke had prompted him to ask about the summit, so it was not the unplanned comment that it appeared. History has been rewritten on this issue, along the lines that Hawke was caught on the hop by Maumill's question, but it seems that Hawke sprang the summit as a way of avoiding outright confrontation with Keating over the consumption tax. And letting the idea fall in the course of a radio chat show pre-empted discussion about the pros and cons of a summit, an event more in the style of Hawke than Keating. The summit would mean a delay, and there would barely be enough time to implement the tax changes even if parliament ran to its full three-year term.

Also part of the strategy for keeping the tax debate on the back burner was the announcement by the government of its nine principles of tax reform. These were drafted in a team effort by staff from Keating's and Hawke's offices. They were published well ahead of the election and essentially set the terms of reference for the summit. They included sweeping undertakings:

- there would be no increase in the overall tax burden;
- any reform should provide for further cuts in personal income tax;
- tax avoidance and evasion would be smashed;
- any reform must lead to a simpler tax system;
- any reform must bring about a fairer tax system;
- poverty traps should be removed or reduced;
- any reform package including changes to indirect tax must be acceptable to the whole community;
- tax reform should provide the best possible climate for investment, growth and employment;
- any reform package must have widespread community support,

including support at a widely representative National Tax Summit of economic organisations and community groups.

The long campaign and the costly open position on tax took their toll on Labor. Hawke seemed depressed by that 1984 election; despite the victory, his morale was dented. The year 1984 had been a good one: the government had nailed down several key planks in financial deregulation, brought in tax cuts and Medicare, held wages growth and been voted into a second term in office. Again, though, the government was to have little chance to rest on its electoral laurels.

9 Tax: a crusader crossed

There is no magic pudding—there must be winners and losers.

PAUL KEATING AT THE TAX SUMMIT, JULY 1985

REFORM OF the Australian tax system became Keating's goal in the second term of the Hawke government. Despite earlier assertions that changes to the tax system were still some way down the track, tax dominated the political agenda for a large part of 1985. And it dominated the treasurer's time. A huge amount of energy, persuasion and brain-power—from government, Treasury and various sectors of the community—was devoted to the tax question. Problems were already developing in the balance of payments but were not to emerge, or to be recognised, until later.

The government had gone into the December 1984 election with the question of tax reform hanging in the air. Hawke's announcement on talk-back radio that a tax summit would be held later in 1985 provided a breathing space, a hiatus that allowed the government to keep the details of tax reform off the election agenda but at the same time not to appear to duck the issue. The summit was also a way for Hawke to dodge or at least delay confrontation with Keating over the treasurer's proposed consumption tax. Hawke blew hot and cold on the consumption tax question. Initially he appeared to give his personal support to an increase in indirect tax. He could see the benefits it would allow, in the shape of cuts in the marginal rates of tax. He knew Treasury was wholly supportive of consumption tax. But as the summit approached, Hawke—heavily influenced by his advisers and by the Department of Prime Minister and Cabinet—became less enthusiastic about the move. The government, though, was firmly committed to reforming the tax system. By early 1985 the momentum was building.

Tax reform has always been heavy going for government. However appealing it might be on economic grounds, it is an electoral minefield. And Australia's three-year parliamentary term leaves little room for manoeuvre. A government bent on reform has to grasp the nettle early in its term to get tough measures through, settled and out of the public mind before the next election looms. Changes to the tax structure have, over the years, become restricted to piecemeal measures and fiddling with the marginal rates rather than wholesale overhaul. By the middle of the 1980s the combination of salary increases (to keep in line with the cost of living) and high tax rates had created the absurd situation where some 39 per cent of full-time workers paid a marginal tax rate of 46 cents or more in the dollar, compared with around one per cent thirty years ago. And the top marginal rate of 60 cents cut in at only 1.6 times average yearly earnings, compared with the mid-1950s when the top rate of 66.7 per cent applied at income levels around 18 times average yearly earnings. And there was little incentive to push for an increase in salary if much of the rise went in tax through what the economists dubbed 'bracket creep': with a 'progressive' tax system the higher the income the higher the tax paid, so that a salary rise might merely push the earner into a higher tax bracket, thus wiping out much of the dollar gain. It was also argued that the high rates of personal tax encouraged schemes to minimise or even evade tax.

The objectives in any serious attempt to reform the tax system include the maximum degree of 'equity'. A good tax system is one that is fair, as well as efficient. No one group should be advantaged or disadvantaged. Ideally, the system should also be simple. The idea of changing the tax mix by putting more weight on indirect tax, such as a consumption or value-added tax, gains support as one method of levelling the tax burden and ensuring less revenue slips through the net.

A consumption tax in one form or another has existed for a number of years in several countries. The European Economic Community adopted a broad indirect tax on consumers, known as a value-added tax (VAT), in 1962. The UK introduced VAT in 1973 and more recently New Zealand invoked its Goods and Services Tax (GST). The chief concerns raised by a consumption tax are the effect it has on inflation, through adding to prices, and its so-called 'regressive' nature. Studies by the Australian Bureau of Statistics on household income and expenditure have shown that lower-income earners consume more than those on higher salaries, which suggests that they carry more of the weight of a consumption tax, although such a tax is usually adjusted for the necessities of life. With these concerns in mind, the architects of the doomed consumption tax proposal in 1985 went to considerable length to devise compensatory measures that would redress the balance so that the needy would not be worse off with a consumption tax. A further worry concerning a consumption tax, however, was its potential effect on general economic activity. In the *Report on the National Tax Summit July 1985*, compiled by the Australian Business Economists in conjunction with Peat Marwick, authors professor Tom Valentine and David Collins commented: 'The real flaw in the Treasury argument is the implication that a dollar raised in income tax would have the same effect as a dollar raised by a consumption tax.' Valentine and Collins argued that even though a tax change does not alter revenue, different taxes have different effects on demand. In their view a switch to a consumption tax would depress demand. They found the White Paper's examination of the macro-economic impact of consumption tax inadequate.

Although 1985 goes down as the year of the Hawke government's big push in the tax area, it had in fact been busily changing the tax system since it was first elected. The summit was a way of accelerating a process that had gone on for some time. The first May statement, in 1983, had set the scene with two significant changes—one to the treatment of lump-sum superannuation payments and the other to the tax status of friendly societies. The introduction of the prescribed payments system followed in September 1983, and that provided a salutary lesson for the new government in the psychology of implementing tax changes. It demonstrated that each new tax measure sparks a backlash of opposition for about two months before the change becomes effective, but the hostility dissipates once the tax is in place.

The prescribed payments system provided a fine example. Under this system, tax is deducted at the source of payments for some services, particularly for sub-contracted labour and transport services. The building industry predicted its own collapse, and with it the end of the affordable home. The real result was a streamlined system and 35 000 new taxpayers. The Housing Industry Association in Canberra acknowledged that opposition to the proposed tax had been overstated and that there had been far wider abuse of the tax system than they realised. Four months after the new system had started in 1983, the then national executive director of the association, Bill Kirkby-Jones, and his deputy (later successor), Ron Silverberg, took Keating's tax adviser, Greg Smith, and principal private secretary, Tony Cole, to lunch by way of apology.

The hysterical reaction to the proposal that fringe benefits—including the leisurely business lunch—be taxed is another illustration of how the furore rises, peaks and then subsides. Restaurateurs forecast widespread closures if the fringe benefits tax and a consumption tax were introduced—it would be the end of civilised eating, said one. But life has gone on, and the adaptable credit-card class remains well-fed. These were useful blooding experiences for the tax reformers.

Keating was dedicated to tax reform but cool on the idea of a summit. He, and Treasury, knew it would be impossible to get consensus from the various groups that would attend. What he had in mind was to push through what Malcolm Fraser and his treasurer, John Howard, had tried, and failed, to get in 1980: a broad-based consumption tax. Considerable work had already been done on this concept by Treasury and the Tax Office, but a huge workload lay ahead. Planning began in earnest on Sunday 13 January 1985 when Hawke, Keating and their advisers gathered at The Lodge to map out their strategy, the timing of the summit, the timing of the reforms and the contents of the draft White Paper. David Morgan, later a deputy secretary of the Treasury and at that time head of the secretariat of the task force on tax, recalls:

> From then on it was really a race against time, because of the lead time with the consumption tax. We had to have decisions by mid-1985 if there was going to be a consumption tax, so that it could be settled down and the one-off inflationary impact could be washed out of the system before the government went into an election. It was a pretty hectic exercise.

The tax summit, originally intended for later in 1985, was fixed for July, giving a very tight time-frame in which to prepare the groundwork and sell the concepts. A task force was established under the chairmanship of Ted Evans, later a deputy secretary of the Treasury, which included Treasury officers, staff from the Department of Prime Minister and Cabinet, from Keating's office and from the Tax Office. The main players from Keating's office were Tony Cole and Greg Smith, both seconded from Treasury. The members of the committee which prepared the White Paper were Ted Evans, David Morgan, Ed Visbord from the Department of Prime Minister and Cabinet, Brian Nolan from the Australian Taxation Office, Ross Garnaut, then an adviser to the prime minister, and Greg Smith. Support was drawn from several quarters where specific advice was needed and considerable intellectual effort came from Treasury. The focus on tax had awakened Treasury to the need to commit more resources to that area. Until that point Treasury had operated with merely a branch running tax—a reflection of the back seat that tax had taken under previous governments—but now decided that tax had be built up into a separate new division with 30 people instead of half a dozen. David Morgan was the first head of the new division. Those involved in drafting the White Paper look back on that period as one of the great bureaucratic efforts of all time, given the work that was demanded in a short time. The White Paper drew on the work of the Campbell Committee's report, which had highlighted the integrated nature of all aspects of the financial system, to propose what was to be 'the rejuvenation and restoration of an institutional framework for Australian business.' The White Paper, the tax summit and the associated discussions were the first steps towards significant tax reform in Australia since the Asprey Committee had reported on the tax system more than a decade earlier. And the emphasis was on tax *reform*, not merely on cutting tax rates.

By March Keating could reveal to caucus the key elements of a tax-reform package. These included a consumption tax—at that stage tipped to be 10 per cent but already being criticised as too low at that level—a fringe benefits tax, and cuts in marginal tax rates. It was on the cards that the indirect tax level would have to be lifted if the government were to be able to remove existing sales tax and provide compensation for the needy, to balance the prices rises brought about by the new tax. In that month the ACTU issued its 56-page background paper, *Tax Reform in 1985*, in which it stated that it would agree to increases in indirect tax only if the regressive nature of such taxes could be offset. Keating knew that the ACTU's attitude was crucial to the success or otherwise of the broad-based consumption tax he proposed. Protracted meetings followed, involving Hawke, Keating and ACTU leaders, with the ACTU demanding proof that their members would be better off under a system based on a new consumption tax and lower rates of personal tax.

Chapters of the White Paper were drafted by April and presented to the revenue committee of cabinet (which is the expenditure review committee plus a few other heavyweights in the ministry). By May Keating was able to come up with new figures showing that a consumption tax pitched at 12.5 per cent would be sufficient to support substantial income tax cuts and provide compensation for those on social security. But opposition was continuing to mount in the Labor Party against the consumption tax, particularly from the Centre Left faction, which, in the absence of foreign affairs minister Hayden (who was out of the country much of the time) had turned to senator Peter Walsh as its spokesman. Walsh's Department of Finance had opposed a consumption tax before, when former treasurer John Howard was pushing for it, and now could fight another round. The department prepared its own plan for tax reform, which Walsh presented to cabinet for consideration as an alternative to the arguments presented in the White Paper. Whereas the White Paper strongly supported a trade-off between a consumption tax and lower personal tax rates, the Department of Finance's paper blew holes in its arguments by highlighting problems associated with areas such as compensation. This underscored the view of the Left and Centre Left that not all of the problems associated with a broad-based consumption tax had been solved. But the Department of Finance's work did not include the possibility of significant cuts in personal rates of income tax, which reduced its appeal.

By late May cabinet had endorsed Keating's proposal of a 12.5 per cent consumption tax. The government was on track to take three choices to the July summit, and these became known as Options A, B and C. Supporters of Option C were in what was dubbed Keating's 'tax cart'. Option A aimed at broadening the income tax base through a capital gains tax, a wealth tax, a scheme to crack tax avoidance and evasion, a move to end fringe benefits, and revenue measures to finance modest income tax cuts. Option B was a combination of Option A plus a 'soft' consumption tax, set at 5 per cent, which would operate with a modified version of the existing wholesale sales tax. This called for operating two indirect tax systems and would be administratively expensive. Option C, the government's preferred package, was the big full-scale tax switch, combining the features of Option A, with its own centrepiece, a 12.5 per cent consumption tax which would raise enough funds to allow a 30 per cent average reduction of income tax plus a generous scheme to compensate those hit by the new tax. Wholesale sales tax would be abolished under Option C. Options B and C were constructed to bring all taxpayers significant cuts in personal income tax. The benefits of Option A were pitched more towards those on higher taxable incomes. A fourth option, based on Senator Walsh's proposed consumption tax that would hit mainly middle-income earners, plus capital gains and inheritance taxes, was dismissed by cabinet. That result was seen as a victory for Keating, who was still faced with quelling ACTU unease.

Meanwhile, more than 200 submissions were made to the Economic Planning Advisory Council from a range of industry, welfare and special interest groups. These submissions argued either for less reliance on income tax, with revenue supplemented by broadly-based indirect taxes, or greater reliance on income tax but with a wider definition of income. Leading contributors, whose spokesmen became key participants at the tax summit, included the ACTU, industry organisations such as the Business Council of Australia, Confederation of Australian Industry and the Australian Chamber of Commerce, and special-interest groups such as the Institute of Chartered Accountants, Australian Retailers Association, National Farmers' Federation, Bureau of Industry Economics, the Australian Council of Social Service and Women's Electoral Lobby.

The draft White Paper was issued early in June and Keating started an exhaustive round of campaigning, selling the government's preferred approach, Option C. Keating journeyed around Australia, canvassing support for Option C through interviews and discussions, talking with a passion to anyone who would listen.

The White Paper surveyed the chief issues in tax reform that the government planned to address: tax avoidance and evasion; personal income tax rates; a consumption tax, including compensation for those who would be worst affected and who could least afford to be; a wealth tax; and business tax. Keating's preference was to talk in terms of various 'approaches' rather than options—he felt the government should be seen to be leading, not presenting choices. In the White Paper, Option C was analysed in the greatest detail. The rest of the paper appeared as a discussion paper to avoid the impression of an attempt to pre-empt the debate. Option C, though, was the government's predigested compromise, providing some pain and some pleasure for all. An editorial in the *Australian Financial Review* on 5 June 1985, headlined 'Too good for its own good', described the White Paper as 'sensible and moderate':

> The worst thing about the draft White Paper on Reform of the Australian Tax System is that it is sensible and moderate. This means that it will appeal to no major sectional interest or constituency in the Australian community.
>
> The White Paper depicts a scheme for reform of the tax system which is by no means perfect. Nor is it the best conceivable. But, as it stands, it is probably the best that has a chance of being put through an Australian Parliament.
>
> Unfortunately, due to the silly commitment of a 'summit' conference at the beginning of next month, the White Paper will

> have to go through the experience of being debated, reviled, torn apart, and condemned by sectional interests without being presented clearly to the Australian public as what it is, a tax reform which would make the tax system more equitable and efficient.

Option C would be an innovative switch in the balance of the tax system, taking the tax impact off dollars earned in income and putting it on to dollars spent through consumption. Economists approve the sense of this but the idea attracts criticism from the equity point of view. The White Paper's support for Option C rested mainly on the expectation that it would help catch some income that had avoided tax, as income would attract tax when spent. Further, it would enable tax cuts so that there would be less of an incentive for people to try to avoid or evade tax and it would allow the government to streamline the present indirect tax system. Aware of the opposition to consumption tax in principle, the White Paper spelled out the conditions necessary for the introduction of the tax. These included maintaining the overall progressive nature of the tax system, cushioning the inflationary impact of a consumption tax and compensating income-earners, particularly low-income groups, for the price increases.

Keating has been criticised for taking too purist a stance on consumption tax, and for swallowing the Treasury line and going inflexibly for a rate of 12.5 per cent. Treasury has been criticised for pushing for so high a rate, knowing that once Keating had taken it on board he would fight for it to the hilt. Treasury by then should have known that once convinced of the rightness of a move, Keating fights for it and does not go to water, or compromise as they had seen so many previous treasurers do. But the high rate was needed to fund the tax cuts, to make sure all the welfare cases and lower-income earners were going to be better off. Tony Cole comments:

> The higher the rate [of consumption tax] the higher the 'fiscal dividend'—the tax you got from the people who didn't pay any tax on income. You needed a big fiscal dividend because there was so much over-compensation on' average to make sure the extreme cases were still fully compensated. It was the overlay of welfarism that killed it. That forced you to have the higher rate—to accommodate the drop in the marginal rate, the increase in welfare, social security benefits and a generous family assistance program.

The welfare sector, which presented a more unified front than business, rejected the consumption tax, partly through a lack of trust and partly out of ideological commitment which left them hostile to the concept in principle. Emotive arguments were used to persuade delegates of the unfavourable effects of a consumption tax for people on a pension. A broad-based consumption tax was seen as bad for migrants, women and the handicapped and was opposed by the ACTU, ACOSS and WEL. They did not feel comfortable about trusting a government to maintain the compensatory features—they could agree to the consumption tax as part of a package but find a future government taking away the social security benefits and leaving the consumption tax.

These groups supported the general thrust of Option A and its moves to broaden the tax base and limit the opportunities for tax avoidance, although they felt Option A did not go far enough. In the end the welfare lobby, by allowing either their blindness or confusion to prevail, probably did not act in the best interests of their constituents. Their negative attitude lost them the chance to broaden the tax base and to have a larger base, in the shape of the increased pensions and other social benefits that formed the sweetener in Option C, to index to the CPI. Business and industry rejected Option A. Option B, modelled on a scheme that had been proposed in Japan, came under little discussion and the debates on Option C focused almost exclusively on the broad-based consumption tax, with insufficient emphasis being given to the personal income tax cuts that it could provide.

The unions had been hostile to the idea of consumption tax all along, and had been pushing for exemptions. They supported a capital gains tax (with an exemption for the family home) and a wealth tax and a restructuring of the personal income tax scales. In the end the unions got much of what they wanted: a capital gains tax, no broad-based consumption tax, and fringe benefits tax to be carried by employers, not employees.

But the group that still carries the blame for torpedoing Keating's Option C into oblivion is the business sector, represented at the tax summit by the Business Council of Australia. In common with the many other interest groups at the tax summit, business focused on the negatives. The Business Council did not present a cohesive front. Up to the last minute it was struggling to decide what to say, and changed foot from one day to the next.

The summit proved to be an exercise in self-interest. Option C badly needed the support of the business sector; without that there was little momentum. But while business supported the consumption tax, it did not like the rest of Option C. Hawke and Keating, and the officials working with them on tax had gone to extraordinary lengths to woo the trade unions and the social security lobby over to their side. They had expected opposition from these sectors but had hoped that the strengths of other groups, especially business, would be enough to push the arguments over the line. Early support from business was crucial to building momentum. Instead, business presented a disorganised front that carried no really clear message; it supported the expansion of indirect tax but rejected the idea of a capital gains tax and a fringe benefits tax to be borne by employers. And business and the Confederation of Australian Industry wanted guarantees that the inflationary effects of the broad-based consumption tax would be excluded from wages rounds. The ACTU laughed that provision out of the negotiating ring.

All the big players were present among the 160 delegates on the opening day of the tax summit. State premiers, business leaders, industry and special-interest groups were all ready to deliver keynote speeches. Keating exuded optimism at the beginning of the summit. But the event went terribly wrong. The summit was virtually killed on day one. Hawke opened the proceedings with a speech intended to quell doubts about Option C:

> I now give this undertaking: under Approach C the government would establish an independent monitoring authority to gauge carefully the effect of tax reform. Its function would be to ensure that should there be any unforeseen effects to the detriment of those in the lower-income areas, they would be drawn quickly to our attention, to be rectified at once. We believe that all the necessary protections have been included in the [Approach C] proposal. But we recognise that all Australians require an assurance that the least privileged among us will not suffer as a result of the changes. And I give that assurance unreservedly.

The first speaker after the prime minister was Bob White, then managing director of Westpac Banking Corporation and president of the Business Council. He launched into his infamous 'We're not in any cart, not A, or B or C' speech, saying:

> We are not on the government's cart . . . we have argued from the start that a package of reforms is essential but each component must be right. There are unacceptable aspects of approach A to which are added other negative aspects in approach B which are then incorporated in approach C. This makes it impossible for us to support, without any major qualifications, any of these. Accordingly . . . it is not possible to limit the debate to the relative merits of the three White paper options.

White's opening remarks dealt a psychological blow to consumption tax. Much of the blame for the tone of his remarks has been laid at the door of Sir Noel Foley, then chairman of Westpac and a staunch

Liberal Party member. Certainly White's speech soured relations between Keating and the banking sector, particularly Westpac. It is still arguable whether Option C could have recovered from that point. Treasury bureaucrats curse themselves for being silly enough not to have realised fully just how silly and inept business could be. Perhaps events would have turned out differently had business been coddled and convinced. As it was, people were working round the clock to get the ACTU on-side. With hindsight, the proponents of reform feel they should have spent more time talking with business. Business had indicated support for the broad-based consumption tax, but finally turned its back on Option C because it did not like the other 'nasties' contained in that approach. Perhaps, at the last moment, business felt it could not be seen to be overly supportive of a Labor government, even one that had taken its interests so much into account. It is unlikely that business intended that White's speech be the kiss of death for Option C—business's intervention was an attempt at endorsing Option C with several 'buts'. The attempt failed.

The loss of the much-needed support from the business sector, whose representatives made up about one-third of those present at the tax summit, was all that was needed to tip what had always been a delicate balance. Hawke began again to believe his advisers, who had warned that the introduction of a broad-based consumption tax would cost Labor the next election. The unions could sniff which way the wind was blowing. From then on, Keating was on his own with Option C. At the end of the day Keating was pleading with participants to put sectional interests aside. But one noteworthy result of the summit's first day was that not one of the 25 speakers supported a 'do-nothing' approach. If Keating had consensus on nothing else, he had it for the broad principle of tax reform.

The fate of the summit was sealed on that first day but delegates went through the motions of following the formal agenda. Each day, officially, was to address a different area but it was clear from the start that the shadow agenda was to carry more weight than the official program. The result of the summit would be determined not by the scheduled gatherings in the House of Representatives but by the meetings on the side to see what winning points could be extracted from the exercise. By the end of the second day it was clear that the ACTU had taken a strong line against the consumption tax. Business Council was horrified at the turn events had taken and tried to rectify matters. Eric Mayer, chairman of National Mutual Life and of the Business Council's taxation review task force, gave a vigorous speech in support of indirect tax, though in the form of a value-added, rather than consumption, tax, in an attempt to strengthen Keating's position. But his efforts were too late.

Day Three brought a strong attack on consumption tax from Eva Burrows, a commissioner of the Salvation Army, who was totally opposed to the proposal and dismissed Keating's outline of compensatory rebates as of minimal interest to those she represented. Hawke was carefully taking stock. And he was worried by the revelations of a Morgan Gallup poll showing the government's popularity had slumped below that of the opposition. Andrew Peacock was beating Hawke in the popularity stakes.

The events leading to the demise of Option C and Keating's defeat have been well-documented. Hawke's meeting with senior ACTU officials at the Canberra International Hotel, on the evening of Wednesday 3 July, following a reception at the Institute of Sport, snuffed out any chance of Keating's victory. While Hawke was negotiating with the ACTU. Keating was holding a press conference, unaware of the events at the Canberra International.

Thursday 4 July 1985 opened as the fourth day of the tax summit. It was to be its premature end. Hawke, who had been chairing the proceedings, was absent and Keating took the chair. The ACTU group was also absent. Keating disappeared and deputy prime minister Lionel Bowen took over. Speaker after speaker took the platform but the events had lost whatever interest they had held. Hawke and Keating reappeared around midday and said the summit would adjourn for lunch and that there would be an announcement immediately after the break.

The corridors of Parliament House were even more than usually abuzz with speculation. After lunch in the parliamentary dining room the prime minister summoned a number of business and industry leaders for private discussions; during ten-minute sessions with each Hawke outlined the outcome of the summit. Keating had been abandoned. The final session of the summit played to a packed press gallery. There was a yawning gap in the gathering below in the House. Business Council, except for Alan Coates and Bryan Kelman, was absent, conferring whether or not to attend. Coates and Kelman, who had long been in favour of consumption tax, sat in solitude, taking no part in the discussions of the final session. The rest of the Business Council eventually arrived.

Hawke thanked delegates for attending. The summit ended at 4pm on Thursday afternoon, a day ahead of schedule. And although sectional interests were muted during the final session the conference closed on a sour note. The government announced that it was working on a revised tax reform package. Hawke said that Option C had not met the ninth principle—community support—and that a new package was to be designed that was basically a variant of Option A. Hawke paid an emotional tribute to Keating: 'No prime minister could have asked for better, closer, more effective co-operation than I have enjoyed with Paul Keating.' Keating pressed his arm. The audience applauded.

Keating showed all the flexibility of a skilled politician that day. He changed tack like a yachtsman trying to catch the wind. Option C had been knifed and by lunchtime of that day it had been clear that the summit was, to all intents and purposes, over. Keating's performance, though, was not over. Before the day was out he managed to salvage two significant measures—the 49 per cent corporate tax rate and full imputation of company dividends. Despite having lost Option C Keating had kept the pressure on and fought. Tony Cole says:

> Keating climbed back by convincing himself that what he was going to do was worthwhile anyway. I think as a result of losing Option C he was absolutely determined to get through the 49 per cent maximum tax rate which was one of his major targets and to get full imputation. He used up what was owed to him to get them. And that's what got him back up.

The Hawke government got a reasonable proportion of what it set out to achieve in tax reform. The tax summit, though, did not reflect well on any of its participants and probably bore out Keating's most pessimistic assessment of the value of such gatherings. 'There is no magic pudding,' he told delegates. 'There must be winners and losers.' In the end the summit was seen as little more than grand-standing, something that gave a warm glow to those in the limelight but did little for anyone else. Hawke government critics dismissed it as merely another macho circus that did the government little good in the eyes of the electorate. Andrew Peacock called the summit a 'futile sham'. The Business Economists/Peat Marwick report had this to say:

> No government in the past has contemplated implementing such a comprehensive package [of tax reform] and in this sense the process of tax summiting may turn out to have been a successful one. When measured against what might have been, however, the National Tax Summit was a debacle and little of the blame for this can be placed on Messrs Keating and Hawke. The Summit was destroyed by self interest, by doctrinaire posturing and by inadequate economic analysis.

Keating had gone a long way out on his own on tax. He had shown determination and guts, and that was recognised. He had mustered some support but had to contend with considerable opposition and uncertainties, who was in the cart, who not. The complex debate was being conducted in a short time and canvassing an enormous area. Keating was criticised later for not having sold the difficulties of watering down the consumption tax, so that the lobbyists were more able to get everyone's ear. But Keating's time was finite: during June 1985 he was travelling the country, carrying out interviews and radio talk-backs, selling the consumption tax and fighting on all fronts—unions, welfare, business and, in the end, even Hawke.

But while Option C had been dumped, the government did bring in capital gains tax, though in the softer approach supported by Hawke, with the exemption of family homes and no retrospectivity. It has been argued that Labor is safer with a capital gains tax than without it, as the spectre of the tax has often been used successfully to turn the electorate against Labor. But it is in, and accepted. The tax that can be tracked to the Treasury was the tax on fringe benefits—what the bureaucrats refer to as 'the next sewer after the nefarious evasion schemes'. Again, business has adjusted to the new tax, though after some modifications were made in its application. In the end, despite the huge effort that was put into selling the tax packages, a lack of understanding had helped deal the final blow, vindicating earlier warnings that there simply was not sufficient time available to ensure widespread community support for such a new concept in such a sensitive area as tax.

The collapse of Option C ranks as one of Keating's worst moments. Day One of the tax summit ended on a bad note; by lunchtime of the second day Keating thought he was winning; then he was sold down the river. He had felt that the logic of his case was so strong that he had to win. He was probably right about the logic but the debate that was worrying the prime minister and his staff was whether Labor would lose the next election if Option C were put through. In any event, Keating did not get the opportunity to give Option C an effective hard sell during the week of the summit. By the end of the summit Keating felt betrayed. A tense weekend followed, marking what was indisputably the low point in the Hawke–Keating relationship.

The tax summit is a shining example of Keating as the consummate politician. Those who were at the summit recall him looking gaunt, sullen, crushed by the turn of events. But he never stopped thinking politically, figuring what best to do next, following the maxim that in politics you are never finished until you are gone. By Thursday morning he had turned his back on the history of Wednesday and was marking out the territory he could still win.

Full imputation—which ensures dividends are tax-free in shareholders' hands, provided full company tax has been paid—was not in the draft White Paper, which had nevertheless highlighted the problem of the so-called double taxation of dividends and canvassed a system of half-imputation. Business favoured imputation; it felt it would lead to more people investing in shares. Keating supported imputation and felt that something had to be thrown business's way, offsetting the body-blows of fringe benefits tax, capital gains tax and an increase in corporate tax from 46 to 49 cents in the dollar. The 49 per cent rate and full dividend imputation were the two main features that Keating pulled out of the fire at the end of the tax summit.

It took considerable time after the tax summit for the Hawke–Keating relationship to warm up again—which it did, out of necessity. The episode illuminated a problem that many, including Keating, had identified in Hawke at that time. The prime minister seemd to be wavering, unable to make up his mind, and to be in some kind of crisis of confidence. It also demonstrated a difference in approach between Hawke and Keating. The treasurer wanted to implement policies that he believed were beneficial and would work; the prime minister wanted to be re-elected. Keating the veteran politician later rationalises that in 1985 the government tried 'omnibus change, tacking everything on'. That was too much. He says:

> I think one of the real legacies of the Option C debate is that people don't understand the importance of the changes that are in. These are, in a sense, in behavioural terms, far more significant than Option C. Option C was about whether Australia had a more secure tax based on consumption and that was a laudable enough thing. But what will change the way Australians behave and how they invest will be lower marginal rates of tax, the relief of the double tax on dividends and the taxation of capital gains. That's going to change the way Australia is. Consumption tax would never have changed the way Australia is. It might have provided a better basis for the revenue in the non-direct area but these things go right to the heart of tax policy. And, of course, the changes are all broadly paid for by cleaning the direct system up by wiping out the shelters. I mean the breadth of our direct side reform is so wide that you can hardly think of a shelter we should address. It's easy for a government to move against some tax avoidance scheme: we find out about it, we draw up an amendment, we put it through the House of

Representatives and the Senate and it's over. But try and take their credit cards off them, or their tax-deductible Mercedes or their discounted home loan—and that's hard. And then tax their capital gains into the bargain—that's reform.

10 Win some, lose some

And they said it couldn't be done.

PAUL KEATING IN FEBRUARY 1985, ANNOUNCING THE ESTABLISHMENT OF SIXTEEN NEW BANKS

KEATING RECALLS 1985 and 1986 as the years in which he exploited every political trick he knew. He used every ounce of the experience he had gained from the party, from parliament and from his many years in committee rooms, negotiating and extracting hard bargains as he fought through what ranked as his worst setbacks.

When 1985 opened the Australian dollar was worth 82 US cents. Within six weeks it was to fall below 70 cents. The currency had begun to make front-page news. Under a fixed exchange rate, the government could tinker with the rate to suit its policies, creating damaging distortions along the way, whereas with a cleanly floating exchange rate the currency was left to find its own level.

The Australian dollar had been regarded as overvalued and ready to lose some ground, but in the event its dramatic decline came as a shock. A number of factors combined to produce a collapse that lopped 13 per cent off the $A's value against the $US in less than three weeks, and reduced its worth against other major currencies such as the deutschemark, yen and sterling.

The slide in the $A had begun after the release of a disappointingly large figure for M3 (money supply) growth in January (which was bad for the outlook on inflation). By the end of the first week in February the Australian dollar had tumbled to 77 US cents. The dollar was also pushed lower by an announcement by treasurer Keating on 29 January that the government would abandon trying to achieve a specific level for the M3 monetary aggregate in the current financial year. The move was logical, as the previous monetary categories had been rendered meaningless by financial deregulation, particularly the move on 1 August 1984 to allow the trading banks to pay interest on overnight deposits. M3, which included the deposits of savings and trading banks, had been bloated as a result and would be further distorted as additional banks entered the system. Since these previous money measures, ranging from the narrow M1 to the broader M3, no longer had the same relevance, it made little sense to target them. The old yardsticks were replaced with a Reserve Bank 'checklist' of main indicators which included money and credit aggregates, interest rates, the exchange rate, external accounts, economic activity and inflation.

Keating stressed that the change did not mean the government had thrown control of monetary policy to the winds, but was conceding to the realities of a deregulated market. In announcing this move, Keating incensed some money market economists, who were vigorously against abandoning what had become comforting signposts along the way. Keating's response was that the money market would have to learn to live without the security blanket of a monthly money supply figure. Domestic misunderstanding of the move paled compared with the overseas reaction. Australia was still little-understood in international markets which, wrongly perceiving a government turning its back on prudent monetary management, gave the Australian dollar the thumbs-down.

Much of the fall was expected and initially even welcomed, because the lower dollar made Australia's exports more competitive overseas. The government gave the impression that it was happy as long as the dollar remained above 75 US cents, although alarms would start to sound if the currency fell below that level. Meanwhile, there was no perceptible change in policy, such as forcing up short-term interest rates to support the dollar. This was soon to change. During early February, short-term interest rates were unusually low because public service work bans had held up the quarterly corporate tax cheques that should have been processed into government coffers. The result of this was a surplus $1 billion in the banking system and money rates as low as 5.5 per cent. This was a further depressing influence on the dollar. By 18 February the Australian dollar had fallen below 75 US cents. But the day of reckoning was 19 February, when the currency dropped to 71 cents and lost 3.6 per cent off its trade-weighted index in one day. By 20

February the Reserve Bank was tightening monetary policy, putting a floor under the cash rates in an effort to prop up the dollar.

Two other factors played a role in the Australian dollar drama at that time. One was a growing awareness of a worrying increase in the current account deficit. The other related less to the realities of the market place and more to perceptions about the Hawke government. On 1 February the government announced that it had agreed to the US's request to use Sydney as a base to monitor test splashdowns in the Tasman Sea of the new-generation MX nuclear missile. The Left, already irritated by what it perceived as Hawke's pro-US attitude on nuclear issues, was incensed. Hawke was under pressure to back down. But his position was complicated by a forthcoming visit to Washington. He was already overseas, in Brussels, when he confirmed a change of heart that would avoid an unsuccessful confrontation in caucus. Australia withdrew its support for US testing in the Pacific. Coincident with these events, New Zealand was thumbing its nose at the US, rejecting requests for warship visits and banning all nuclear-capable ships from its ports. The future of the ANZUS defence alliance was in doubt.

The connection between the MX missile debacle and the tumbling Australian dollar may have been irrational, but at the time the financial markets took to heart what seemed like disarray in the government. There was deep concern that the US would become suspicious of the Labor government and that this would be bad for investment and the currency. By the time Hawke reached Washington, on 7 February, the Australian dollar had lost five US cents in four days. US and Australian relations surived but the appearance of instability in the government touched financial market nerves, domestically and overseas.

Keating's contribution to the MX missile furore was to tell party members to 'shut up' and to accuse several of behaving like 'fourth-graders'. Accusations flew round the corridors of Parliament House that the ALP was polarised between an elite group of 'prefects' and the rank-and-file, with policy decisions made by the prefects who rode roughshod over the the juniors. Writing in the *National Times* on 15 February 1985, political correspondent Alan Ramsey painted this picture:

> I remember when Treasurer Paul Keating was what he now characterises as a fourth grader in the Federal Parliamentary Labor Party. I do not recall that the Paul Keating of 15 years ago ever acted as if he saw himself as anywhere but in the first form. Nor was he very good at 'shutting up' . . . it did him no great harm. In six years Keating was a minister at the age of 31.

Ramsey pointed out that Keating believed in so-called 'fourth-graders' paying their dues—'the political environment of the NSW ALP machine is one where everyone has their place; you serve your apprenticeship by doing as you're told by those who hold the position of power and privilege'. But in Ramsey's analysis this gulf between the ruling elite and the ordinary folk was a chief reason for the disruption in ALP ranks that was provoked by the MX missile issue.

Storm clouds were gathering over Australia's horizon. The tax debate was beginning to gain momentum and alleged splits between prime minister Hawke and treasurer Keating were making news. The balance of payments figures were showing a persistent deterioration in the trade and current accounts. While the performance on this score was disappointing, it had not plummeted to the depths it was to hit the following year. But the figures were bad enough to prompt the government to revise upwards its forecast 1984/85 current account deficit. Taken all round, Australia's image seemed shaky and this was reflected in a lower currency. Perceptions had quickly changed.

Keating had not allowed the MX missile arguments to divert his attention from financial reform. While that issue preoccupied much of the ALP he seized the opportunity to float the possibility that about a dozen new banks might be authorised, not the six or eight that had been suggested earlier. Keating had been working doggedly since 1984 on the issue of admitting foreign banks. Throughout that year he had lectured the various caucus committees. His most telling argument, which he used to caucus, to cabinet and to the June 1984 national ALP conference, was that the existing system of banks had brought no benefits to Labor voters. Drawing on his knowledge of Labor history, on details learned from Jack Lang, he drew a vivid picture of the banks as historical enemies of the ALP, institutions which had done nothing to help the ordinary worker in terms of home finance and loans to small business. It was a clever strategy that wrenched the initiative away from the Left. In arguing against foreign banks, the Left was made to appear to be defending Labor's most bitter enemies, a sector of the establishment that had contributed to the downfall of the Scullin government, driven Curtin to an early grave and destroyed the Chifley government. Keating used his intricate grasp of the past to determine future policy. He turned the Left's arguments on their heads, insisting that there was no reason for a Labor government to protect powerful banking interests by blocking competition. His own personal hostility to the banks cannot be dismissed. He had watched his father try, and fail, as a small businessman to obtain bank finance to expand his promising business.

Keating began working on caucus early in 1984. He honed his arguments in succcessive performances to the different committees and invited speakers from the general community to contribute to the debate. He made a point of attending all the meetings of the large caucus economic committee, which involves all the factions. Caucus also invited speakers so that members could hear all arguments. Keating thumped home his points, wearing down the opposition. He took the issue to the June national conference, where he thundered at the audience: 'Banking is the artery of the economy and we've had hardening of the arteries for too long in this country.' He won a general endorsement of his bank policy at the conference. The matter then had to be thrashed out in cabinet, again in caucus, and with the unions. It was a major fight at all levels.

On 28 February 1985 Keating staged a triumphant press conference at which he announced the government's approval for 16 new trading banks. 'And they said it couldn't be done,' was his boast. Many, indeed, had thought that it would not, could not, and should not, be done. Here was a Labor treasurer overturning Labor tenets. Banks were the enemy of hard-line Labor supporters. Two years earlier, when abruptly pitched into the shadow treasurer's role, Keating had issued a press release warning that interest rates would rise if foreign banks were allowed into Australia. In doing so, he was delivering a statement prepared for his predecessor, Ralph Willis, which reflected the party line. Now Keating had successfully argued for an expanded banking sector where the domestic banks would have to compete with new entrants. In admitting sixteen new banks Keating had given the banking sector more rope than it had expected. The final figure of sixteen owed much to political horse-trading. Had Keating held to around six new banks, as suggested by the Martin review group, he ran the risk of offending a country or bank by exclusion. And all the Australian states were eager to share in the new business rather than see new banks concentrated in Sydney and Melbourne. There had to be sufficient new entrants to cover the ground.

Keating does not regard the admission of foreign banks as 'selling out' to the financial community. He sees it as a way of shaking up the local private banks, but by a method they cannot challenge. The banks had long supported freeing up their sector and were well prepared for a more competitive market, to the extent that the new banks have found life in Australia's well-banked community remarkably tough.

The Left's argument was that allowing foreign banks into the country linked Australia irrevocably with overseas trends and possible instability at a time when several international, particularly US, banks were experiencing severe problems with non-repayment of loans to Mexico and some South American countries. What this argument missed was that Australia had for years been linked with overseas markets through a multitude of foreign-owned, Australian-based subsidiaries in finance and business, which operated as part of a worldwide network. And internationalisation had intensified since the Australian dollar was floated and exchange control regulations dismantled.

The structure which the foreign banks have been compelled to adopt in Australia has gone some way to ensuring that problems are not imported along with the foreign shingles. Foreign banks setting up business in Australia have had to establish themselves as locally incorporated subsidiaries, not as branches, which means that they have to bring capital into the country and produce annual reports and financial statements. They also fall under the supervision of the Reserve Bank of Australia and have to comply with whatever guidelines are imposed on the domestic banks in areas such as gearing (the ratio of borrowings to shareholders funds), holdings of specific assets (the prime assets ratio or PAR) and the maximum amount that can be lent to an individual client.

The move to allow foreign banks into Australia was part of the gradual internationalisation of the country's economy. Australian banks, confronting the limits of a domestic market of sixteen million people, had been expanding overseas for years but were restricted in some countries by the need for reciprocity. An Australian bank could establish in some countries only if those countries' banks were allowed to do business in Australia. The world economy had opened up, and if Australia was to move forward it had to participate in that trend.

The move to grant licences to new banks marked a high point in Keating's status with the financial community. He was constantly in demand, addressing business seminars and opening new banks. The banking sector has always enjoyed being massaged by its hero. Keating readily complied with requests, and contributed to the opening celebrations of a number of new establishments, including the Bankstown branch of the UK Barclays Bank. But even as the bankers were toasting the reformer with champagne in March 1985, events were unfolding that were to have a radical effect on the lives of all Australians and to present treasurer Keating with possibly his most formidable challenge.

By April of 1985 Keating was in one of his favourite cities, New York, where among other events he participated in a one-day conference on the Australian economy and US-Australian investment relations, organised by Westpac Banking Corporation and the Asia Society. His address to a well-heeled audience of business people at the Asia Society auditorium in Park Avenue was warmly received. Keating the tactician had delivered precisely the soothing words that the Americans had wanted to hear; they had been uncertain about Australia in the wake of the ANZUS crisis and the decision to abandon monetary targeting, and in the light of the growing current account deficit.

In May, Keating was the target of praise from an unexpected quarter. Former Treasury secretary John Stone took the opportunity when addressing a Melbourne gathering to describe Keating as 'one of Australia's best post-war treasurers . . . he had a degree of clout that not all treasurers have had'. Stone recorded his approval of Keating's initiatives in financial deregulation but added:

> I don't think I should get into a ranking game of treasurers for whom I have worked but I have no hesitation at all in saying that I personally found in the nearly eighteen months that I worked for Paul Keating that he is an excellent minister, a hard-working minister, an intelligent minister, a minister who learns very fast.

Keating, deep in preparations for the tax summit, faced with the annual state premiers' conference and Loan Council meeting and with minimal breathing space between those events and the budget, appreciated the comments. Stone later took a harsher line. Profiling the former Treasury secretary in the *Sydney Morning Herald* in October 1987, Craig McGregor quoted Stone:

> Keating's gone rotten. He began reasonably well; his first serious mistake was the budget of 1984/85, which was the budget just after I resigned. It was one of the factors in my resignation; incomes were up, and the opportunity was missed to make a major reduction in the deficit . . . [Keating] is a person of considerable abilities but he carries the seeds of his own destruction . . . arrogance, lust for power . . . he's always playing the political game.

But in 1985 relations between Keating and his former Treasury secretary were genuinely warm.

Trouble was brewing on a different front: reports had surfaced since Easter of renewed strain between the treasurer and his prime minister. Keating had been portrayed as the tough, unwavering politician during the MX missile debacle while Hawke had appeared to dither and change his mind. Keating's firm resolve on tax matters, including the consumption tax, contrasted with Hawke's vacillating approach, which was largely attributed to his staffers' opposition to a consumption tax. The *Australian Financial Review* in an article on Friday 31 May, commented on mounting tension between the two and talked of Hawke being annoyed that Keating was taking too much of the credit for the government's achievements. Hawke had overruled Keating in a cabinet discussion about the annual premiers' conference held at the end of May, with the prime minister pushing for a tougher line on states' growth. The *Sydney Morning Herald*'s political correspondent, Mike Steketee, described the *Review* article as 'bearing all the signs of a strategic leak' and commented: 'It seems Mr Keating does not blame Mr Hawke for the leak to the *Financial Review*. He is not so generous to some of the Prime Minister's staff.'

Hawke and Keating were keen to hose down rumours of dissension which they both felt were not in the interests of the government's status in the country. In a subsequent *Financial Review* article on 3 June 1985, entitled 'Hawke dismisses reports of rift with Keating', Hawke was described as being at pains to point out the different roles carried out by a prime minister and a treasurer. The prime minister used the opportunity when appearing on the Channel Nine program *Sunday* to say: 'The truth has been from the beginning of this government that we've worked closer together probably than any other prime minister and treasurer in the history of this country.' Hawke talked about himself and Keating working 'hand in glove . . . standing shoulder to shoulder' on the issue of tax reform and in selling the government's preferred package. The prime minister was eager, on the eve of the release of the draft White Paper on tax reform, to smother any suggestions of disagreement between him and his treasurer.

Throughout June and early July the debate over tax reform dominated the headlines and much of the government's time. The dollar took a battering early in July when rumours that Keating would resign swept the currency markets. The tax summit was drawing to an end and the markets were abuzz with speculation that Keating had decided to quit when the consumption tax for which he had fought so hard was clearly doomed. The effect that even a rumoured Keating resignation had on the dollar was spectacular; only vigorous denials from Keating's office allowed the currency to settle. The *Sydney Morning Herald's* report quoted a foreign exchange trader: 'If Mr Keating had resigned you wouldn't have been able to find the Aussie dollar—it would have gone down the plughole.' By late July the dollar had staged a small rally and reached about 72 US cents, encouragingly higher than its 66 US cent level at the beginning of the month. With the tax summit over, Keating's next hurdle was the annual budget, brought down on Tuesday 20 August. The budget deficit for 1985/86 was pitched at $4.9 billion, down from the previous year's $6.7 billion. The figure was to prove unachievable and the failure was another dark thread in the dismal economic tapestry of 1986. Reaction to the budget was initially positive because the projected deficit was lower than expected. But feelings turned negative as it was recognised that the reduction in the deficit was due to benefits in revenue that resulted from an improvement in the economy rather than an attack on spending.

And Australia was not alone in having problems grappling with a volatile exchange rate. The Plaza Agreement of September 1985—so called because it resulted from a meeting at the Plaza Hotel in New York—marked an attempt by the world's chief central banks to come to some arrangement that would reduce the fluctuation in exchange rates which was so disruptive to world economic performance and trade. The meeting was attended by senior central bankers and finance ministers of the US, UK, West Germany, Japan and France (known as the Group of Five or G5). It took place after the US Treasury secretary, James Baker, had persuaded his government that the high $US was inflicting damage on the country's export industries and succeeded in bringing the $US value down. Exchange rates and the need to help solve the debt problems of countries such as Brazil and Mexico dominated the agenda at that year's IMF/World Bank meeting, held in Seoul, South Korea. The US Treasury secretary launched his 'Baker plan' whereby the chief commercial banks would agree to provide $US 20 billion to the debt-ridden countries. Keating, absorbed in hammering new tax measures into place, missed that year's meeting. Australia was represented by Chris Hurford as acting treasurer.

Back in Australia, the government was shaping the September 1985 agreement with the ACTU that came to be tagged the Accord Mark II. This agreement was the product of a series of meetings between Keating and Willis and the ACTU, and provided for full indexation of wages to continue, except that the March–April 1986 wage increase would be discounted by two per cent to help offset the effect of the depreciation of the Australian dollar. Accord Mark II was an attempt to preserve the advantages of the $A's fall, in terms of the competitiveness of Australia's trade, and not have these advantages cancelled by a surge in wages. The extent of the Australian dollar's fall had raised the question of how to adjust wages in the light of the currency devaluation. If wages were fully discounted to reflect the effect of the fall in the Australian dollar, thus restraining production costs, then the benefits of the fall—in terms of international trade—would be preserved. If wages were not discounted for the fall in the dollar then the benefits of the currency's depreciation would be lost. The trade union movement was against full wage discounting but was prepared to accept an initial discount of up to 2 per cent, to be followed by a further 2 per cent in the next wage case. As had been the case when monetary targeting was abandoned, and when the MX missile argument arose, the compromise over wages was interpreted wrongly overseas as a sign of a weak government caving in. The problem was compounded because the deal was seen as being too late, in that earlier effects of the depreciation had been allowed to slip through.

By September 1985 Keating looked exhausted, his eyes puffy and rimmed with black circles of fatigue. The work on tax reform, the long hours spent persuading, arguing and haranguing around the continent, followed by the tax summit, the budget and cabinet sessions on the revised tax package had taken a toll. He had fought, and won, cabinet battles to get the tax reform through. Few, by that stage, felt in any position to oppose him. It was small consolation that there were already expressions of regret that his cherished Option C package had been rejected. That month he announced the government's tax package in a comprehensive statement that included the controversial fringe benefits and capital gains taxes. The reform of the Australian tax system also introduced full imputation of company dividends and a hike in the corporate tax rate, from 46 cents to 49 cents in the dollar, to help offset the cost to government of allowing the dividends on which full company tax had been paid to be tax-free in shareholders' hands. Keating announced the end of the tax deductibility of business entertainment expenses and tougher rules on the substantiation of allowances. Provisional tax was to shift to quarterly, rather than annual, payments. Personal tax rates would be progressively reduced, to achieve a top marginal rate of 49 cents in the dollar by July 1987. The statement foreshadowed the introduction of a national identification system—the doomed Australia Card. The thrust of the package was to reduce marginal tax rates and curtail tax avoidance and evasion.

Keating played safe and had a sandwich in his Parliament House office rather than brave a restaurant on 19 September, the day that the new regime became a reality. He appeared on television that evening, in the *Carleton–Walsh Report*, with a discussion panel that included Andrew Robb of the National Farmers' Federation, Eric Mayer of the Business Council of Australia and John Howard, by then leader of the opposition. Keating rejected the suggestion from Max Walsh that the business community had been heavily hit by an increased tax burden which included a higher rate of corporate tax and a foreign tax credit system, as well as a fringe benefits tax to be borne by employers on cash and other non-salary benefits to employees. He pointed out that business had got what it wanted—imputation of dividends.

Keating later in the TV program defended the introduction of full imputation on dividends as a trade-off against the fringe benefits tax. He also argued that the fringe benefits tax was not unfair to business. 'Business has had an enormous advantage by walking around the tax system arm-in-arm with its employees by providing fringe benefits . . . We are changing that. We are putting that tax on business at a time of enormous increase in company profits,' he said. Andrew Robb put forward his view that 'some key elements of the package are going to be very harshly received in the bush and in particular the capital gains tax proposal and the limits to writing-off of farm losses'. The National Farmers' Federation was squarely against taxing capital gains, believing it would discourage long-term risky, but productive, investment. Keating responded:

> Well look, there's one thing about the National Farmers' Federation, you can never please them. Never please them. Every single farm at this moment is exempt from the capital gains tax. No existing asset will be capital gains taxed and Mr Robb just completely forgot to mention that little fact, that no existing farm will be capital gains taxed . . . The fact that some people have been able to take their income as capital, has meant for the last twenty years we've been putting our money into real estate instead of productive plant equipment investment, and he must understand that. But the most unbelievable assertion he makes is that in some way we shouldn't be legislating against the Pitt Street farmer. Because, from my understanding of rural Australia, the Pitt Street farmer has driven up land values at the expense of genuine farmers for years . . .

Robb's response was that the 'paranoia with Pitt Street farmers had led to a provision which discriminates against a whole range of farmers'. Next day Keating flew to another round of media interviews, in Sydney and then Melbourne.

Keating was rarely out of the headlines in September and October 1985, for one reason or another. He shared the limelight with the

NSW deputy opposition leader, Mrs Rosemary Foot, whose earlier allegations that he was involved in state government land 'deals' cost her $47 500 in settlement. Defamation actions by Keating and the Sydney businessman and property developer Warren Anderson against Mrs Foot resulted in a payment of $17 500 to Keating and $30 000 to Anderson. The *Sydney Morning Herald* reported:

> Mrs Foot . . . read out in court an apology to Mr Keating and Mr Anderson admitting comments she made about them last year were 'unjustified and unwarranted'. The defamation action centred on allegations Mrs Foot made at the beginning of last year that the State Government had arranged to sell Mr Anderson foreshore land within the Hermitage Reserve in Vaucluse for about $550 000 less than its real value. She alleged Mr Keating was part of a corrupt 'network of favouritism' involving the NSW Labor Party which had resulted in Mr Anderson being offered the land at a reduced price. In her statement Mrs Foot said she accepted there was no basis for the allegations and she regretted having made them.

October brought a significant addition to Keating's personal staff, with the arrival of Seamus Dawes, assistant secretary of the NSW branch of the ALP, as Keating's political adviser. Dawes' arrival followed the departure in April 1985 of Barbara Ward. He brought the skills of political, rather than economic, advice. His appointment was interpreted as an attempt to bridge the gap that many believed to be widening between Keating and the NSW right-wing party machine. As Keating's political strategist, Dawes would bring the flavour of Sussex Street to the Canberra office, whose atmosphere many in New South Wales believed contributed to Keating's isolation and distance from political realities. Dawes would also provide balance in a staff that was otherwise largely culled from Treasury.

Meanwhile, with an eye to the international as well as domestic scene, and the need to bolster Australia's flagging image overseas, Keating decided to visit New York towards the end of October. He planned to discuss financial markets and especially exchange rates, in what was to be his second address in six months to the Asia Society. The New York correspondent for the *Australian Financial Review* at that time, Glenda Korporaal, asked the Asia Society's director of corporate programs if it were not a shade unusual for someone to request a second appearance so soon, and at fairly short notice. The director replied: 'I guess he's got something he wants to say.' US investors were beginning to turn cold on Australia and business publications were highlighting the country's heavy load of debt, falling currency and general economic difficulties. Keating delivered a message designed to allay their doubts and moved on to London as part of this mission to try to lift Australia's international profile.

The Australian dollar confirmed pessimistic predictions and slid to 65 US cents around mid-November. This followed a 3.8 per cent wage increase, with no discounting for the depreciation of the Australian dollar, and an alarmingly high inflation figure for the September quarter. By then the Reserve Bank was tightening monetary policy to support the flagging dollar. The result was a substantial hike in interest rates. The 90-day bank bill rate briefly hit 20 per cent in December and banks were charging between 19 and 20 per cent for overdrafts. There was a concern that if interest rates remained at these levels they could choke off growth. But if rates were allowed to ease too soon the dollar might take another tumble. The treasurer was walking a fine line.

By the end of November monetary policy was being used to such an extent to prop up the dollar that Australia no longer had a 'clean' float—that is, one in which the currency responds to market forces and the central bank does not interfere. Australia had started to live with a 'dirty' float. This was not unique—most countries which had floated their currencies found their floats 'muddied' from time to time as the central banks attempted to keep the currencies within acceptable ranges. With a fixed or managed exchange rate, the central bank has to try to swim against the tide, then when pressure gets too much, concede with a sizeable devaluation or revaluation that may bring only temporary relief if the basic problems that forced the move have not been solved. Almost inevitably, speculation starts to mount again. The float might not be the perfect answer but, among other things, it ends the disruptive cycle of a massive build-up in speculation that leads to a big increase or decrease in the value of the currency—in which speculators frequently make profits at the expense of the central bank.

There was little cheer for Australia's treasurer as what had undoubtedly been his most demanding year drew to a close. Much had been written about Keating's lost battles but he was acknowledged as being valiant in defeat. Commenting in the Melbourne *Herald* on 4 November 1985, Peter Costigan wrote: 'There is no doubt that Paul Keating is the political star of the year, if only because he absolutely refuses to accept that the numerous policy defeats he suffered during the year are anything but the flick of the wings of inconsequential flies.' Costigan's article also told of Keating's virtuoso performance as guest-of-honour at the Canberra press gallery's annual dinner, which that year was a no-spouse, off-the-record event. He wrote:

> For the record, it is fair to say that over recent years Bob Hawke and Andrew Peacock were boring at off-the-record Gallery dinners, Jim Killen was amusing at an on-record function and Malcolm Fraser resolutely refused to attend any, under any rules. Gough Whitlam did, hilariously, and Sir John Kerr did too, the year adjoining Whitlam, more hilariously, but without humour.
>
> It breaches no pledge of silence to report that Paul Keating delivered a performance at the 1985 Press Gallery Dinner without peer since the last time Gough Whitlam appeared, more than ten years ago, as Prime Minister . . . His speech ran to nearly an hour, encompassed black Irish humour about most of the Cabinet and a fair portion of the Press . . .

The article's tone became more serious at its conclusion. Costigan made the frequently heard comment that Keating was a man to watch as a potential leader, but cautioned that 'two things, apart from fate, are hurdles in his path'. One was the risk that Keating might believe too much in his destiny. That, Costigan wrote, would be a great undoing. The second danger was that Keating would continue to believe too much in what Treasury bureaucrats were telling him—potentially, in Costigan's view, an even more likely disaster.

Just how far the Hawke government and its treasurer had travelled in the previous twelve months could be gauged from such comments. By the end of 1985, speculation about the party's leadership succession was being fed by the oft-reported differences between prime minister and treasurer over policy matters, and comparisons between the apparent vacillations of one and the single-mindedness of the other. The year 1985 ended on quite a different note from the buoyant 1984 which had seen good results in employment, inflation and economic growth—a performance that was crowned by the government's re-election for a second term, although with a far smaller majority than it had expected. The 1985 downturn in Australia's economic fortunes, reflected for all the world to see in its weaker currency, cast the government's policies into doubt. Keating's predicted J-curve—the illustration of the performance of a country's balance of payments after its currency has been devalued—had not arrived. According to the J-curve theory, manufacturing industry gets a boost from a depreciation after initially being hit by higher import costs. After a time, exports start to rise in volume because they are cheaper, and imports start to fall because they become more expensive. And the current acount should turn from showing a deficit to a surplus.

Bachelorhood ends. Keating, 31, marries 26-year-old Anna Johanna Maria von Iersel, known as Anita. The wedding was in January 1975 at Oisterwijk, in Anita's native Holland. Many politicians would see her qualities as valuable political assets but Keating, on the contrary, has been almost obsessive about keeping his wife and children out of the spotlight. The trip to their son's wedding was the first European visit for Min and Matt Keating.

An unusually casually dressed treasurer Keating chats to a more formally attired Malcolm Fraser in Newport, Rhode Island, USA. It is September 1983 and political differences come second to Australian camaraderie at the America's Cup, won that year by Alan Bond's twelve-metre yacht.

Above Keating's assistant Barbara Ward whispers advice in her boss's ear at the July 1984 ALP conference. Ward was hired early in 1979 as general adviser and was Keating's sole staffer in Canberra until Labor won election in March 1983. Her unusual mix of economic literacy and electoral savvy made her invaluable, so much so that Keating, ever wary of the unfamiliar, was reluctant to rely on new advisers. But the weight of the treasurer's role forced him to expand his staff well beyond one assistant. Ward remained until April 1985. *Below* September 1984 was Keating's second visit as Australia's treasurer to the annual meetings of the International Monetary Fund and the World Bank. That year he was named finance minister of the year by the prestige bankers' magazine, *Euromoney*, an accolade that brought him under the international spotlight as a world political figure.

Keating in a reflective mood ahead of what was to be a doomed tax summit in July 1985. Over the four-day summit he saw his cherished plan for tax reform, including a consumption tax, attacked and dismantled from unexpected quarters. But he picked up the pieces and salvaged what he could. Three years later he had broadened the tax base without needing to rely on the consumption tax he had so passionately espoused in 1985.

A pair of torcheres and candelabra on loan from Keating to the National Gallery in Canberra. Keating brought them to the gallery as examples of the neo-classical or French empire style he so much admires. The mahogany torcheres were made about 1805, from a design by Thomas Hope. The candelabra date from about 1797. Both take their form from the ancient monuments of Greece and Egypt.

Day one was the beginning and the end of the tax summit. Keating's initial confidence fades to doubt, then to clear anxiety as he seems to be wondering in disbelief where events were heading — until finally it dawns on him that he is being defeated.

The Hawke government scored a record third term with its July 1987 federal election victory, but there were strong signals of disenchantment from the electorate, including a 7.4 per cent anti-Labor swing in Keating's Blaxland electorate. Nevertheless Keating was able to enjoy a celebratory beer at the Bankstown Sports Bowling Club.

Hawke and Keating share a joke for the camera — though the relationship has not always been so cheerful. Behind them caucus poses for a final shot on the steps of the 'old' Parliament House on budget day, September 1987, when Keating later delivered a triumphant balanced Budget, the last to be read in the old House.

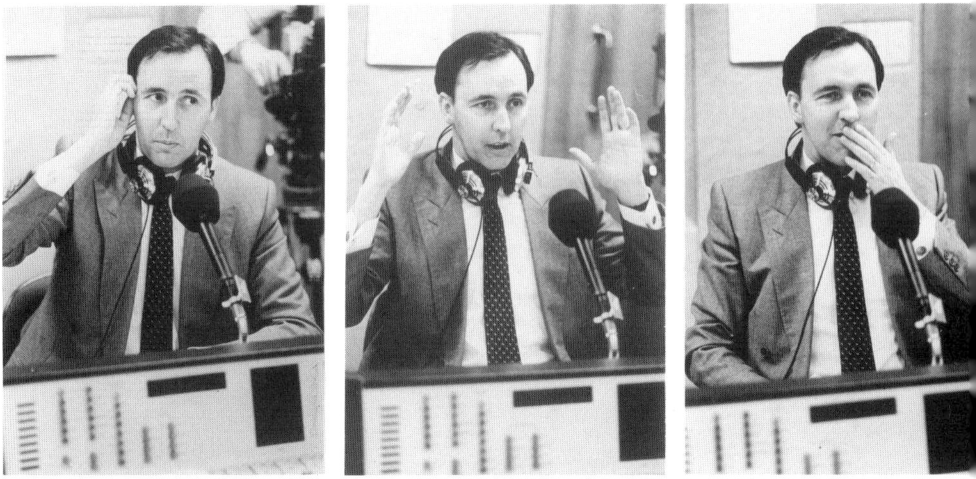

Keating relaxes with radio host John Laws in the 2GB studio in Sydney. It was on Laws's program in May 1986 that Keating made his famous 'banana republic' comments which signalled the gravity of Australia's economic problems and marked a turning point in government policy.

Keating is crowned as the first 'Australian Irishman of the year' at a $250 a head inaugural dinner of the Ireland Fund in Australia held at the Regent Hotel in Sydney. The then senator Susan Ryan joins in the occasion, where Keating confessed to being a typical Irishman, 'sentimental to the last teardrop'.

Anita and Paul Keating and their four children — Patrick standing next to his mother, father Paul with daughters (*from left*) Katherine, Caroline and Alexandra. Many a politician would capitalise on such a photogenic family; Keating prefers to keep them away from the public stage.

In fine rhetorical form, Keating addresses a lunch to open Victory House small business centre at Blakehurst in May 1988. In the same month he delivered an economic statement that cut corporate tax rates and attacked sacred cows such as the tax-free status of superannuation funds and the exemptions from corporate tax of gold-mining companies. That month also brought a resurgence of comment and speculation about not *whether* but *when* Keating would succeed Hawke as prime minister.

The ALP biennial national conference at Hobart. Newspaper photographers could not resist the opportunity to make effective use of the background slogan — *the Australian Labor Party: working for Australia*. Keating delivered a speech in which he described the ALP platform as drawing together 'the philosophic and economic principles which underpin the government's economic policy. . .'.

John Leard, the prominent conservative businessman with whom Keating had regularly chatted about the economy and who was now a strident critic of the Hawke government's policies, reminded a group of business people at a Securities Institute lunch in Sydney in December that it was a little more than twelve months since Keating had been crowned *Euromoney's* finance minister of the year. 'I wonder whether you know the treasurer of Mexico won it the year before,' Leard said.

Keating at that time seized the chance to set on the record his views about the Hawke government's philosophies and achievements, and their place in Labor history. Delivering an address at the inaugural Whitlam Conference of Labor Historians in Sydney on Sunday 1 December 1985, he cited reforms such as Medicare, youth employment, improved social welfare and additional funds for public housing as important achievements. He explained the moves to deregulate the finance industry and reform the tax system as part of Labor's strategy for achieving economic growth; they were not, as some had accused, a sign that Labor was adopting conservative, right-wing thinking.

> I maintain today that in continuing to pursue this growth objective, the Hawke Labor government is operating completely in concert with the tradition of the Labor movement . . . in adopting practical, pragmatic measures to create growth and jobs, the Labor Party of 1985 is doing nothing out of the ordinary from what the Labor Party in government has sought to do throughout its long history. Those who allege that the current administration has questionable Labor credentials fail to understand the very essence of the Labor tradition and have been misled into thinking that the views and objectives that developed in the party's aberrant period of the 1950s and 1960s more correctly reflect the party's true direction.

Keating's twenty-page speech included a potted history of the origins of the ALP, the chief aim of which became, as the historian Bede Nairn terms it, 'civilising capitalism'. Keating described the Labor Party as a pragmatic party, traditionally interested in economic progress and practical social reforms. He quoted the opening words of the Labor platform: 'The Australian Labor Party had its origins in the aspirations of the Australian people for a decent, secure, dignified and constructive way of life.' In that address, as elsewhere before and since, Keating referred to Labor's 'aberrant philosophies', to a 'minority of activists' whom he has blamed for rendering the party irrelevant. 'It is in overcoming such a period of irrelevance that Gough Whitlam's greatest achievement lies,' said Keating 'His great and enduring legacy was to refurbish the party, to breathe life into it . . . Whitlam and the government which he led played the central role in Labor's emergence from its long period of irrelevance in the 1950s and 1960s . . . when it was racked by self-indulgent, ideological conflict.' The Whitlam government, he said, had 'rehabilitated' Labor.

Keating quoted Whitlam's own summing-up of his government's impact, delivered two weeks earlier on Channel Nine's Sunday program on the eve of the tenth anniversary of his dismissal: 'I was the person who made the Labor Party credible.' Many of the Whitlam policies have endured—his foreign policies were largely adopted by the Fraser government, Medibank was demolished but revived as Medicare by the Hawke government, his contribution to education has been preserved, as have his landmark law and electoral reforms which established the principle of one vote, one value, and regular redistributions. Keating moved from praising Whitlam's contributions to pointing out the flaws of his government (though less harshly than he was to do two years later when addressing the Victorian branch of the Fabian Society).

> The one area where the Whitlam and Hawke governments have a different perspective is in economic policy. The agenda Whitlam set himself did not emphasise the primacy of economic growth because his government came to power at a time when growth in Australia had long been taken for granted . . . Whitlam entered government believing he was in a position where he could take abundance for granted and instead concentrate his energies on distributing it. In comparison, the current government gave primacy to the growth objective on taking office. That there was such a difference . . . was largely a result of circumstance rather than philosophy. But I emphasise that this was a difference upon taking office. The Whitlam government's greatest failure was its belated recognition that the economic sands had shifted beneath it.

Keating went on to outline the problems that ensued in the economy as the Whitlam government 'abandoned economics . . . in favour of an undisciplined dash to implement a decade's worth of reform'. Wages blew out and budget outlays surged in what he referred to as 'tragic confusion of objectives and means'. He attributed the Hawke cabinet's expertise to the lessons of the Whitlam years. Keating had put his case in more forthright language in an earlier interview in the *National Times:*

> In terms of the Labor agenda, this government has left every other Labor government before it bare-arsed. No other Labor government even gets within cooee of it. We have a Cabinet which

> has a degree of economic sophistication which puts the Whitlam government into the caveman class in economic terms.

If Keating had harsh words for that government's economic mismanagement, he was even more scathing about the coalition government that followed. Malcolm Fraser's seven years in office, he said, were among the 'most barren this century'. In criticising that government for fostering hopes of a resources boom as a solution for Australia, Keating was echoing the views of the late US physicist and futurologist Herman Kahn. Kahn, founder of the Hudson Institute, the US think-tank, and co-author of a book on Australia's future, *Will She be Right?*, had earlier commented that resources-rich countries end up being intellectually lazy because they do not try hard enough to make their real resources work for them. A month earlier the *International Herald Tribune* had quoted Keating as saying that the notion that Australia could dig up another mound of rocks and sell them to someone had gone on for too long.

The purpose of Keating's address was to lay to rest the notion that the Hawke Labor government had somehow been invaded by a gang of demons since it came to power in 1983; rather, it had adopted sensible, in some instances bold, policies aimed at ending distortions and improving efficiency as well as lifting Australia's position internationally.

So 1985 drew to an end. One year into its second term in government Labor had been faced with steering Australia through one of its most challenging times. The OECD put some icing on Keating's Christmas cake with its forecasts of another year of good economic growth for Australia, and a drop in inflation and unemployment. But problems in the current account were to dominate the coming year. Keating was going to need all his steel.

11 The banana republic

If this government cannot get the adjustment . . . and a sensible economic policy, then Australia is basically done for. We will just end up being a third-rate economy . . . a banana republic.

PAUL KEATING TO RADIO HOST JOHN LAWS, MAY 1986

FOR PAUL Keating, 1986 was dominated by the need to tighten fiscal policy. Tension built through the year as economic problems intensified and financial markets reacted by dragging the Australian dollar lower.

The trade account had been gradually worsening for months but the decline suddenly accelerated in January 1986 when the Organisation of Petroleum Exporting Countries (OPEC) decided to let the price of oil fall. The move was to shake out the non-OPEC producers and allow the OPEC countries to regain their market share. The ramifications of that move took some time to flow through to other energy products but over the next few months their impact began to show up as the fall in the price of oil triggered a drop in commodity prices generally. For a commodity-exporting country such as Australia, this was bad news.

The Hawke government was in an unenviable position. It was faced with the worst trade collapse since the second world war, at a time when it had already undertaken to make big tax cuts over the following two years and to reduce the budget deficit. The tax cuts had to be delivered as they formed part of wages policy and tax reform. The deficit had to be trimmed as part of a policy aimed at restraining domestic demand, reducing imports and encouraging lower interest rates. The government had to demonstrate fiscal reponsibility to the international community. At the same time the government was reluctant to abandon its published growth targets and employment objectives. It was to be a tough year.

Paul Keating was confronted by a challenge of a different nature when parliament opened in February for the first session of the new year. From day one it was clear that the opposition had decided to attack. Who better to launch a vitriolic verbal assault than Western Australia's member for O'Connor, Wilson 'Ironbar' Tuckey, described in one press report as 'Shadow Minister for Getting Under Ministers' Skins'? What better target could he pick than the government's best performer, Paul Keating, renowned for his own quick and often vicious tongue and for his ability to shoot back when under attack. The exchanges between the two men did nothing to lift the quality of parliamentary debate, and would have passed into the record with minimal comment had not one of Tuckey's shafts so rattled the normally imperturbable Keating.

Tuckey began by objecting to Keating's referring to John Howard as 'his oiliness' and delivered a scarcely veiled warning: 'If you want me to talk about Kristine you keep up with this "his oiliness". I will give it to you any time you want it. You play it straight.'

Tuckey's reference to Kristine involved the story of Keating's broken engagement in the early 1970s, and the subsequent breach-of-promise action brought against him by his then ex-fiancee. Friends recall Kristine as 'a nice girl but wrong for Paul'. She had little interest in politics and did not understand his commitment. But the romance had its own momentum. The two had become engaged, then the engagement was broken off, after much agonising on Keating's part, only weeks before the wedding. Some time later Kristine sued for a number of items including, for some reason, a bar stool which she had earlier given her fiance. The press gallery was well aware of the story—a list of items for which she had reportedly sued had circulated around Parliament House the previous year. This was said to be an extract from a statement of claim against Keating filed with the NSW Supreme Court. It was an old story in the corridors of Canberra.

Tuckey and Keating went into battle. The deputy speaker, Leo McLeay, called for order. His words went unheeded. Keating fired back: 'The honourable member for O'Connor is a member with a criminal intellect, and is a criminal in my view.' The words were calculated to fan the flames. Tuckey demanded a withdrawal. 'I do not mix with criminals,' he said.

Keating goaded Tuckey further. 'I do not get someone to hold somebody against a wall while I belt him with a trucheon,' he threw back—a reference, often used by Labor, to Tuckey's conviction in 1967 for assaulting an Aboriginal in a West Australian town.

The deputy speaker asked Keating to refer to the leader of the opposition by that title, and to withdraw the remarks made about Tuckey. Keating said: 'Mr deputy speaker, in deference to you I withdraw but I point out that the leader of the opposition hurls all sorts of abuse at me, and all through Question Time those two pansies over there want retractions of the things we have said about them. They are a bunch of nobodies going nowhere . . . '

The interchange of abuse continued. Keating scathingly referred to the opposition as 'the animals on the other side', the deputy speaker chastised the opposition for interrupting, but to little effect, and when Jim Carlton, then shadow treasurer, got up to speak Keating greeted him with the barb: 'Here is old Rosie again.' Carlton objected to what he said was unparliamentary language. It made entertaining if hardly informative copy for the press gallery.

The protagonists went into round two the next day. Tuckey kicked off with another threat to mention Kristine. Keating's rejoinder was that ' . . . the loopy crim from O'Connor is at it again'. Tuckey waded in deeper: 'Kristine had a little girl called Paul.' Keating was furious: 'You stupid foul-mouthed grub . . . you piece of criminal garbage.' The opposition raised objections to Keating's language. The chair said it had not heard Keating's last sally above the racket and called for order. Tuckey kept up his taunts: 'The treasurer has not yet withdrawn. I request that he withdraw. Now I know how Kristine felt.'

Keating accused Tuckey of hurling 'what he believes to be personal obscenities at me privately across the chamber' and then demanding a withdrawal when Keating retaliated. The second day's exchange made more headlines. 'Rafferty's NSW rules as Keating tucks into a bovver boy Liberal' ran the *Sydney Morning Herald's* column from the press gallery. The *Herald* reported that it had asked Tuckey to explain his 'mysterious references' but he had declined, saying: 'The campaign I have been running against Keating is to say, "Lay off personal abuse of other people" or I will extend that debate day by day until he does.'

What so stung Keating was that Tuckey's words implied there was more to the story. Keating was riled by the slur and rang Howard to protest about Tuckey's behaviour and language. Tuckey later claimed he had intended to say 'Paul had a little girl called Kristine', but had mixed his words. He repeatedly refused requests to exercise his right as a member of parliament and have the Hansard altered, although he admitted that the recorded words were not what he meant to say. Keating's undisguised fury kept the episode alive long after it should have faded from the news pages.

Political commentators were surprised that this usually cool politician, this parliamentarian *par excellence* who had built over twenty years a reputation as a champion verbal duellist should allow Tuckey's taunts to pierce his guard. Keating was incensed at what he regarded as below-the-belt insults that intruded on his personal life and dragged an innocent third party into the limelight. Never shy about lashing the opposition or using vulgar invective to get out of a tight spot, he nevertheless adheres to an unwritten code that stops short of offending wives and families. Keating employs what he calls 'the corporate slur'. He later said: 'I don't appreciate people saying that I've got an illegitimate child when I don't have such a child.' He defended his own colourful language as 'hard political repartee' and not personal abuse. 'When you start talking about someone's actual personal life that's a personal attack and I just don't see any place for that,' he said.

Political parties have always gathered evidence—or scurrilous rumours—about opposition members but generally the information remains locked in filing cabinets or muttered about in bars rather than aired in the House. It was Tuckey's clumsy outburst that breached this code but it was Keating's reaction that won the story huge coverage. Writing some weeks later in the *Sydney Morning Herald*, political commentator Peter Bowers said: 'Letting Wilson Tuckey . . . get under your skin is worse than catching a galloping dose of scabies. The itch is terrible; you're liable to tear yourself to pieces.'

At the end of the Tuckey–Keating clash the speaker of the House of Representatives, Mrs Joan Child, rebuked members on both sides for their language and behaviour. The legacy of those first two weeks of the 1986 parliamentary year showed in two ways: there was a flurry of speculation that Keating might prove to have a less-tough hide than had been supposed, and the easy relationship that had existed between Keating and Howard was irretrievably damaged. Certainly Keating's regard for Howard had diminished as his conviction grew that the Liberals had utterly failed economically. But the two men, despite being on opposite sides of the political fence, had enjoyed a friendship over the years, sharing plane trips between Canberra and Sydney and the common ground of the weird world known only to politicians and their staffs.

But that had ended. Keating blamed Howard for Tuckey's behaviour. He told a group of journalists outside Parliament House that he had learned that Howard had taken a deliberate decision to use Tuckey's aggressive behaviour to the full advantage of the oppositon. 'The cost of this to Mr Howard is going to be very expensive,' Keating warned. 'From this day onwards Mr Howard will wear his leadership like a crown of thorns and in the parliament I will do everything I can to crucify him.' Howard's response indicated that while he might not wholeheartedly approve of Tuckey's words and methods he was not about to rebuke him publicly. 'I don't like any personal references in the parliament and it's not my style,' Howard said, 'but I am certainly not going to desert, censure or criticise one of my people for raising it when you take into account all the personal abuse hurled at our people which in many cases has been worse.'

Tuckey remained jubilant and unrepentant. 'I have chucked out half a prawn and caught a bloody mackerel,' he crowed. The *Sunday Telegraph* tracked down Kristine and her mother and reported that Kristine, now happily married and living in a well-to-do Sydney suburb, would prefer to forget the whole matter. The *Sun-Herald* profiled Keating, and talked of the treasurer's warm personality and rarely-shown passionate nature. The public had been allowed a glimpse of this passion. But even in the throes of rage Keating remembers to play politics. The *Sun-Herald* reported that he was busily doing the rounds of the press gallery telling his story:

> [Keating] was in the *Age* bureau confidently putting his case when he happened to glance at the television set (with volume turned down) on which Mike Willesee was conducting an interview. A woman appeared on the screen. Keating saw her out of the corner of his eye and thought it was Kristine who had gone public with her side of the story. He gave a nervous shout: '(Expletive deleted) Turn it up.' To his relief he saw it was someone else and had to furiously cover his embarassment. 'Christ, I don't remember what she looked like,' he said lamely. 'It was a long time ago.'

By the time parliament resumed sitting on 3 March a different kind of news was keeping Keating in the headlines, in the form of renewed criticism that he was out of touch with his NSW power base and no longer listened to their political advice, preferring to soak up what Treasury told him. That offended his mates in the party, to whom solidarity is everything. Keating seemed to have strayed too far from the disciplines of Sussex Street, Sydney, the heartland of NSW Labor. Senator Graham Richardson, known as the principal right-wing numbers man and for years a close ally of Keating's, was visibly cooler towards the treasurer. Richardson laughed off suggestions of a real quarrel, telling a group of inquiring journalists that the NSW Right was 'like a large Irish family . . . members have tiffs, even brawls, but the blood is wiped up quickly and no-one outside should know the details'.

Speculation also revived that relations between the prime minister and his treasurer had grown less cordial. This view was fed by the opposing approaches taken by the two men on the question of whether or not the government should intervene in the attempted takeover of Australia's biggest company, BHP. Robert Holmes à Court's Bell Resources had launched a $1.92 billion bid for 250 million shares in BHP—a move which, if successful, would take Bell's stake in BHP from 18.8 per cent to almost 40 per cent. Keating's view—which became a wedge between him and his factional mates in Sussex Street—was that takeovers were best left to the market to sort out. Hawke supported the notion of government intervention. Cabinet had its chance to block the Bell bid by stalling the relevant amendments to the Trade Practices Act that were at that time before the Senate. The cabinet decision not to put any obstacles in Holmes à Court's path was read as a victory for Keating.

Keating's approach was not merely contrary to that of the prime minister—it was roundly criticised by many of his supporters within the ALP. The most publicly outspoken critic of Keating's attitude was John MacBean, secretary of the Labor Council of NSW and a man whose personal and political relationship with Keating stretched back for years. MacBean claimed that Keating had forfeited his title as spiritual leader of the NSW ALP machine. The *Sydney Morning Herald* of 4 March 1986 reported MacBean's disappointment at the absence of a government inquiry and his criticism of what happened. MacBean said three significant points had been raised by the episode.

> First, it has shown that the current legislation governing takeovers and monopolies is grossly inadequate, and offers no protection for public interest, shareholders and employees. Secondly, it has highlighted the absurd position in which people like Mr Holmes à Court can raise $2 billion and the interest charges on that are tax deductible . . . Thirdly, it has shown that the trade union movement has been able to establish that they are an important factor in takeover bids.

The point that interest on borrowings of the magnitude of Holmes à Court's, and for purposes such as takeovers, could be claimed as a tax-deductible cost was to haunt Keating for most of

1986. It was a topic frequently raised and dissected by Max Walsh in his regular columns in the *Sydney Morning Herald*. And it fed the hostile perception that was growing in some quarters of a disillusioned electorate that government decisions seemed to benefit wealthy entrepreneurs such as Robert Holmes à Court. The Hawke government's image was starting to suffer from its apparent closeness not just to the financial community but to the growing 'club' of the new rich. Hawke's friendship with Sir Peter Abeles, chief executive of TNT, was well documented. He was known to be on good terms with Kerry Packer. Keating's admiration for entrepreneurs such as Holmes à Court and Alan Bond, and his distaste for the 'established rich' was never concealed.

It had fallen to the Hawke government to implement radical changes to Australia's financial system at a time when the country's economy was experiencing enormous difficulties and the entire world was going through a prolonged sharemarket boom. It was not only in Australia that financial services, rather than manufacturing, were attracting attention; the phenomenon was world wide. Every country with a sophisticated capital market had produced a generation of yuppies, earning huge salaries in banking, investment and merchant banking and stockbroking. Australia—and New Zealand—had also produced a crop of professional investors, entrepreneurs who based huge businesses on share trading and takeovers, who did not concentrate on *making* anything useful but accumulated paper wealth. This paper wealth could be obliterated as quickly as it was acquired, as the sharp correction in the sharemarket in October 1987 was to show. But in 1986 the boom seemed never-ending.

The Hawke government was faced with a peculiar situation—the paradox of implementing change in a country that was at the one time racked by economic problems and fostering a thriving financial sector that helped the concentration of enormous wealth. The fact that financial deregulation was accompanied in Australia, and in New Zealand, by a sustained boom in the sharemarket has distorted the effects of the changes. The easy access to finance to fund takeovers or buy shares was not merely a product of fewer government controls; it was fuelled by the prevailing mood of buoyancy in the sharemarket. Even though, by 1986, the commentators and economists were predicting a downturn in the sharemarket, many of the key players were still borrowing and trading as if the gravy train were going to last forever. Keating, ever the economic rationalist, stuck to the view that it is best to leave the market to resolve its own problems.

The tension in senior levels of government that was revealed in March 1986 was not what the government needed. Hard decisions had to be made on crucial issues and the government had to be seen as in command and in agreement. Keating was furious that a preliminary budget outlook paper had been leaked to the *Sydney Morning Herald* and talked threateningly of what he would do to the culprit if found. The thorny question of home-loan interest rates emerged in March 1986. The banks were losing deposits as investors turned to outlets that paid higher rates of interest, such as cash management trusts. The loss of depositors' funds meant the banks' pool of available finance for lending was dwindling. The banks argued that they could not attract more funds by paying higher interest rates to depositors because they were fenced in on the home-lending side by a maximum rate of 13.5 per cent.

The banks, spearheaded by the Australian Bankers' Association, proposed to Keating that the interest-rate ceiling be lifted from home finance. In return the banks would increase the amount of funds lent to home-buyers and would examine ways to increase the flexibility of loan repayments. Keating met the chief executives of the four main banks, ANZ, Commonwealth, National Australia and Westpac. He was receptive to their argument. It fitted with the general tenor of deregulation. In fact, the remaining control on home-loan rates was an anomaly in a tapesty of interest-rate deregulation, and favoured the home-buyers who succeeded in organising such finance over other categories of borrowers. It was a relic of the 'sacred cow' attitude to home-loan interest rates.

Any move that threatened to increase the cost of home finance spelled electoral disaster. The reaction to press leaks that the Hawke government was contemplating lifting the ceiling on home-loan interest rates showed attitudes had not changed. The government retreated. Hawke said in parliament on 19 March 1986: 'The government remains committed to the retention of the ceiling on housing interest rates.' Keating was more equivocal and next day told a group of journalists that the whole of the housing issue was to be examined. Work continued on what was to become a package of proposals on housing finance which saw the ceiling lifted on new home loans and the banks agreeing to provide additional funds for lending to home-buyers. Existing loans were protected—their interest remained at 13.5 per cent—but these loans would gradually disappear from the banks' books as they were repaid or refinanced. The last regulatory fence on interest rates had been removed.

By April the collapse in Australia's terms of trade was taking its toll.

Export prices were down and, given the lower currency (which was destined to fall even further), the price of imports had risen, widening the gap on the current account. A report from the influential US investment bank Salomon Brothers pronounced Australian bonds a good buy and this gave the Australian dollar a respite, boosting it to around 74 US cents early in May.

Keating's public message during April was of continued optimism. But behind the scenes, the treasurer had been receiving advice from several sources, most notably the Reserve Bank, that the outlook was far from rosy. A lengthy discussion paper, prepared by the bank and presented to Keating in April, was a vital element in persuading the government to change its tack. The paper gave a base-line projection of the balance of payments, under certain assumptions and over a period that stretched into the 1990s. It was presented at a special meeting in Canberra attended by senior bureaucrats from the Reserve Bank and Treasury as well as by Keating and staff from his office. Keating and Treasury were initially dismissive of the paper, saying the assumptions were unrealistic. The Reserve Bank conceded that some of the assumptions could be changed but that would not alter the outcome—the government would have to shift its concentration from domestic growth to concern for the external situation and the level of overseas debt.

The meeting convinced Keating that serious economic problems threatened the country. The seeds of his famous 'banana republic' speech, in which he forecast dire consequences if Australia did not lift its game, had been sown. The true dimensions of these problems were revealed on 13 May 1986 with the release of the April trade figures, which, with a $1.35 billion deficit on the current account, were far worse than had been expected. Mid-May 1986 goes down as a pivotal point in Keating's career, a juncture where the Hawke government was forced to change course, abandon the high growth targets and knuckle down to solving the country's deep-seated economic problems. The gospel of growth to which the Labor government had clung since gaining office in 1983 would be replaced with more sober economic rhetoric and action. The government was persuaded of the gravity of the situation facing the country; the next challenge was to spell out the message to the broader community.

Hawke departed for a two-week trip to Japan and China on 14 May, the day after the April figures had been released. He had encouraged Keating to provide some comment on the bad figures. It was not incumbent on the treasurer to elaborate on the monthly trade figures but the gravity of the numbers demanded some statement.

Keating also left Canberra that day, for a round of engagements in Melbourne. Hawke and his entourage were out of Australia when Keating went public with his views. By the time he had finished the Australian dollar had dropped four cents. Speaking from Melbourne by phone to the Sydney talk-back radio host John Laws, Keating set out to tell the story:

> I get the very clear feeling that we must let Australians know truthfully, honestly, earnestly, just what sort of an international hole Australia is in. It's the prices of our commodities—they are as bad in real terms since the Depression. That's a fact of Australian life now—it's got nothing to do with the government. It's the price of commodities on world markets but it means an internal economic adjustment. And if we don't make it this time we never will make it. If this government cannot get the adjustment, get manufacturing going again and keep moderate wage outcomes and a sensible economic policy, then Australia is basically done for. We will just end up being a third-rate economy.
>
> Laws: Is this situation that exists now the worst situation that has existed economically in Australia since the Depression?
>
> Keating: It is in terms of our export prices—absolutely.
>
> Laws: If we don't get out of this economic hole, as you described it, what is the prognosis? In simple terms.
>
> Keating: The prognosis is, the only way you can deal with the massive current account imbalance is to close the economy down. You cut all growth to zero, you stop all the imports growing and unemployment starts rising again, and profits fall apart, and we go back to being the kind of economy we were in 1982 . . . or worse.
>
> Laws: Or worse. I mean that's a perfect description of a depression.
>
> Keating: If in the final analysis Australia is so undisciplined, so disinterested in its salvation and its economic wellbeing, the fall-back solution is inevitable because you can't fund $12 billion a year in perpetuity every year, and then the interest on the year before that, and the interest on the year before that. The only thing to do is to slow the growth down to a canter. Once you slow the growth under 3 per cent, unemployment starts to rise again.
>
> Laws: And then you have really induced a depression.
>
> Keating: Then you have gone. You are a banana republic.

The words made headlines. The impact reverberated around the country and around the world. Keating had in fact used the banana republic analogy earlier that year in London, when delivering a lunchtime address to an audience of prominent City people organised by the leading investment bank S.G. Warburg. It was a private lunch with no media coverage, and the colourful analogy was heard without comment. Keating's second reference to Australia's possible banana republic fate created a sensation, and signalled a sea-change in mood. Keating had mixed feelings about the banana republic speech. It was certainly effective in ramming home the message to caucus, cabinet and the trade unions as well as the wider community, that Australia faced serious problems and that belt-tightening and wage restraint lay ahead. But it also sent a note of panic through the narrower area of the financial markets, which reacted by savagely marking down the Australian dollar. Bernie Fraser, secretary of the Treasury, believes the banana republic outburst was successful in fostering an acceptance in the broad community that the country was in difficulties. 'The trade unions have a greater acknowledgment now that they need to be more responsible. Business no longer wants hand-outs. Keating has fostered a market psychology,' he says.

Hawke, visiting Japan and then China, was annoyed by reports that indicated the treasurer had taken hold of the reins of policy in his absence. Distance added its own dimension to the misunderstandings and exaggeration. The press corps, travelling with Hawke ostensibly to cover his trip for an audience at home in Australia, were trying to report on a story that was taking place 5000 kilometres away in Canberra. Hawke faced a press conference in Tokyo just as reports filtered through that Keating was planning a mini-economic summit. The Australian journalists were keen for some comment but Hawke wanted to steer the discussion away from the domestic and on to the international scene. He almost succeeded. But it was hard to hide the fact that Hawke was trying to avoid talking about a situation of which he knew little and did not control. His advisers did not like the turn of events. Geoff Kitney, one of the journalists travelling with the prime minister, filed what was billed as the 'inside story' for the *National Times:*

> Hawke went on to an official dinner. His advisers, with time to reflect on what had happened, concluded that Keating had acted appallingly and that Hawke was in an invidious position. When Hawke returned from the dinner, the decision was taken to direct deputy prime minister Lionel Bowen to set up a meeting of senior ministers in Hawke's Parliament House office on Monday morning, which Hawke would address by phone from Beijing. In an 11.30pm call to Bowen, Hawke told his deputy to take charge of events and to tell ministers to hold their tongues. After speaking to Bowen, Hawke was satisfied that the matter was under control. But that was not the public perception. The next day, Saturday, saw Hawke go from golf course to sumo wrestling, apparently oblivious of the storm breaking around him . . . By Sunday morning, as the prime

> ministerial party packed and set off for China, his silence had become absolutely peculiar. All requests from the press to get a word from him were refused. He was too busy, was the response. But . . . the press applied pressure . . . When he reached Beijing, Hawke . . . was told by his advisers that correspondents travelling with him were prepared to write highly critical reports about his apparent failure to exercise leadership. The strong advice to Hawke was that details of the phone calls to Bowen should be released, to show both that he had acted decisively and that he, and not Keating, was the leader of the government. Hawke took the advice.

Hawke's telephone conversation with the assembled ministers created its own small storm. His words were not news—the main points were already in print for all to see, on the front page of that day's edition of the *Australian Financial Review*, in an article filed by Greg Hywood who was with the travelling entourage. Keating was far from impressed. Old ghosts returned to haunt him. Not only was Hawke surrounded by his 'minders' but in Beijing he was also in the company of Ross Garnaut, a former adviser to the prime minister, a former staunch opponent of Keating's consumption tax and now Australia's ambassador to China. Hawke seemed out of Keating's reach, kept that way by those whose business it was to advise the prime minister. Keating did not keep his grievance to himself. 'Keating slams Hawke staff—"Manchu Court" who think they are elected' shrilled the headline of the *Daily Telegraph* on 30 May, the day after Keating had criticised the prime minister's staffers on the ABC radio show *PM* and on Mike Willesee's television program.

It was no secret in Canberra that Keating's particular nemeses were Peter Barron, previously press secretary to the former NSW premier, Neville Wran, and Bob Hogg, formerly secretary of the Victorian branch of the ALP. Keating believed they pushed vote-catching rather than policy moves. He said on air that he and Hawke got on well together, that he considered Hawke to be a great prime minister but that he had been having a 'permanent stoush with Hawke's minders for years'. Keating said:

> They are always my trouble. They've never been elected or anything but they think they have, and every now and again I remind them they haven't. And he [Hawke] should remind them every now and again as well . . . The prime minister and I have been at cross purposes over the last week or two mainly because of the difficulties of communicating our position while he was in China . . . I couldn't get his ear because I was a long way away and they were nearby . . . they keep bobbing up and I keep knocking them over. It's the Manchu court, they sit around like courtiers.

It was another time of strain between prime minister and treasurer, although not as severe as the tension between them after the tax summit of the previous year.

Hawke decided to soothe national nervousness about Australia's economic future by delivering an address to the nation, given on 11 June 1986. Couched in emotive language, it was designed to turn the national mood, but failed. The address was badly received, largely because it was seen as too vague to be constructive. It seemed to highlight the government's problems without suggesting that it had specific policy remedies. Hawke outlined the reasons for Australia's dramatically increased difficulties: the country's national income had fallen in line with lower prices for its exports, while import prices had continued to rise. 'This most recent turnaround in the terms of trade has slashed 3 per cent off our capacity to maintain existing living standards,' he said. Hawke foreshadowed tough decisions in the budget, and at the premiers' conference to be held a few days later. And he praised the launch of the 'Buy Australian' campaign.

The 1986 premiers' conference fulfilled the prophecy of a tough stance by the government. The states accepted the argument supporting the need for restraint and took a 10 per cent cut in their borrowings and in general purpose payments from the commonwealth. The blow was softened by the two per cent increase the states had enjoyed that year in general revenue.

The weight of economic problems threatened to keep Keating away from the biennial ALP national conference, held that year in Hobart. But he put in a late appearance and gave a speech which provided entertaining theatre for the delegates and journalists reporting the events. Discussing the debate about takeovers and the tax-deductible status of interest on funds borrowed by business for such purposes, Keating defended the government's stance:

> There's been more column inches in the *Age* and the *Sydney Morning Herald* on this than you could ever imagine. At 9.30 almost every second night on the ABC there are glazed eyes across the dining rooms of this country on the same issue and everyone's revved it up; they've all revved it up that there's a new demon out there—it's interest deductions—and it's bringing us all unstuck. I tell you this: that is basically fraudulent . . . when next you see [talk] about interest deductions, well, you know what you want to do. Put it on the spike in the back toilet, because that's where it belongs.

July 1986 seemed to bring nothing but bad news. An announcement on 1 July that the government would remove the exemption from withholding tax that was enjoyed by bearer bonds, and which was seen as critically important to the appeal of the bonds, went down extremely badly with overseas investors. (Bearer bonds are securities issued with detachable coupons, which the holder presents for interest payments. The name of the holder of the bond is not registered. Withholding tax is levied on dividends and interest sent abroad. Their exemption from this tax made bearer bonds attractive to foreign investors.) The financial markets seemed to be tired of waiting for good news, or at least a turn in the tide, and sold the Australian dollar down to an extent that the currency went into a virtual freefall, hitting an all-time low of 57.30 US cents on 28 July. The markets had overshot and sent the dollar down too low, but it is in the nature of markets to over-react. And the mood was brittle. Keating was swept along by the panic. Policy had to be shaped in a way that kept the financial markets happy, otherwise an outflow of capital and rising interest rates would compound the existing problems.

The government rushed out some desperate decisions to try to stem the run on the dollar, freeing up foreign investment policy and revoking the ill-advised move to lift the exemption from withholding tax that applied to interest earned by bearer bonds. The decision to lift, and then reimpose, the withholding tax exemption is one of Keating's few regrets. It was said at the time that he was badly advised. He counters: 'Not badly. But I don't think the advice comprehended the market.' Keating says that was one decision that he let pass since he has been treasurer with which he basically did not agree. 'It just proved the point that you can never afford to let one go by. After a while you start saying to yourself, "Am I too sensitive in these issues?" You think maybe you are, so you let something go by. But I was right—so that was when we turned it around.'

Critics who say that Keating had by then stopped listening to outside advice, that he was relying overmuch on Treasury counsel, point to the withholding tax episode as symptomatic of a treasurer who had lost touch with the reality of the financial markets. If domestic market operators were startled by the move, overseas investors were appalled. The Japanese, whose funds have played a crucial role in financing semi-government and government borrowings, talked for some time about the peculiarities of such a rapid change of heart. The about-turn on withholding tax showed that Keating was capable of changing his mind. He has been accused of being overly stubborn, resisting or stalling on advice to change course. At the same time the episode showed the risks at stake when a politician does have a change of heart, how hard it is to concede that a move was wrong when publicly one has hung one's hat on it.

Adding to the government's problems was an overrun of $700 million on the budget, taking the deficit to $5.7 billion. The increased shortfall was largely due to the effect of the falling currency on the cost of imported defence equipment. It was the not the type of news the government needed. Nor was the threatened airline pilots' strike, prompted by concern over the arrival of promised tax cuts and superannuation changes. The strike was called off when Keating met the pilots' demands for written confirmation that the tax cuts would eventuate. But the episode added further to Australia's tottering international image. Australians travelling overseas were frequently the butt of jokes about living in a banana republic, needing food parcels, bargaining with the South Pacific peso and now unable to get home. The fact that the airline pilots' strike did not eventuate was irrelevant. Internationally it was 'bash Australia' time.

It was late in July 1986, as budget preparations were underway, that the *National Times* contacted Keating for his co-operation with an article that would examine his friendship with Warren Anderson, the wealthy property developer whose interests include the Coles New World shopping centre sites. *National Times* writer Brian Toohey had sent Keating a list of questions, some of which related to Anderson's business interests and problems with the Australian Tax Office, which he wanted the treasurer to answer as part of the paper's investigations. Keating declined to co-operate. In a written rejection his office told Toohey the treasurer had little wish to talk to him, even if he had the time. The *National Times* article appeared on the Sunday before budget day, and was to feed Keating's growing conviction, bordering on paranoia, that elements of the Fairfax press were gunning for him personally.

The 1986/87 budget went further than the government had initially intended, providing for deeper cuts in expenditure and, in particular, more tax increases than had been planned. The books had been closed off on Labor's fourth budget, due to be handed down on Tuesday 19 August when the Australian dollar, which had recovered from its low levels of late July to around 62 US cents, fell once again to 60 US cents. The currency's fall sent the architects of the budget back to the drawing board. The budget deficit was pitched at about $3.5 billion but the figure got a rough reception, reflecting a general disbelief that it was attainable. At $3.5 billion the deficit projection was lower than had been expected but the government missed out on the psychological impact usually associated with such news. The market just did not believe the figure. Time was to prove the scepticism wrong—the deficit for that year came in at $2.7 billion. But in August 1986 the mood was still pessimistic and the market took the Australian dollar down to 60 US cents. Only Reserve Bank defence of the currency prevented it from falling further.

Meanwhile, Australia's national ego was dealt another blow when the US credit-rating agency, Moody's Investor Services, downgraded the country from the coveted AAA status to AA+, citing the ballooning current account deficit and the country's dependence on commodities as the cause.

It was a rocky time for treasurer Keating, who was coping with tremendous challenges in his professional life and unusually demanding times on the personal front. His wife, Anita, who a year earlier had given birth to their fourth child, Alexandra Johanna, had been unwell and was admitted to hospital for a gallbladder operation. Keating, having delivered the budget, was closely involved in wage negotiations, travelling between Canberra and Melbourne. Finding time to visit his wife in hospital was not easy but he did—and once fell asleep while there.

By October 1986 the current account deficit had reached a peak of $1.8 billion, highlighting the extent to which Australia was living beyond its means and borrowing to support its fairly high standard of living. The Hawke government's earlier moves to free the dollar and lift exchange controls became a popular target for critics who blamed much of the country's woes on those deregulatory moves. What the critics seemed to ignore was the damage that had been done under the Fraser government, when rigid adherence to anti-inflation policies had seen the government set the Australian dollar unrealistically high, so that manufacturing had become uncompetitive, while at the same time promoting expectations of future earnings increases, buoyed by the belief that a resources boom would occur in the early 1980s. Australia was busy enjoying bread that was yet to be baked.

The states embarked on an ambitious borrowing program to finance the infrastructure needed for future resources projects. Once the states have secured a borrowing allocation, that level becomes the minimum to be raised. If a state raised less, its allocation could be cut back. Borrowings were well in place when it became evident that the much-touted boom was not to be. But enthusiasm about its arrival had swept along the business community and the unions. Wage rises had been sought and granted on the basis that prosperous times were on the horizon. The demand for funds spilled beyond the resources of the domestic capital market. Borrowers turned to international markets.

Australia's rising international debt was the subject of considerable academic criticism in 1985 and 1986 but it was not until the full blast of the deterioration of the trade account hit home that the extent of the problem became clear. The country was caught on a dangerous treadmill. The borrowings undertaken to offset the deficit in the current account grew in foreign exchange terms (because the weaker Australian dollar bought less foreign exchange); similarly, the cost of interest on foreign borrowings rose when expressed in terms of the Australian dollar. Overseas markets saw the ballooning debt and marked the Australian dollar down, setting off the treadmill once again.

Australia has been dependent on a healthy world demand for its exports, such as meat, coal and wool, for decades. Whenever demand for and prices of these goods fall, they take Australia's living standards down with them. If the international markets turn cold on a country, so that it can no longer easily borrow, it is faced with deflationary moves domestically to repair its difficulties. Australia so far has been lucky in that it has been saved from time to time by a boom in the demand for minerals or other commodities. In the absence of this demand, it has had to face tougher options, such as cutting government spending and trying to increase its savings and investment.

The situation was already delicate when the downturn in world commodity prices dealt its heavy blow in 1986. The vicious circle of bad trade figures and a weak currency, which was pushed lower by continued disappointment on the trade front, meant that the cost of servicing Australia's foreign debt, in Australian dollar terms, was $9 billion or 20 per cent of export earnings. It was to be a long haul to get Australia back on track. After the high point of $1.8 billion in October 1986, the current account deficit began an improvement, initially exaggerated by a change in the Customs Department's method of reporting, but nonetheless a turnaround. Selling pressure on the Australian dollar slackened and was gradually replaced by buying demand. But it was not until well into 1988 that the current account delivered encouraging news and the dollar significantly increased in value. The fluctuations in the current account weigh on Keating's thinking. He explains:

> Seeing the current account change continuing, that's the biggest challenge. Investment and import replacement are by far the biggest and most fundamental change facing the government,

> facing Australia. And it's happening as we thought it would, but it's a slow process. When you break your secondary structure, it takes a long time to get the whole thing back. In a sense our productive culture had sort of gone and we're now in the business of building the culture *and* the machinery and it won't be accomplished quickly. But that is without a doubt the big challenge—and all of the structural things which the government has been involved with in the past few years are geared to meeting that basic challenge.

Keating did not allow the problems at home in 1986 to dampen his performance at that year's IMF/World Bank meeting in Washington. His speech at the interim committee meeting turned heads, ruffled some feathers and pleased many of the delegates. His vigorous speech, pointing out that the IMF was long on rhetoric and short on action, made headlines in Australia. He succeeded in irritating many at the Washington meeting, not so much by what he said as by the way he said it. And, as usual, he enjoyed the chance to say something forcefully to a group of significant people. Representatives of the larger countries were clearly rattled at being told off by someone who, in their eyes, represented a small upstart country. Others, such as Canada, related well to what Keating said and were complimentary about his performance.

The treasurer is more entitled than most to be critical of mere rhetoric. He can take much of the credit for the Hawke government's rhetoric being matched by its actions. The Fraser government was free with words but baulked at putting much of what it said into action. It talked a great deal about deregulation but in reality the Fraser years were marked by considerable government meddling that was often at variance with the rhetoric. And Keating is bent on delivering what he is convinced is right. In that regard, according to Bernie Fraser, he is a 'unique animal'. The Treasury secretary explains:

> Once Keating makes up his mind about something he goes all out to achieve it, he believes in doing it. So often in the past ministers have been persuaded or believe that something is worth doing, they make an attempt, fail and say, well, they tried but couldn't get it through. Keating's not like that. He *wants* to deliver. The foreign bank issue is an example, so is tax, even though the consumption tax did not eventuate. He pressed on with subsequent reforms. He had to contend with opposition within and without.

As treasurer, Keating is involved in several aspects of government policy. Bernie Fraser says that Keating's great strength is that he has what he himself calls the 'broad picture'; he knows how it fits together and understands the linkages. Says Fraser:

> Keating knows how far he can go in monetary policy before problems start to occur in the economy—unemployment and so on—and how critical wages are to addressing the current account problems and inflation. He has a good feel for how hard he can press—on Kelty, on his colleagues, on the fiscal front and how hard he can press on monetary policy—without causing problems.

Not everyone is as impressed by Keating's talk of understanding the 'big picture'. When he used this line of defence, saying it was his concern about the broad canvas that had allowed him to overlook details such as filing his 1985 and 1986 tax returns, he was roundly ticked off. 'That big picture you're on about will be hanging over John Howard's mantlepiece if you're not careful,' was one caustic warning. Keating's staff were not surprised that he was behind with his tax returns—they had seen his disorganised approach to paperwork at first hand. Papers on his desk might be straightened into neat piles to look ordered but there would be no logic to the piles. Barbara Ward says: 'Paul's not a good paper man. You wouldn't leave him with paper. You went in with stuff and sat in front of him while he read it and signed it. You didn't leave him with something. Otherwise kiss it goodbye.'

In the past, though, Keating had been careful that tax returns were filed on time. He was conscious of his position. The late tax returns were an indication, along with his over-reaction to the Tuckey jibes, of how stress and pressure were taking their toll. He told parliament on 27 November 1986:

> I received a letter from the honourable member for Mackellar [Mr Carlton] asking me to comment on a letter from the Deputy Commissioner of Taxation in Sydney that had come into his possession. This letter from the Deputy Commissioner of Taxation, dated November 3, was to advise me that my income tax return for 1985 was overdue and that I should now lodge a return for 1986 as well. I never received the letter from the Deputy Commissioner, which was obviously stolen from the mail. The first knowledge I had of its existence was on Tuesday morning of this week when I received a telephone call from the Commissioner of Taxation telling me that he had had an inquiry regarding the letter. I took the opportunity to tell the Commissioner that I had prepared my return for 1985 and that I was in a position to lodge it that day, which I did . . . I am a PAYE taxpayer and my PAYE deductions are such that I expect to receive a refund . . . As a consequence any cost . . . is borne by me and not by the Commonwealth . . . This is not to say that I should not have lodged the return earlier; obviously I should have and I regret not having done so. I fill in my own tax returns and

> unfortunately, through oversight, I failed to lodge it on time . . . I might add that in this matter I have been treated no differently from any other taxpayer, but I appreciate the manner in which the honourable member for Mackellar chose to raise the matter with me.

The following day the subject of Keating's late tax returns was raised again. Jim Carlton talked of Keating's failure to comply with the procedures that apply to ordinary people, saying: 'At the heart of all this is the question of double standards and the question of decency.' He called for both the prime minister and treasurer to be censured. Keating's retort was that the question of ministerial responsibility was not at issue; it was a private matter between him and the tax office. He reminded the House that he aired the matter in 'unequivocal and unambiguous terms' the previous evening. 'I said then, and I repeat, that I regret having not filed the return. There is no excuse for me. The return should have been filed. I do not walk away from that whatsoever.' He then swung into unmistakable Keatingspeak:

> I did make a mistake but, unlike the leader of the opposition, my mistake did not cost half a million people their jobs. My mistake did not retard the economy for twenty years. My mistake did not induce a massive domestic recession, unlike his mistake which almost destroyed the fabric of the Australian economy. And he sits up here as a failed treasurer asking, as he did absurdly this morning, for my resignation over something that is of course entirely a private matter between me and the Tax Commissioner.

Keating subsequently demanded that the opposition explain how it came by the letter addressed to him from the tax office. He pointed out that intercepting correspondence between the tax office and a taxpayer is a serious matter. 'It is not a copy from the tax office because tax office duplicates do not carry the masthead,' he said.

> Let us hear about the opposition's role, if any, in this criminal offence against the Post and Telegraph Act. Let the lawyer with the silk handkerchief in his pocket over there tell us about criminal offences under that act, let old unctuous over there, the shadow treasurer, tell us how he came by this letter, and let the leader of the opposition tell us how he came to this letter.

Tuckey threw in his contribution, objecting to Jim Carlton's being labelled 'old unctuous'. In the ensuing brawl Keating needled Carlton about the timing of filing *his* tax return. The speaker called for order several times. Keating weighed in again:

> We heard from the leader of the opposition about me, about my travelling allowance, about the suntanned windows and about the white car. These are snide remarks thrown around by the leader of the opposition. But I will never get to the stage of wanting to lead the nation [like Howard] standing in front of the mirror every morning clipping the eyebrows here and clipping the eyebrows there with Janette and the kids.

It was the last day of that session of parliament. Keating dredged up every grievance he could throw at the opposition, winding up with:

> Let me conclude by saying that I regret having not filed my income tax return. My future tax returns will not be overdue. All tax payers should file their returns on time and there can be no excuses—that must be said. But that does not cover the deceitful approach of the opposition for standing against every decent piece of taxation law that this government has tried to introduce and every decent piece of economic policy that it has pursued. No amount of personal attacks on me will ever confuse the parliament about that fact.

News of Keating's late tax returns broke not long before Christmas, when Australian families were juggling their budgets to cope with the cost of the annual festivities. The revelation provoked considerable resentment: here was the country's treasurer, who had waged a relentless campaign for tax reform and, in the name of economic rationalism, introduced measures that carried some pain as well as some pleasure, ignoring his duty as a taxpayer. Keating's oversight provided his critics with a fresh supply of ammunition; they declared that his action smacked of the arrogance of someone who felt above the common throng. Talk-back radio programs buzzed with indignant callers, ready and eager to bucket the treasurer.

Another issue that was probably less clearly understood but potentially more damaging politically was Keating's travelling allowance. He undoubtedly lost points over this question, which rested on the $30 000 or more he had claimed over the previous two years for accommodation costs while away from home. The travelling allowance is intended to cover the costs of MPs' travelling from home base to Canberra and accommodation while in the capital city. The opposition made considerable mileage out of the fact that Keating and his family live in Canberra, although the family home is in Sydney, and that Keating felt justified in claiming a travelling allowance when in reality he was not away from home. He was living in Canberra. Keating defended his travelling allowance claim as legitimate: he was within the definition, living in Canberra, away from his home base, defined under the legislation as 'principal place of residence' which, he said, was the house he owns in Sydney and not a rented house in Canberra. In claiming the allowance he was not behaving any differently to many other MPs. But having set himself up as such a vigorous opponent of so-called 'rorts' he had placed himself on exposed ground. Accusing others of abusing fringe benefits and then claiming a travelling allowance when he lived in Canberra smacked of a double standard.

Keating's retort was that it was Howard who had advised him to move his family to Canberra—that it was impossible to carry out the treasurer's job by fax from Sydney and to keep any semblance of family life. And Keating does not want to miss seeing his children grow up. He has seen what harm the peculiarities of political life can inflict on a marriage and children. He wants his family happy, intact and nearby. So he moved them to Canberra, where he had to live to do his job. 'I don't do it in a tent on the front lawn of Parliament House. I live in a house here,' he said. And he pointed out that the allowance went towards the rent he paid to live in Canberra to do the job of treasurer. But the row stirred up significant public resentment at a time when people had been lectured about belt-tightening and the need for austerity. There was potential for huge political damage. Politicians are placed on high pedestals. When they are found capable of human error the lapses makes headlines. Ministers have to be especially on their guard.

Changes were foreshadowed that would prevent a repeat of accusations that Keating was defying the system, but it was not until December 1987 that the remuneration tribunal handed down a decision which resolved the difficulty. The tribunal redefined what could be claimed as a home base. The opposition called the change 'the Keating amendment'. An additional provision was made so that the home base became defined as the principal place of residence *and* the place to be maintained and to which the minister would normally return if he or she were not required to spend continuous periods in Canberra on official business. If Keating were not occupied with work in Canberra, he would return to Sydney.

If 1986 ended on a mixed note for Keating personally, at least he could enjoy good news on the economic front—welcome relief at the end of what he often described as the government's worst year. The current account appeared to be improving and the OECD had forecast healthy growth of 3.25 per cent for the year ahead. A state by-election was looming in Keating's electorate of Bankstown in January, and was to provide the excuse for one of his least favoured newspapers, the *Sydney Morning Herald*, to write about the growing gulf between Bankstown and its former son. By the end of 1986 Keating was paying increasing attention to the media, but for another reason: his involvement in the proposed media ownership legislation.

12 Princes, queens, and a king hit

You're either queen of the screen or prince of print . . . now there is no major network owned by a print proprietor.

PAUL KEATING

THE YEAR 1987 brought a radical restructuring of Australia's media industry. Newspapers, television channels and radio stations changed hands at an unprecedented pace and at unrealistically high prices as the market sought to keep one step ahead of the new legislation and operators fell over each other to position themselves in the new environment. By the end of 1987 no media operation was as it had been at the start of the year. Television was in the hands of new owners, such as Christopher Skase, a former financial journalist turned entrepreneur, Alan Bond, better known for his property and brewing business interests, and Frank Lowy's Westfield Capital Corporation, built on suburban shopping complexes. Rupert Murdoch dominated in print, Kerry Packer had sold out of television, Robert Holmes à Court looked to be gaining influence in newspapers, and the ultimate fate, shape and size of John Fairfax Ltd, the media empire most shaken-up by the year's events, was still in question.

The new generation of television barons had paid high prices for their acquisitions. The prospect of changes in the legislation affecting media ownership had pulled a vital thread in the tapestry of Australian media companies and plunged the owners into a frenzy of activity even before the ink was dry on the draft rules. A chief consequence was the division of ownership between print and broadcast—the diversified media conglomerate with a range of communications activities spanning newspapers, magazines, television and radio would no longer exist. With the dismemberment of the Fairfax corporation, Australia lost such a group. In its place are a number of businessmen-turned-media-owners whose interests are not confined to publishing. Paul Keating played a leading role in the legislative changes which brought about the restructuring of the media industry.

Keating's fascination with the media was not new. He had been critical of Australia's media legislation, and of the concentration of ownership in the industry, since the early 1970s. The issues that came to a head in 1986 and 1987 had been simmering for decades. Probably the most significant triggers that brought them to the boil were the launching of Australia's domestic communications satellite in 1979 and subsequent reports by the Australian Broadcasting Tribunal into cable television (1981/82) and satellite program services (1984) which recommended sweeping changes in the broadcasting industry.

By the time the issue was in full debate, in the second half of the 1980s, Australian media power was firmly held in a few hands. The chief names were Fairfax, Packer, Herald & Weekly Times and Murdoch. The Fairfax group held a strong position in print—as publishers of successful papers such as the *Sydney Morning Herald*, the *Age* and the *Australian Financial Review*, and a healthy group of business and general-interest magazines—and had significant holdings in television and radio. The Herald & Weekly Times group also had major holdings in both print and broadcasting, as did Rupert Murdoch's News Corporation. Kerry Packer's Consolidated Press ran a successful stable of magazines and a network of television stations. These major players dominated the industry under a system of government regulation which in fact had made their corporate existence remarkably comfortable and profitable. Under the rules, no individual or company could own more than two television stations and eight radio stations in Australia. The twenty-year-old two-station rule had been designed to restrain the concentration of influence in television ownership. But in reality the rule had fostered concentration: two stations were two stations, irrespective of their size, so that an operator owning two small regional stations was no more able to expand than a larger player with a station in each of two capital cities.

Keating had fired his earliest arrows at the structure of media ownership in Australia in 1971, when he criticised the extent of the

Melbourne *Herald*'s controlling interest in channels HSV7 in Melbourne, BTQ7 in Brisbane, ADS7 in Adelaide and TVT6 in Hobart, calling this a contravention of an act of parliament. He then highlighted the rule that no single organisation should control more than eight radio stations in Australia and argued that the Fairfax group was in contravention of the act through its ownership of stations including 2GB in Sydney, 2WL in Wollongong, 2CA in Canberra and several smaller country stations in New South Wales. His criticism mounted in the following year. In May 1972 he accused the government of the day of being a 'lackey to special interest groups . . . particularly a lackey to the media'. He told parliament on 18 May 1972:

> . . . no other country would stand for those multi-media combinations . . . In the United States of America the Federal Communications Commission busted the newspaper and television monopolies but this government has done nothing in that direction. A couple of months ago the Postmaster-General [Sir Alan Hulme] introduced legislation . . . to extend the provisions of the Broadcasting and Television Act so that a Labor government on taking office at the end of this year would not be able to interfere with the provisions of licences granted to television companies or radio companies during what is expected to be Labor's first three years of office. I assure the government that ingenuity will not cease and Labor will at least attempt to break up the multi-media combinations.

Labor won office in the federal election of 2 December 1972 but it was not until 1976, when once again in opposition, that Keating made news with his mission to streamline media legislation. On 4 November 1976 he put forward a media bill which would forbid present and future investment by newspaper publishers in radio and television—the basis of his later 'prince of print or queen of screen' definition. Keating, who had only some months earlier been given responsibility for the minerals and energy portfolio, again told parliament that the Australian media was dominated by three groups of companies to an extent that would not be tolerated in other countries. He continued:

> What also makes the situation frightening is that most of the proprietors who operate these groups share a common social background and, in political terms, share a common point of view. Divestment must occur . . . newspaper groupings should not be permitted to take over other groupings with holdings in radio and television.

The bill was defeated by 81 votes to 31.

Around the time that Keating was presenting his doomed bill to parliament, one of Australia's media barons, Kerry Packer, was successfully selling the concept of a privately-owned domestic communications satellite to prime minister Fraser. It is an irony that Kerry Packer, the chief driving force behind the satellite, had sold out of television by the time—ten years later—that national networking had become a reality. Back in 1976, Packer had commissioned a study of the feasibility of the satellite. He passed on a report to the government, which then established a satellite task force. By 1979 the government had decided that it would, in principle, support the idea of the satellite. The announcement brought widespread opposition from telecommunications unions and from regional television owners who saw themselves being pushed off the scene by large operators such as Packer. The birth of the satellite was the trigger that unleashed a whole range of pent-up pressures that were to prove too much for a family-dominated industry.

In establishing the satellite the Fraser government had bitten off more than it could chew. It could not resolve the diverse problems created by the satellite. A good concept had been wrongly sold from the start on the basis of being used for broadcasting, which could never pay for it. The satellite should have been sold as a step to improve communications, not just to service broadcasting needs. The agreed aim was to try to make better use of the satellite but no-one had figured out a way to achieve this. The challenges of satisfying country viewers and the big networks, and at the same time allowing smaller television operators to expand and to get regional television operating well, were part of the legacy inherited by the Hawke government when it won office in March 1983.

The problems that related specifically to media issues fell to the lot of Michael Duffy, minister for communications. Duffy, a lawyer with a reputation for pragmatism, outspokenness and courage, became a popular figure with the media executives with whom he dealt. He quickly gained an understanding of the industry—no small achievement, given the proliferation of broadcast legislation and policies that reflected the absence of a coherent government policy. The industry appreciated Duffy's attitude: he was not there to please everyone, but he was prepared to listen to everyone, including the smaller regional players who generally found it difficult to get a minister's ear.

A milestone on the path that led to the ultimate industry shake-up was the report delivered in July 1984 by the Australian Broadcasting Tribunal on satellite program services, which recommended that the government undertake a complete restructuring of the broadcasting system. Some months later, in February 1985, Duffy revived the issue of national networking and commissioned an inquiry into how best to provide services around the country.

A hurdle that stymied progress for most of 1985, though, was a growing rift between Hawke and Duffy, over defining the 'reach' level to be allowed television owners; that is, the percentage of the national audience they could reach. Rupert Murdoch and Kerry Packer each reached 43 per cent of the national audience with their existing television stations. Duffy's view was that 43 per cent should be established as the maximum level, so that the two existing operators could hold their share and newcomers could work towards that level. Hawke wanted a top access level of 35 per cent, with a 'grandfather' clause that would allow Murdoch and Packer to retain their existing 43 per cent but restrict newcomers to the lower market share. Such a notion was untenable, from the political or equity point of view. Hawke's stance was seen as blatant favouring of his 'mates'. 'Tell us what Kerry and Rupert want and we'll work around that,' was one minister's sarcastic response. The clash between the prime minister and Duffy became a serious strain within the government. Duffy had logic and principle on his side, and widespread support in caucus, but was sticking his neck out against his boss. A committee was appointed, consisting of Hawke, Duffy, Keating and senator John Button, to examine the issues.

Keating's solution—borrowed from the US legislation that he had praised more than a decade earlier—was to place no limit on television ownership but to introduce a new rule banning cross-ownership between print and electronic media. Keating broadened the debate into the area of media, rather than merely broadcasting. Whereas Hawke was fascinated by the power of television, Keating's obsession was the power of the press. He lobbied hard during 1986 to win widespread backing for his compromise solution, which he had to get past Duffy and through caucus and cabinet. He whipped up support among the Labor Left by reminding them of the Melbourne *Herald*'s hostility to Brian Howe, the minister for social security. The *Herald*'s campaign against the assets test for pensions was seen as an example of the newspaper's animosity to Labor. No tears would be shed in the Hawke government if the HWT group fell victim to the new legislation. In fact, the government was anxious to apply the new rules in advance of any takeover move against the perennially vulnerable HWT.

By October Keating's proposals had won the acceptance of

most of his colleagues—although Duffy remained unconvinced. He had had his portfolio hijacked, and he knew he could not win against Keating. He dug his heels in nevertheless, resisting Keating's policies despite considerable persuasion from the senior minister. Keating pointed out that Duffy would make his name in history if he took the proposals to cabinet as his own. But it was not in Duffy's nature to ride on someone else's coat-tails. He stuck to his insistence on a maximum reach limit of 43 per cent, knowing it was in vain. Cabinet's decision to implement Keating's proposals went to a caucus that, however much it might dislike the deal, was expected to endorse it. Keating worked up momentum by forecasting that the HWT group would be carved up as a result of the changes, and that that would be no bad thing as it was not 'one of us'.

Duffy announced the new rules for television ownership on 27 November 1986. The existing two-station rule was to be replaced with one which limited the reach of any one television station owner to 75 per cent of the Australian population and which limited cross-ownership among television, radio and newspaper interests. Duffy's announcement read:

> Lifting the two station rule would adversely affect competition if it simply allowed interests to own a television or radio licence and a newspaper in the same area and thereby have an exaggerated influence over local affairs. For this reason the government has decided, in principle, to regulate cross-ownership of the media in Australia . . . Of course we do not intend to penalise those who have acquired their licence under existing rules. There will be no forced divestitures. Interests held at the time of this announcement that would be in conflict with the cross-ownership rules will be grandfathered.

The legislation was to be introduced during the autumn session of parliament in 1987. At that stage, the government, desperate to push the legislation through, buckled to a National Party amendment cutting the reach limit to 60 per cent. The legislation was passed in June 1987. The changes were immediately identified as favourable to Packer, with his focus on television, and to present serious obstacles to the more diversified groups, such as Fairfax and Herald & Weekly Times, both long regarded as anti-Labor.

The new rules were a catalyst in a cauldron that had been fermenting for decades. Within days of Duffy's announcement Murdoch launched his assault on the Herald & Weekly Times. It was widely known in political and journalistic circles that the HWT group was vulnerable. Murdoch and Holmes à Court had made sharemarket forays against the group years earlier, but their bids had come to nothing. Murdoch's $2.3 billion bid for HWT on 3 December 1986 lifted the curtain on the first round of a drama that was to be played out, with multiple climaxes, in the media industry over the ensuing twelve months.

The next event of interest was Kerry Packer's move to acquire television stations in Perth and Brisbane, a development that triggered Alan Bond's media subsidiary into offering Packer $1 billion for his Sydney and Melbourne stations and associated radio interests. Packer, who ten years earlier had been pushing for the satellite, and for television networking, accepted what was acknowledged as an offer too good to refuse, and bowed out of the industry he had helped towards the shape it was about to take. 'Satellite booster cashes in his great network dream', ran the headline in the *Australian Financial Review* of 21 January 1987.

Meanwhile, all was far from finished in the HWT camp. Murdoch did win control of the HWT conglomerate and began to dismantle it. Under the new cross-ownership rules, Murdoch could acquire either the print or the electronic arms: he was to be the first to choose to be either a prince of print or a queen of the screen. It was no secret that the government would be pleased with the break-up of HWT. As one Fairfax newspaper executive observed: 'They danced on its grave.'

The Fairfax group, desperate to pull something out of the HWT carve-up, plunged in with the $318 million purchase of the group's Melbourne television channel, HSV7. Their entry to the media melee was late and costly. Fairfax turned a bad situation into a worse one with some clumsy handling of industrial relations problems and programming at the Melbourne television station. Ratings fell. And Fairfax's hopes that the government would relax its new stance on cross-ownership between print and television were dashed when the company found it could hold only 5 per cent of HSV7, not the 25 or 30 per cent it had hoped. Fairfax's ownership of its Sydney and Brisbane television channels was quarantined, as that had been established before the rules changed. What Fairfax had in mind was to create a full east-coast network with the addition of the Melbourne station. Keating's new rules blocked that. In July 1987, Fairfax reversed what had been judged an ill-conceived purchase when it announced the sale of HSV7 as part of a package that delivered all of Fairfax's television interests to Christopher Skase's Universal Telecasters for $780 million. Skase was now firmly placed as one of the new breed of television owners.

Fairfax's announcement of the decision to sell out of television and concentrate on print was worded in a way that highlighted the high price received for the network and drew a veil over the loss made on the earlier, impulsive acquisition of HSV7. Rival newspapers, though, chortled at what they saw as a commercial blunder and published columns of comment about the ill-fated television purchase. Arch-adversary Kerry Packer made an unwonted sally into print, saying: 'They were aiming to shoot themselves in the foot. In the event they blew off both kneecaps.' The sharemarket reacted positively, however, and pushed Fairfax's share price up by 62 cents to $5.22. One significant plus of a deal that ended Fairfax's 30-year involvement with television was that it left the company virtually debt-free, and thus well-positioned to borrow if necessary for future expansion in print, its traditional strength.

But the events of 1987 had brought another player on to the field—26-year-old Warwick Fairfax. Young Warwick, as he has been known since childhood, is the youngest son of the late Sir Warwick Fairfax and his third wife, Lady (Mary) Fairfax. The weight of family history and maternal ambition shaped his thinking. Educated at Sydney's select Cranbrook School, a short distance from the family's waterfront residence, Fairwater, in the wealthy suburb of Double Bay, and then at Oxford, Warwick was groomed to shoulder the Fairfax mantle. His aspirations were fed by those of his mother, an ambitious, effusive woman who contrasted vividly with the traditionally reserved Fairfax wives. History will debate the extent to which the Keating legislation pulled Fairfax apart or merely provided Warwick Fairfax with a fertile backdrop and incentive for action. Politicians like to take their share of the credit. Many ingredients, though, went into the recipe that produced a radically changed Fairfax—ambition, impatience, family dissension and rivalries. The 157-year-old newspaper company that operated from its bleak headquarters on Sydney's Broadway provided a running drama of soap-opera dimensions that was distinctly at variance with the restrained style the Fairfax family had clung to for generations.

Ultimately, Warwick Fairfax's ambitions to privatise the family's media empire turned sour and his heritage was savagely diminished. The outcome was less a result of the new media legislation than a combination of impetuosity and poor forecasting. Fairfax's $2.5 billion takeover attempt, hailed by some as courageous and by others as foolhardy, faltered when the worldwide 1987 sharemarket crash slashed the value of the company. The young pretender was forced to sell off assets and close unprofitable newspapers to try to reduce his takeover debt. After his competitors had picked over the offerings, Fairfax was left with a drastically shrunken company and unresolved debt and cash-flow problems.

Keating knew the effect the legislation would have on the Fairfax group. In dumping the tidal wave of reregulation on the Fairfax sandcastle Keating was settling a few old scores, on his own behalf and on behalf of other Labor luminaries such as the former NSW premier Neville Wran. At a later meeting with Fairfax executives Keating gloated: 'I've hurt you more than you hurt me.' Politicians of all persuasions have their own peculiar view of the media, particularly print media, often ascribing a degree of power to them that they do not, in reality, enjoy. But feelings can, and do, run deep. Staunch Labor left-wingers turned their backs on Murdoch after his paper's treatment of the Whitlam government in November 1975 and many boast of never having bought a Murdoch paper since.

More than a year after Murdoch had first thrown down the gauntlet with his bid for HWT, the media industry in Australia had been completely reshaped. Keating is quick to point out his long-standing interest in media ownership and to emphasise that the role he played throughout the protracted debates on Labor's media policy was not a mere whim or calculated vindictiveness against Fairfax or any other part of the media. He says:

> The satellite was in the sky but we couldn't deliver the regional television. It was a breakdown in public policy. We had the equipment, we had the technology but we didn't have the policy. Because we had this crazy two-station rule—two stations were the same whether they were Sydney and Melbourne, or Mount Isa and Broken Hill. So to get rid of that we had to come up with how much of a network you could own. Well, we came up with 75 per cent but you couldn't own any new TV where you had print. Because what I said was, you're either queen of the screen or prince of print. And that's as it came to pass. So there is now no major network owned by a print proprietor.

And Keating also stresses that pushing for regulations is not his style—he is not a great believer in regulations, in telling companies what they can and cannot own. But he is firmly convinced that had he not forced through the cross-ownership rules, the Australian media would have been carved up in a way that left Murdoch owning everything that was not held by Fairfax. His attitude towards Murdoch had been that he could own the Melbourne *Herald* but he could not stay in television. Fairfax had been left protected—existing television interests were grandfathered or quarantined, so that Fairfax could have maintained its existing network in television, although it could not expand it.

His hostility towards the Fairfax group, however, cannot be ignored. Part of it may be explained by the fact that Fairfax does not belong to the 'new money' club which attracts Keating so much and by its historical attachment to the conservative side of politics. More important, in Keating's view some of the Fairfax publications and journalists became obsessively interested in his private life and finances, in what seemed a relentless search to unearth the kind of unsavoury details that could topple a politician. Keating was furious with the *Sydney Morning Herald* for publishing the address of his Elizabeth Bay 'mansion', so that busloads of tourists could peer at his house. And he resented articles published in January 1987, to coincide with a state by-election in Bankstown, which included interviews with former neighbours in Condell Park who talked of the growing gulf between Keating and his origins. Fairfax's response was that Keating's complaints were representative of long-standing Labor perceptions of anti-Labor bias in the group's newspapers. Dispassionate observers have said there was a degree of paranoia on both sides.

The fact that some of the Fairfax newspapers, particularly the *National Times* (later *Times on Sunday*), were running articles that Keating saw as gunning for him personally would inevitably have coloured his thinking. On 17 August 1986 the *National Times* ran an article by Wendy Bacon, Colleen Ryan and Brian Toohey which drew attention to Keating's friendship with the property developer Warren Anderson. It was two days before the 1986 budget, at the height of Keating's behind-the-scenes lobbying for his solution to the arguments on media legislation, and at the start of a week that was to see Anita Keating in hospital for a gallbladder operation.

The article documented Keating's real-estate investments, the purchase of his first house in Condell Park and its subsequent profitable sale—described as the real-estate 'leg-up' many Australians experienced in the 1970s—and the acquisition of the four-storey Victorian terrace in Sydney's Elizabeth Bay. The writers detailed his shared investment in a Paddington property with the antique dealer Paul Kenny, and the profit made when he sold out of that arrangement. The article tracked Warren Anderson's success as a developer of properties such as the Coles New World shopping centres, the extent to which his business activities were being investigated by the Tax Office, his collection of *objets d'art* and his luxurious residences at which Keating has stayed. Keating, who met Anderson through a shared loved of antiques, has been a guest at the property developer's rural residence, Fern Hill, at his former Sydney harbourside mansion and at his ski lodge in the Perisher Valley. He likes talking to Warren Anderson about antiques as a relief from the demands of politics. 'You run out of people to talk to in this game,' says Keating. His friendship with Anderson is such that the treasurer provided a character reference when Anderson was charged over allegedly bringing a loaded revolver into Australia following a trip to PNG. Anderson was later cleared of a charge of making a false customs declaration.

In preparing the article, the *National Times* had asked Keating if he had ever discussed taxes with his business friends. Keating declined to answer that or any of the 31 questions put to him in writing. He also declined to be interviewed for the article. He was well aware of the direction of the journalists' inquiries, however. He was kept informed, for example, when builders at the Elizabeth Bay house were rung to see if they were connected with Anderson. They were not: Keating hired them through another antique collector, the advertising and public relations executive Leo Schofield.

The length and tone of the *National Times* articles prompted Hawke to accuse the paper of mounting a vicious attack on Keating. Keating felt the paper was out to destroy him. In his view, his friends are his own business. 'You don't need that kind of stuff,' he says, indicating the article that referred to Anderson buying a clock from him and the difficulties of accurately pricing the French empire clocks the two men admire. The journalists' fixation with Keating's friends and finances seems to be largely a Sydney phenomenon. Keating is bitter at what he says are personal attacks, claiming that no-one has ever taken the same obsessive interest in the wealth acquired by other Labor politicians. Furious at the journalists and the paper for publishing the article, Keating later said to friends: 'Don't they realise it's a jungle out there and I'm a tiger? The only way to get a tiger is to shoot it here,' and tapped the centre of his forehead. 'Those fools hardly hit me.'

Late in 1986 two Fairfax editorial executives met Hawke to discuss the prime minister's protest over the Keating articles. The meeting was initiated by Max Suich, then chief editorial executive of Fairfax. Present at the meeting, apart from Suich, were Hawke and his adviser Bob Sorby, and Robert Haupt, then editor of the *National Times*, whom Suich had, at the last minute, invited to accompany him to Canberra. The two newspapermen were prepared to defend the paper's treatment of the Hawke government and specifically the coverage of Keating. Instead, they were surprised to find Hawke launch a vigorous and emotional defence of his 'own mates', the business tycoons Sir Peter Abeles and Kerry Packer.

Keating defends his personal friendships as his business, but veterans of Labor politics suggest it would be prudent for him—and Bob Hawke—to be seen less with the new rich boys who inhabit the 'big end of town'. Keating's admiration for the 'new rich' is as profound as his distaste for 'established' money. This is another reason for his undisguised animosity towards Fairfax and his relative tolerance for the newer, brasher media barons. He admires goers and achievers in a way that many in Labor see as selling out. His retort is to dismiss the critics as 'anti-achievers, whingers and wimps'. That response does nothing to dissuade some from a perception that Keating has a naive admiration for people who have made money, that he likes to rub shoulders with them.

Keating dismisses accusations that the government's media legislation resulted in greater concentration, rather than diversification, of media ownership. When the dust settled, Australian print was dominated by just one company, News Corporation, which controlled 60 per cent of the market. But Keating points to the increased number of television proprietors and to the separation of print and screen.

A serious criticism of the changes of ownership following the legislation is that more and more newspapers and radio and television stations are now operated by companies with diverse business activities—airlines, mining, brewing, commercial property—and that this threatens the integrity and independence of their news coverage. Australia is an expensive country for media, with 16 million people spread over a vast tract of land, demanding a service that would be equal to that available in densely populated Europe or the US. Operators need deep pockets. But media are no longer in the hands of operators interested solely in media. Something of value has gone.

13 Old clocks and four-letter words

If Paul Keating were not what he is now, he would've been a mad inventor.

MIKE GAVAN, BOYHOOD FRIEND

FEW PEOPLE know Paul Keating. Many claim to know him. Even more, without having met him, form assumptions about him based on what they have read and heard. Most of these people say they do not like him. The likeable Paul Keating is a man the public rarely sees. The public is fed a steady diet of Keating as he is defined by the media. His family and close friends do not recognise the cold, arrogant, even grim figure portrayed in articles. They relate even less to the cartoon caricatures of Keating the saturnine treasurer. Keating has undoubtedly cultivated a tough exterior, as politicians must, and he has trained himself to be a winner in the bare-knuckle arena of parliament. He is undeniably and genuinely a hard politician—that is the public persona, the player who captures the leading roles in the theatre of parliament. To those close to him he is another Paul Keating: a devoted husband, a doting father, an affectionate son, a warm and loving brother, a loyal friend who can be good company. As the Labor historian Michael Sexton says: 'He's one of the small group of people on either side of politics that you'd really want to have dinner with.' The Paul Keating known to family and friends is a private but passionate man for whom family and children are of first importance, who is happy browsing in an antique shop. The politician portrayed as a street-smart, head-kicking product of the NSW Right begins a telephone call to his mother with: 'It's only me, Mum.'

Keating, from mostly Irish stock, is a good hater, but a warm and loyal friend. He was born under the sign of Capricorn, whose children are said to be marked by a cool outside, a passionate inside and huge ambition.

Keating has had phases of interest since childhood, encompassing fob watches, fast cars, silverware, music (classical and rock 'n' roll), French empire clocks and budgerigars. As a youngster, he was interested in mechanical things; he enjoyed himself and irritated his mother by taking a car to pieces and putting it back together on the front lawn. He converted a billy-cart into a motorised go-cart, using a Harley Davidson engine which was too powerful for the small cart. 'It burned the back tyres,' says Mike Gavan, a friend from childhood. He adds: 'If Paul Keating were not what he is now he would've been a mad inventor.' The twelve-year-old Keating wired up the family telephone to the house two doors down the street. Gavan remembers the youthful Keating talking about inventing an automatic potato peeler. The two formed a car rally team, Gavan driving an Austin Healey and Keating navigating—if he was not taking photographs. 'He was a keen photographer,' says Gavan. Keating took spools of film at Gavan's wedding in August 1962. The interest in photography replaced an earlier fascination with birds. Keating had built an aviary and, when the preoccupation with birds waned he turned the aviary into a darkroom to develop his pictures. His teenage enthusiasm for an aviary continued into an adult interest in breeding budgerigars. Keating talks proudly of his two black-and-white budgerigars. Friends teased him, they're pee-wees, or budgies that fell in your toaster. But two dark grey and white budgerigars share their perch with the bright blue and green birds. Keating likes his children to have pets. Asta, the family's almost-collie, has been around for most of the children's lives.

Music has long been a passion. It was one of Keating's early outlets. His sister Anne can still picture him, late at night, listening to classical music with headphones on, waving his arms, conducting. The adult Keating is developing an impressive collection of compact discs and talks enthusiastically about his favourite pieces. He also enjoys the 1930s numbers, the songs of Fred Astaire, the show tunes of Cole Porter and Irving Berlin, but he offends Elvis Presley fans by dismissing their idol as 'a fake'. Jazz does not interest him. Relaxation for Keating after a long day at Parliament House is to soak up music, to unwind to the stirring chords of Elgar or Rachmaninov, to Otto Klemperer conducting Mahler or Wagner. When his carefully-positioned speakers are dispensing the soothing notes a striking change comes over this hard-edged politician. The face that is mostly seen in serious mood cracks into a broad grin as he savours and absorbs the sounds, his foot tapping in time. He draws everthing out of the music as though it were a well he had to drain dry. It inspires and fortifies him. 'Others listen,' he says. 'I'm doing something else.'

That is the Keating the world does not see. At home after a tough day, unwinding to a favourite piece of rousing music, the heavy wooden lounge-room doors closed so as not to disturb sleeping children, he soaks up the sounds, arms waving, conducting, losing himself in the music.

Of the passions—other than politics—that have punctuated Keating's life, the most enduring has been his enthusiasm for the artwork, furniture, architecture and clocks of the neo-classical or French empire period, from the late eighteenth century to about 1840. Keating's attachment to the architectural history and *objets d'art* of this period is a consuming interest that takes him into a different milieu from that which surrounds him day-by-day in Canberra. More than a hobby—he describes it as 'an intense, not just a moderate, interest'—it brings him into contact with people in the world of art and antiques who can provide a refreshingly different emphasis and outlook to a man normally constrained by the routines of political life and the pressures of government. Keating's approach to collectables shows the same depth of concentration and ability to absorb detail that characterise his professional life. His critics, though, claim his obsessive interest in antiques is further evidence of an elitism which increasingly distances him from his Labor roots, his electorate and his voting support. They dispute his qualifications, suggesting that his enthusiasm disguises a merely superficial grasp of a narrow field in which few can challenge his knowledge. Keating's deep interest in this period, though, is symptomatic of his approach to any task—never to do anything half-mast. What Keating does, he does with determination. It is a boots-and-all approach.

He is attracted to the art and furniture of the French empire because they represent a period that he believes is significant in history, what he describes as a start of a new order. To him it is an academic and absorbing interest in all aspects of a chosen period of history. To his irritation it is frequently written off as a peculiar obsession with old clocks.

His associates in the antique business talk of Keating as a fount of information, a man with a genuine feel for a fascinating and substantial period of history. The people he meets through his interest in antiques also see a Paul Keating that the public rarely glimpses—the man with a wicked sense of humour, good company around a dinner table, able to spar and crack a joke. Keating enjoys the company of those in 'the trade' and can relax easily among people whom he can trust to have minimal interest in the topics that normally occupy his mind. Like Keating's family, the people in the antique business cannot relate the Keating they know to the grim figure portrayed in newspaper cartoons as an undertaker.

Bill Bradshaw, doyen of the Australian antique trade and Keating's close friend, says he never asks a question about politics or finance—not out of discretion, but because he is just not interested in these areas. In his company Keating can shed the public image and forget about being on his guard. Bradshaw and Keating communicate on the common ground of the French empire. The two met in 1976 when Keating walked into Bill Bradshaw's antique shop in Queen Street, Woollahra, to inquire about a display in the window—a pair of statuettes holding classical urns of gilded bronze. Keating said he recognised the mercury gilding, and reckoned it dated from 1795 or 1800. His reckoning was accurate. Bradshaw says he warmed to Keating there and then because of his 'wonderful enthusiasm'. He says: 'He was totally appreciative of the objects around and we chatted for hours. I showed him my collection. We became fast friends because of our mutual enthusiasm.'

The neo-classical period which so attracts Bradshaw and Keating has a small number of devotees in Australia but is very much admired in Europe. Most of Keating's collection of clocks—of which he would have about a dozen at any one time—come from France. According to Bradshaw, France offers the best quality. Keating also has a fondness for the candelabra of the same period, and for the furniture. French empire clocks were not always in vogue—Bradshaw recalls that in the 1940s they would be taken apart and the pieces used as paperweights. Fashions change, and with them the prices—Bradshaw says a French empire clock that sold for £11 in 1950 would now fetch between $3 000 and $4 000. The two enthusiasts lay bets to test each other's skill. For example, Bradshaw might challenge Keating to guess the age of a particular French clock. When the clock is dismantled and the date on the mainspring checked, Keating's estimate is usually close to the mark. Bradshaw once tried to trip him with a pair of Carcel lamps from the romantic period (which followed the neo-classical era) and challenged Keating to guess their age. 'They're not as old as they look,' Keating replied, guessing at the range of 1835 to 1840. The lamps were dated April 1837. On occasions Keating has been wrong, and Bradshaw has held him to the bet and won a lunch or a dinner.

Keating was already studying the neo-classical period when he and Bradshaw met. Earlier he had taken a liking to Victorian pieces, but had gradually come back to what Bradshaw calls the 'ageless elegance' of neo-classicism. His tastes have changed since the time when, as a teenager, he bought his first clock as a present for his mother. That German-made clock, a Spelter, might have been of indifferent quality compared with later purchases, but already the young Keating was peering with increasing discernment into the windows of Sydney's antique shops. And by the time he was working with the Municipal Employees' Union he knew every second-hand jeweller in Castlereagh Street by name. John Grayson, who worked with Keating at the union and shared his developing interest in politics, remembers that his colleague had a collection of fob watches at that time. The young collector was already becoming clever in buying and selling antiques. Bob Carr says Keating tried to interest his friends in antique clocks. 'He came around to our house. He had a French empire clock in the boot of his car, brought it up—he'd mentioned this earlier on the phone—and set it up on the mantlepiece then climbed up on the table to redirect the light so that we could see it to full advantage. We didn't buy it.'

Steve Loosley, who knows Paul Keating in the context of politics rather than of art, tells of an episode which gave Keating the chance to lecture him on architecture and history.

> I was single during most of the time he was president [of NSW Labor] and whenever he was at a loose end, if Anita was overseas or at home while he was committed downtown, from time to time he'd ring and ask what I was doing, and if I was free we'd meet for dinner. On occasions we'd go to a restaurant in Woollahra and have a quiet dinner, and then he'd take me on a walking tour of Paddington. He'd give me an architectural history of the place, looking at all the galleries and antique shops, giving me a history of clocks and antiques. It was absolutely fascinating—and that was his way of relaxing. He knew I had an interest in and appreciation of Australian history and culture and he used to like to talk. And he really was like Whitlam in that sense: he immersed himself in cultural pursuits.

At whatever level he is working, Keating is alert to his immediate surroundings, particularly his cultural environment. During a radio talk-back show with the journalist John Tingle, the treasurer thumbed through a stack of compact discs in the studio while broadcasting answers to questions about the economy. The governor of the Reserve Bank, Bob Johnston, says that Keating gazed out of a window at the view over Martin Place and Macquarie Street during a meeting at the bank and announced enthusiastically: 'This is going to be the Wall Street of the south.' On another occasion the two men were in the corridors of the Federal Reserve Board in Washington, waiting to see the then chairman, Paul Volcker. Keating was struck by the *objets d'art*. 'If you had stuff like this I'd come to see you more often,' he told Johnston.

Art and architecture are Keating's way of relaxing. He said in an interview in 1982 with the *National Times:* 'Other people play the neddies—I perv on buildings.' Bill Bradshaw recalls reading to Keating a passage from a book on Greek architecture, in which the Parthenon was described as 'frightening in its finality. It is at once perfection absolute and forever.' The passage so struck Keating that he made Bradshaw repeat it to him—and he has since quoted it several times in interviews. He is eager to share his enthusiasm, to have others get the same appreciation and enjoyment out of works of art that he does. When Steve Loosley was heading overseas in 1982, on his first trip to Europe, Keating made sure he would know what to look for when he arrived in Paris. Loosely recalls:

> I was leaving on the Tuesday after the party conference, on a delegation that was going to the Middle East and then on to Europe. Paul drew me a walking guide to the city of Paris on the back of a conference agenda, to take with me, pointing out different landmarks which he said would not be found on a tourist brochure. He was dead right. I took it with me and followed it. He did that while chairing the conference. He likes drawing on bits of paper.

Journalists also benefited from Keating's doodles. Andrew McCathie, travelling around Australia in June 1985 with the treasurer, who was selling his tax reform package, described in the *Australian Financial Review* how Keating outlined the proposed tax package on an airsick bag:

> Jetting into Canberra after another day on the trail campaigning for tax reform, the treasurer hauled out of the airline seat pocket an air sickness bag (unused) and proceeded to draw all over it to hammer home once again to the travelling press the virtues of his plan to reshape the Australian tax system. It was all there, scribbled on the back and on the front of the bag, how it would affect low-income earners and compensate social security beneficiaries . . . Even after the plane had come to a halt on the tarmac, Paul Keating was still talking tax.
>
> He never stops talking and selling tax. He seems obsessed. Any angle, any time, Paul is willing to talk to you . . . Tax reform has taken up so much of Paul Keating's time lately that one of his great

disappointments was missing seeing the country and western singer, Johnny Cash, when he visited Australia.

Keating uses doodles well. He likes to explain complex concepts graphically. The *Sydney Morning Herald* political commentator Alan Ramsey was given a diagrammatic lesson in the balance of trade on Christmas Eve 1987 when he visited the treasurer in his basement office at Parliament House. Keating was just finishing—the other ministers had started their Christmas break—but it was six hours before he went home. Scribbling frenetically on a makeshift blackboard, Keating illustrated to Ramsey his 'game plan for the Australian economy'. Ramsey reported:

> The commentary overwhelms. 'Look,' he [Keating] says, 'when net exports come through, they tend to come through like this.' (He draws what looks like a very fat tadpole.) 'It starts off as an appreciation. Prices shift. Importers hang on, cut their margins, because they think it might be temporary, right? Later, they realise that's hopeless, give up market share, and what happens is you get this [the tadpole bulge].
>
> 'Now, a coupla other points. When exports really start to flow, it comes through in a blob [scribble]. That's the 2.5 per cent we got last year, this bit here [scribble] is the one per cent we got the year before. We'll get another one per cent this year. But up here [scribble] we need more, another two per cent of GDP, a thicker tail.' (He scrawls a heavy strap from the head of the tadpole.) . . . 'But when the blob comes through, that's about all you get. You then have a whole lot of other handstands to do to get this last bit [scribble], the thicker tail [heavy underlining]. It's like driving a car to 100 mph from 90; it can do it at 90, but at 100 it's got everything blatting full-out, all the [expletive] valves are jumping, you know what I mean?
>
> 'In other words, to make it do THAT [scribble], so that in HERE [scribble] we get, say, another two per cent of GDP, which would get THIS [scribble], we got to pick up another two times 2800 [scribble], that's 5600 million off the current account. Well, roughly $5 billion, right, to get that two per cent of GDP.
>
> 'Now the only way we can do that is by high levels of investment and less demand . . . You know, cutting consumption, lifting savings. And one of the ways of continuing to do this is by further public sector dis-savings.' (He repeats this, slowly, like speaking to a retarded child.)
>
> 'That means the Commonwealth Budget will go further into surplus and we'll start cutting those deficits . . . you with me?' No, not really. But over the next hour Keating . . . makes his point and rams it home. It is, broadly, that if the Hawke government had just 'sat on its bum and done nothing' our foreign debt, through an

> expanding current account deficit, would be growing now at an underlying rate of $25 billion a year. It isn't. It's growing at less than half this rate, or $11.5 billion this year. And it's continuing to slow, to turn around, as investment builds up and Australia begins to trade its way out of trouble.
>
> Exports *are* overtaking imports. This is the fat tadpole . . . The lesson continues: 'We had a nice graph here the other day, our indebtedness graph line.' (He shuffles around in the cards behind the easel). Yes, here it is. That's another thing people don't understand. People say, oh, you shouldn't let Bondy and Elliott and all these blokes go offshore, that's offshore investment. Yet if Bond ends up building up a massive equity in US breweries, and Elliott does the same in English breweries, and you get Boral and all the others; well let's say they end up with $20 billion in gross assets abroad, our net debt abroad is *reduced* by $20 billion. So all this stuff about their offshore investment not coming back as dividends, and so on, it's just bullshit.'

Ramsey's lesson continued. Then Keating went to join his family for Christmas.

Priorities in Keating's life are his family, politics and art. He is known around parliament as the ultimate family man, a devoted husband who is intensely interested in his children. Keating is obsessed with his family's privacy—some say neurotically so. The man who can deliver a spontaneous dissertation on the economy or deliver an off-the-cuff verbal demolition of the opposition, the media, or whatever may be that day's irritation, is far more reserved about his personal life.

He draws a clear line between what is demanded of him through his job, and what is due to him as an individual. He is unwilling to co-operate in what he terms 'open-heart surgery'—articles that dig into his relationships and analyse his personal life. He resents the intrusion of the media into his family life, the TV cameras filming around the Canberra house, newspapers running photographs of his Elizabeth Bay property in Sydney or shots of previous Keating homes in Bankstown.

Photographs of Keating with his wife Anita and their four children—Patrick, Caroline, Katherine and Alexandra—are reserved for pre-budget issues of women's magazines, or the occasional post-budget or pre-election interview; otherwise, the family is kept out of the limelight. He does not carry Anita around like a useful accessory, as politicians sometimes do with their wives. She is an attractive and stylish woman, with a gracious manner. People feel comfortable with her. But she does not chase publicity and he does not seek it through her. He reckons he is the one in the family who has been elected, not Anita. He cops the flak: no-one else in the family should. Keating explains: 'I prefer to keep my family scene as normal as possible. And the best way of doing that is to keep them removed from some of the high and low points.'

An image has been built of a man interested in property and expensive cars, esoteric antiques, pricey clothes and a flashy lifestyle. In fact, Keating does not lead an affluent life; the family lives in a rented house in Canberra and there is little home entertaining or dining out. The antiques are for him a recreation. He defends his acquaintanceship with people prominent in business. In his view he can learn from the non-Labor sector and it is better for someone in his position to know how business thinks and behaves. His association with business people has been built into a larger issue, prompting debate in some quarters about the appropriate relationship between government and big business. The 'ordinary' Labor voters quite like to see their Bankstown boy up there, mixing with the rich and powerful, provided they can feel confident that he is representing their interests. It is question of image and public perception.

Keating's capacity to switch off, either with his family or by polishing a clock, is a great asset. Staffers and colleagues envy him the ability to close the door on the pressures of the job, get a good night's sleep and awake refreshed and ready to take on another day. Neo-classical art became an interest when Keating, as shadow minister for minerals and energy, found he needed something diverting and relaxing to read at night. His colleague Kim Beazley says Keating 'gave himself a fine arts degree by reading in bed at night'. Barbara Ward says: 'He has an uncanny ability to turn off. It's one of the things that keep him sane. The rest of us would stagger home and lie awake thinking, "What am I going to say in that speech tomorrow," or whatever, but Paul goes home and just turns off. He just forgets about politics, starts playing with the kids, polishing the car or his clocks. He completely forgets about work.'

Tony Cole recalls weekend sessions at the treasurer's Canberra home, working on cabinet agenda or preparing for other meetings. 'Nearly every time I went around to his house for that he was playing with the kids or cleaning a clock or mucking around with a car.' Cole agrees Keating switches off easily—but with qualifications. 'He doesn't switch off for long. If he goes off on holiday for a few weeks, inevitably within a couple of days he's on the phone to Canberra. He doesn't cut the knot.' Family and friends agree—Keating will fiddle restlessly while they are talking, or be looking around for a telephone.

The knack of being able to blot out politics, however briefly, is a useful survival aid. Most politicians suffer from Canberra winters, the constant proximity to colleagues, the endless shuffling of papers, the exhausting demands of a job that never seems to end. Ward describes Keating:

> He can keep going during an election campaign or something when he has to but he does not have a lot of stamina. He's not someone who can keep going all day and every day. Paul needs to stop and regroup. He doesn't like heavy itineraries. If he's going on a trip, whether in Australia or overseas, he's not one of these people who pack in every minute of the day. Some politicians' itineraries leave them five minutes for lunch—Paul likes to operate at a more leisurely pace. His health does pack in if he has to keep going under a lot of pressure.

Keating is fussy about temperatures. He never hesitates to complain if the air in a room is too hot or too cold for his comfort. He is aware of the need to stay on his toes: 'When you get tired you lose your edge, your cutting edge, and this job's all about judgments, all about judging right. There are a lot of mechanical parts and they're easy but it's the judgments that count.'

The hours put in by politicians and their staff are punishing. Those who live the strange life of a Canberra politician or staffer learn to cope with minimal sleep and interrupted social and personal life. They get used to it, to putting in long days and still being alert at midnight or later, grabbing sleep when they can. Even the journalists tracking their movements, in parliament, in press conferences, electioneering around the country and travelling overseas, find the schedules exhausting. Keating can sympathise with them. He told one reporter: 'At least we're doing it for the history books—you're doing it for tomorrow's fish and chips.'

To politicians, the attitude of the electorate is complicated, contradictory and fickle. The people want politicians in whom they can have confidence, to whom they can look up, yet at the same time they want their politicians to be no different from themselves. Susan Ryan comments:

> I'm a strong supporter of the egalitarian ethos in Australia but it does create immense pressures for people who aren't the same as everyone else, working the same hours. Politicians work much longer hours, take much more responsibility and public hostility,

> and yet are expected to have the demeanour of someone who has a nine-to-five job.

Keating the family man and doting father is also noted for exercising one of the sharpest tongues in parliament, variously described as 'creatively crude' or merely crude. His most-quoted insults include several aimed at Andrew Peacock: 'Does a souffle rise twice?'; 'All tip and no iceberg'; and 'You've been at the dye-pot again, Andrew'. Keating has adopted some of Jack Lang's favourite sayings, such as: 'In a horse race always back self-interest, you can be certain that horse is trying'; and 'Like a dog, he returns to his own vomit', to add to his own original and forceful language. He has honed a style of rhetoric that owes more to his origins in Bankstown and the rough-and-tumble of NSW Young Labor than to the floor of the House of Representatives in Canberra. Keating never minces words. He uses language effectively, forcefully, colourfully. And he is expert in the purposeful use of vulgarity and obscenity. He is not a debater—his form of argument is to attack and, with a tongue that wounds like a verbal machine-gun, to cut the enemy down.

Ryan says of Keating's 'inventive use of our language':

> He's very funny, but that's not a side of him that the public sees. You see a bit of it in parliament because he uses it in debate and he'll often be more vicious than funny because he's tearing down the opposition. But around cabinet he can just be hilarious. He has a very visual kind of metaphoric mode where he'll describe something . . . he's really very clever and very original. You can't fit him into any stereotype current political leader. Profiles of him have left out so much.

Ryan says there is something almost Swiftian in Keating's powers of invective. And she cites a cabinet meeting where the dependent spouse rebate had been under discussion:

> We'd been discussing, endlessly it seemed, the dependent spouse rebate: could we turn it into a payment that goes directly to the dependent spouse, rather than have it as a tax rebate? That had many attractions. Then there was the question of whether it should be made only to those with children, and Paul would say no, it can't just be to those with children because what about all the white leghorns out at Bankstown? That's a very old-fashioned term for lady bowlers—chooks with white stockings. And it's not just funny, it's actually very compassionate. He went on to say they mightn't have kids now, but they're in their fifties and sixties and they've brought up a family and if we're bringing in a new payment we can't ignore them. And I don't think that's the image of someone who's just interested in Empire antiques.

The opposition collected and circulated a list of terms which Keating had used when referring to them in parliament: harlots, sleazebags, frauds, immoral cheats, cheats, blackguards, pigs, mugs, clowns, boxheads, criminal intellects, criminals, corporate crooks, friends of tax cheats, brain-damaged, loopy crims, stupid foul-mouthed grub, piece of criminal garbage, dullards, stupid, mindless, crazy tenet of the opposition, alley cat, bunyip artistocracy, clot, fop, gigolo, hare-brained hillbilly, malcontent, mealy-mouthed, ninny, rustbucket, scumbag, scum, sucker, thug, dimwits, dummies, a swill, a pigsty, liberal muck, vile constituency, fools and incompetents, rip-off merchants, perfumed gigolos, gutless spiv, glib rubbish, tripe and drivel, thugs of Australian politics, constitutional vandals, stunned mullets, half-baked crim, insane stupidities, champion liar, ghouls of the National Party and barnyard bullies.

Keating is uninterested in physical activities, so much so that he would regard it a bit odd to have a stroll around Canberra or across the city. He sees little sense in walking a golf ball around a course or chasing a football over a field. Does he try to keep fit? No, he says:'I just keep thinking. Keep your brain right and the rest of you will sort of drag along behind you.' The lack of exercise, long hours in a sedentary but pressurised job and late night sessions in bars and restaurants have rounded out many a Canberra silhouette but Keating has added only a few kilos to his tall frame during his twenty years in parliament. He is philosophical: 'It doesn't matter much when they put the lid on you.' He remains a light eater and a recreational drinker who enjoys wine with a meal rather than a session in a pub. Staff know not to give him a second glass of wine in the office if they want to get more work out of him. And if Keating is seen enjoying an after-dinner cigar that is a sign he has eaten and drunk well. Former secretary Jan Kell remembers Keating 'bitching' about her and Barbard Ward smoking in the office and then seeing him indulge in a cigar after a few drinks at dinner. That was a sign he was well on the way to letting his hair down.

The man whom friend and colleague Kim Beazley describes as 'the best family man in politics' has no reputation as a womaniser. Women are friends and colleagues. He might offend feminists by calling them 'love' but he has a respect for women's views and capabilities, which is at odds with what comes across as a very traditional, almost 1950s, view of a woman's role as wife and mother. Ros Kelly says Keating was friendly to her when she arrived in Canberra as a member of parliament in 1980. 'I said to him: "I like you because you never see me as a woman, you see me as a number."'

Keating urged her not to miss out on having children, she says. They are so important, he told her; they bring huge rewards.

Keating tries to involve his children in his work, but very carefully. The oldest, Patrick, has watched his father in parliament, delivering a budget speech. The youngest, Alexandra, has shared the morning drive to Parliament House with her father—but she moves into the back seat once the car comes within a block of the House before riding home with the driver. The separation of politics and family life is paramount.

Keating has said: 'You can become a recluse in this job'. A politician, especially a minister with a portfolio as prominent and sensitive as the treasurer's, has to be careful about whom he spends time with. A social encounter can become a tedious harangue about politics. Subtle sacrifices have to be made, not just by the politician but by his or her family and friends. They all pay a price for the politician's public life—they are constrained and many of the small pleasures that 'ordinary people' take for granted have to be given up, or indulged in only with forethought and safeguards. Dinner parties and guest lists have to be carefully arranged. Spur-of-the moment excursions are unwise. Political advisers must be listened to. Keating keeps in touch regularly by telephone with his family in Sydney, particularly with his mother and his sister, Anne. But they see less of him than they, and he, would like. Families of politicians live a deprived existence.

Politicians inhabit an unreal world. Canberra is the most affluent city in the country, the best-manicured. That is one element. Canberra is also a one-industry town where the public service dominates. And politicians' days and lives have a peculiar pattern: virtual imprisonment in offices in Parliament House, isolation from the public who elected them, separation from their families and old friends. Leo McLeay says:

> In Canberra you're dealing with a whole lot of very intelligent people in the upper echelons of the public service. They're as good as any outside management but work for half the price. So you spend your time working with people like that, it's very stimulating. Everyone's living off each other—the bureaucrats are living off the politicians, the press are living off the politicians, the politicians are living off the press. You're all jockeying with each other for advantage, for the next ministerial ballot, for the next prime ministerial ballot. If you're in, you've got to stop someone else from getting in; if you're out, you're trying to push someone else out so's you can get in. You don't make friends. No-one has friends down here. You have permanent interests. It's hard to be friendly with

> some bloke when you might be asked to go to his electorate and kick the shit out of him. And there's no time for friends outside Canberra. Wives and family provide the balance—and pay the price, hardly see you.

Old hands in politics tend to believe that politicians should live in their electorates. The Labor veteran Fred Daly says that in his day politicians who left their electorates to live in Canberra invariably lost their seats. Keating's choosing to live in Canberra has been criticised as evidence of his 'growing away from his grass roots', distancing himself from his Blaxland electorate, even behaving as if he were the prime minister, living in Canberra. Keating was chastised for moving his wife and young family to Canberra so that he could spend more time with them—a move he was earlier encouraged to make. Keating did not want to farewell his children each Monday morning as he left for the working week in Canberra. Kids do not stay kids forever; he wants to see them grow up. Daly says:

> I always tell the young fellows not to neglect their families. In my book I wrote that I always gave politics number one priority, even over my family, but if I had my time over again, at least one day a week I'd have nothing to do with anyone in the electorate. I tell young members this but they don't take notice—but Paul Keating does and I admire him for that.

Keating has been tipped as a future Labor prime minister since he first set foot in politics. By early 1988 it seemed he was having a long wait and there were hints that he might tire of the life and move on to fresh fields. He had earlier laughed at the idea of staying in politics *all* his life; that would be like a death sentence, he said, life is too interesting for that. Above all, he knows he has made a contribution. In March 1988 he scotched rumours that he might depart for Europe—an idea both he and Anita had considered—or the attractions of Wall Street. He told radio host John Laws he would stay around. 'I won't want to get old in the place . . . but I am not leaving too early,' he said.

McLeay says:'People like myself, and long-term friends and party officials, would put the acid on him to stay. And I suppose one would end up appealing to his love of the party, though that's a bit maudlin, and to his sense of responsibility. One of the strong reasons I came into parliament was so that I could be here to see Keating become prime minister.' McLeay is contemptuous of what he calls 'this bullshit about how he's left Bankstown behind' saying:

> Keating might not live in Bankstown but for someone from Bankstown to become prime minister of Australia, that's great. For

> someone who only got to intermediate certificate of high school to become prime minister has to be a marvellous thing for all those kids out there who haven't got a role model. We ought to be pushing Keating as the best role model this country's got—that in Australia you can succeed if you just work at it. There's no secret, just work bloody hard. He's got tenacity, and he realises that you have to put back in what you get out. And he does put something back in for the people who live in Bankstown.

People disagree over Keating's image and style and approach but no-one disputes the degree of effort he puts into whatever task confronts him. Even the one-liners are polished. Friends and colleagues who have known him since his teenage years comment on the amount of preparation he does. And that is one of the features that makes him stand out from the crowd, they say: take away the investment in preparation and you have a mere mortal, albeit one with an unusually quick and retentive mind.

Keating does not worry about the public image. 'They can take me or not,' he says. 'I've got the levers here and I try to use them as best I can, in the best interests of the place, make the changes as swiftly as I can. At the end of the day you've got to say, "Well, we did enough or we didn't do enough or we did all we could do." I'm not really worried about whether I looked this good or not—because I'll pass off the stage just like everyone else.' Keating is no stranger to just how quickly politicians can pass off the stage; his experience as a minister for three weeks under the Whitlam government gave him an early and unforgettable lesson on the ephemeral nature of political life.

Fred Daly understands Keating's absence of concern about 'image'. 'Treasurers cannot be nice fellows,' he says. 'A treasurer doesn't have to be nasty but he has to be able to say no—and Keating can.'

> If there are shortcomings in economic policy I think it's mainly because the powers-that-be in the party weren't prepared to support him on some very necessary but probably unpopular issues, such as tax. With due respect to the more highly-qualified economic wizards in the party, Keating appeals to me as a treasurer—not that I always agree with what he does—because of his down-to-earth stubbornness, his ability to say no and his preparedness to fight for what he puts up. In the Whitlam government we had treasurers who would't fight for what they were putting up, except Hayden, and he was too late.

Daly defends Keating against criticisms that he is arrogant and obstinate. 'If a treasurer's going to back-pedal all the time you'll all go broke. I'd put Keating in the Chifley line. Chifley wasn't an economist but he was always a student of economics. I said to Chifley: "How is it you know so much when you left school at fourteen?" And he said: "It's marvellous what you bloody well learn after reading books for 30 years." ' Others are less generous in their praise of Keating, saying he lacks the debating skills of a Chifley, who, they say, could take a Treasury line apart.

Feelings about Keating's style are mixed. Some of his colleagues damn him as an electoral liability, pointing to his image of arrogance. But he is acknowledged as the backbone of the government. Kim Beazley says: 'Politically and in IQ he's points ahead of the rest of us. And he dominates cabinet not because of bullying but because he is knowledgeable and competent.' Many see his refusal to 'sell' himself, to soften his image and promote himself and his family to the public through 'staged' media events as a wise approach. Bill Kelty does not believe it would be hard to 'package' Keating: 'He's a tough politician who loves his family. And he's a man of vision. That's not a hard act to sell—but it hasn't been sold.' Susan Ryan says:

> He's probably quite right not to care about his public image. Maybe he should, but once you start worrying about public image there's no end to it; you really make yourself a hostage to the profile writers and the media. Paul's just not into running around promoting a different image. If he wanted to he could exploit his family but I think he's quite sensible. Really, once you've made yourself a hostage to that there's no getting out of it because your image can be good one week and bad the next. You can see with some of our Liberal opponents who've obviously been to image-training school that it doesn't work. Ultimately you're judged on your policies. Obviously you can't ignore it. But trying to manipulate it, getting buddy-buddy with journalists so they'll give you a good profile—that's a bottomless pit.

Keating is fierce in his defence of the Hawke government as a Labor government bent on improving the lot of the Australian people. His views, while strong Labor views, are not straitjacketed by 100-year-old Labor prejudices. Sensitive as he is to comments about his perceived lifestyle, to articles that trivialise what to him are genuine interests, and to speculation about his friendships, the barb that most gets under his skin is the accusation that he has betrayed Labor, that he is no longer a Labor person. Keating sees himself as imbued with Labor principles. He talks of the changes in Australia in recent years as the product of Labor philosophy and as Australia's 'debut into the world.'

> This is the true internationalisation of this economy. There is no more important thing to be accomplished than for that job to be finished, so that we are a country competitive in the world, facing all the pressures of international competition . . . The *Fortress Australia* people, who had the best of motives and who believed that was in Australia's best interests, were in fact selling Australia right down the mine . . . without knowing it. So I regard the completion of this task, seeing Australia face these chill competitive winds, and to be able to see its constitution strengthened by being able to withstand those kinds of elements, as the best thing, as the most important thing that the government could do, that I could do. And we are now well down that road.

Keating says that in doing what it has done the Hawke government has 'changed Labor':

> What a long overdue change it has been, in a sense at least twenty years overdue . . . changing it back to what it once was, and that was not a party driven by single issues but a party addressing the broad problems that affected most people. That was what it was like in its best years; it was like that in its state governments particularly. Now we have a Labor party presiding over one of the highest employment growth rates in the western world, yet restructuring the place so that everyone is going to have a better chance of a job and a higher living standard over time—and if that's not basic Labor philosophy, what is?

He points out that he could hold whatever views he liked but would not get anything off the ground if his cabinet colleagues were not sympathetic to the arguments. 'What has been accomplished has been put through by a very responsible cabinet,' he says, 'and by a PM prepared to face the hard issues, the ones that are fundamental to the structure, to the fabric, and in that environment it's possible to do something.' He talks of a 'unified cabinet . . . and constructive, clear thinkers in the ERC'.

> One of the nicest things, I'm sure, however long I stay in politics, without any shadow of a doubt, one of the most enduring, nice experiences I would take away would be the sense of purpose and *esprit de corps* of this cabinet and particularly the ERC ministers. You do get a shared sense of accomplishment which you need in politics. Politics is all about issues and pressures, and if you can get sanity about the issues and courage in facing the pressures, you've got all you're going to get.

Paul Keating has frequently said he would not stay in politics forever. Despite having spent almost all his adult working life in politics and being acknowledged around Canberra as the ultimate political animal, living and breathing politics, he is not a political junkie. To stay in politics all one's life would be a death sentence; there are too many other interesting things to do, he says. His belief is that 'you can only be around when you're ahead, useful, you've got the leads in your hands'. Public life is a wearing experience and no-one can be effective forever. He has other interests and he is convinced that he can move on.

Being comfortable with himself, with his family, his work and his other interests, is one of Keating's real strengths. It is a rare enough quality, but particularly so in the frenetic, lunatic world of politics. Keating says he is a 'man at peace with himself'.

> I like what I'm doing. I'm not acting any lie, I'm doing it as I see it and I'm doing it without trying to overblow it, but I'm trying to do this as I think it ought to be done for Australia. Now you're never after perfection, and you never get it. But you do your best in the political and economic circumstances and in doing that there is a certain sense of accomplishment.

14 The yellow brick road

It restores your faith.
PAUL KEATING ON LABOR'S FEDERAL VICTORY
IN JULY 1987

THE MOST damaging issues to dog Paul Keating were more personal than political. As 1987 began wounds were re-opened by articles that dimmed Keating's star by focusing on the events of late 1986. The influential *New York Times* published a profile representing Keating as a politician under attack, his future under a cloud. The forgotten tax returns and the questionable travel allowance were irritations that would not go away. These issues, still fresh in the electorate's mind, were further revived by press articles which highlighted those and other questions that suggested the treasurer had lost touch with his political home-ground. The peg used for continued discussion was the state government by-election to be held in Bankstown on 31 January. The *Sydney Morning Herald* published photographs of Keating's former Condell Park home and interviewed several locals who volunteered compliments about Keating-the-former-neighbour but who were critical of Keating-the-politician who chose to live away from his electorate.

Keating, along with the Labor government, might have been out of favour in the suburban backblocks of Sydney but he was still winning points among the domestic and international financial communities. Much newspaper space was given to explaining why Keating, the so-called electoral liability in what was likely to be an election year, was really the government's most indispensable political asset—and how prime minister Hawke was well aware of this. Hawke's recognition of the contrasting but complementary styles of himself and his treasurer lay behind his decision to have Keating chair the expenditure review committee sessions, leaving Hawke more time to be a highly visible, highly public, prime ministerial figurehead. That way, each man was able to make the best use of his individual skills: Hawke, the people's prime minister, talking to the throng; Keating steering the government's economic policy.

With a federal election due within twelve months, the government was taking careful stock of the outlook in early 1987. It was to prove a big year but at that point all did not look bad. The economy seemed to be improving and the sharemarket was still strong. Hawke could boast that his original ministry of 27 was still intact, four years after it had been first elected. And NSW Labor's win in the Bankstown by-election was hailed as a victory for the party. The then ALP federal secretary, Bob McMullan, made sober mention of the 'consistent pattern of people being prepared to vote for minor parties in by-elections', but his warning did nothing to diminish Keating's exuberance. The treasurer was pleased that the Liberals' slogan of *Give Keating a beating* had proved a damp squib. He returned early from holidays and called a press conference. 'Every now and again we all have a good day in politics and I have had one today. It is a great victory,' he said.

And the Hawke government had learned from the mistakes of the 1984 election. It would not again run an over-long campaign and give the opposition the chance to muster its forces and the electorate time to become bored with the issues and slogans. The big question was when to go to the polls. The government's second term in office had begun on 21 February 1985 so that its final date in the three-year term was 20 February 1988. Two people were pushing Hawke to go early in the year. Bob Sorby, the prime minister's staff political adviser, and Richard Farmer, who had previously worked for Hawke and Hayden, now in the wine trade but retaining a sharp nose for politics, were both convinced of the wisdom of an early election. That, they said, would allow the government to exploit the divisions in the coalition ranks and get the election out of the way before tough economic decisions had to be taken later in the year. No-one else took this view. Hawke flirted with the idea. Keating vigorously opposed it, saying it was important to have the May economic statement out, to demonstrate the government's economic credentials. Hawke, never entirely convinced of the merits of such an early poll, decided against it.

Talk of an early election was officially off. Hawke said so publicly, at a press conference on Wednesday 1 April, going as far as to commit himself to a late 1987 or early 1988 poll. Keating deplored this, saying the prime minister should keep his options open. Hawke was attracted to an election in the summer of 1987–88 for several reasons. To go earlier might smack of panic. Hawke liked the idea of an election in 1988, the bicentennial year, against a background of a festive country celebrating its 200th birthday. The pageantry appealed. Summer is regarded as a more propitious season for electioneering and February and March seemed to be months with a favourable aura for Hawke—he had won Labor leadership in February 1983 and federal office in March that year. If he remained as prime minister until January 1988 he would become Australia's longest-serving Labor prime minister; if he led Labor into a third successive term he would set a record. Keating was unimpressed by these arguments. He does not share Hawke's faith in the power of pomp and ceremony. To him the May mini-budget, not the bicentennial celebrations, was the springboard to launch an election.

By this stage Keating had concluded that the optimum time for an election would be after the May statement but before the August budget. No-one supported this proposition. A winter election was considered out of the question. But convinced that a July or August election was the way to go, Keating directed his energies to the May economic statement, now widely touted to contain a considerable range of measures that would normally be associated with an annual budget. This expectation gained credence when the weight of work forced Keating to cancel an overseas trip at Easter that would have included the interim meeting of the IMF in Washington and some time in Europe. Anita Keating flew out of Australia with her parents, but without her husband, on Thursday 16 April for a few weeks overseas.

During April and early May Keating continued to canvass the idea of an election in July or August, slotted in between the May statement and the August budget and timed to capitalise on the tax cuts that came into effect on 1 July. Hawke was not enthusiastic. Neither were most other ministers, advisers or party officials. Keating had not been keen on a May election when Hawke had earlier supported an autumn poll, so why was he pushing for a July/August election now? Keating's response was the government would look good after the May statement and should go to the polls while that, and the tax cuts, were uppermost in the electorate's mind. This renewed support for an early poll flew in the face of Hawke's April commitment to wait. But the idea was tempting—Labor's standing was good and the opposition was savagely divided. Keating wanted to exploit this split in opposition ranks. Hawke was unconvinced. Prime minister and treasurer were at loggerheads.

Keating delivered the May economic statement in the House of Representatives on Wednesday 13 May. Sartorially elegant, as usual, in a dark suit and white shirt, he dominated the parliamentary stage and played his role to the limit—the role of a serious, tough, economic repairman. His performance was pitched as much at the thousands in his TV audience as at his colleagues and opponents in the House. Anita Keating, back from her trip, brought Patrick, their eldest child, to the parliament to watch his father in the spotlight. The May statement included many of the tough measures that might normally appear in the annual budget. The budget deficit was to be slashed by $4 billion, almost double the figure originally considered. Keating was paving the way for a winter election. Later that night, he deserted the prime minister's party to join the journalists drinking downstairs in the non-members' bar. It was vintage Keating behaviour. Even as federal treasurer he did not send his hounds out to sniff which way the press gallery wind was blowing—he went himself, getting the feel of the gallery as he had done since he first arrived in Canberra in 1969.

The economic statement was well received as a positive step along the budgetary path. Its good reception turned government thoughts back to an election. Within days conjecture was rife that a date was about to be set, probably for July. Hawke was being urged from all sides to go to the polls. Speculation mounted. Meanwhile, Keating was off working hard at selling the May statement. There were plenty who wanted to hear what he had to say. The Securities Institute of Australia organised a lunchtime address on Monday 18 May at Sydney's Sheraton Wentworth Hotel. Almost 600 people came to hear Keating; some 200 had to be turned away.

The next event on the agenda was the annual premiers' conference and Loan Council meeting. There was every sign that the government was determined to take a tough line with the states. In his statement at the premiers' conference on 25 May Keating announced that commonwealth funding for the states and state borrowing would fall by about 7.5 per cent in the following financial year. Hawke took the opportunity provided by the conference to sound out the state premiers' thoughts about the timing of an election. The four Labor premiers were unanimous: go.

As election speculation grew throughout May, another topic began to preoccupy the media—a debate about the Hawke government's credentials, particularly its credentials as a true Labor government. The debate took place mainly in the pages of the *Sydney Morning Herald*. The protagonists were, on one side, the social commentator Craig McGregor and former prime minister Gough Whitlam, and, on the other, Paul Keating. On Saturday 2 May the *Herald* ran an article by Whitlam, titled 'Where Hawke went wrong', and one by McGregor on 'Hijacking middle Australia'. Whitlam criticised the Hawke government's media legislation and talked of a 'want of federal will rather than federal power' regarding the transfer of media ownership. He criticised the government's 'prevarication on Aboriginal land rights', its policies on workers' compensation and 'general failure to correct longstanding weaknesses in Australia's political and economic structures'. McGregor proclaimed: 'The Hawke government is being dragged remorselessly to the conservative end of the political spectrum . . . the good politics are over . . . the pragmatic and non-reformist character of the present Labor government will remain'. McGregor talked of the 'middle-classing of the Australian electorate' and said that the ALP had responded by shifting its position towards the centre to gain the middle-class votes it needs. And, in a stab guaranteed to rile Keating, he included the treasurer in a 'small group of pragmatists trying to hold the centre . . . creatures of their time, not scruple-less (as the cynics think) but faith-less . . .'

Keating retaliated a week later, under a banner proclaiming 'A basic flaw damns Whitlam's attack', in a reply that was larded with unmistakable Keating invective. The treasurer accused both writers of providing a 'massive dose of superficiality . . . It was a contest as to whether the heart on the sleeve outweighed the chip on the shoulder. There certainly was a shortage of cerebral ballast to maintain any equilibrium.' Keating took both to task for failing to recognise the achievements of the Hawke government, in the process dismissing McGregor's assertion that the government's reforms were merely 'paler versions of opposition policies'. Keating reminded his readers that Labor in the 1980s could no longer take wealth creation for granted, as could governments in the 1960s and early 1970s:

> By 1982–83 we had experienced our first negative growth in 30 years. Despite a boom in commodities, particularly in energy, John Howard managed to give us the deepest recession since the Great Depression. It does not matter how clever a party is—or thinks it is—it can't get blood out of a stone. There was no point in 1983 trying to shift income shares to the less well-off or to reverse unemployment until there was an adequate increment of wealth

> from which to draw. That's not a philosophical view or an ideological view, just plain sense.

It was not the first time that Keating had turned to the pages of a newspaper to shoot down critics of the government. Earlier in the year he had been stung into writing a lengthy reply—virtually a litany of every move the Hawke government had made—in response to a series of articles in the *Herald* which, he said, shared a common theme: 'that the present Commonwealth Labor Government has been overtaken by some alien and unorthodox philosophy, which is not only un-Labor, but is also deleterious to its constituency and the nation.'

Keating's reply was directed at arguments put forward by Hugh Stretton, Jim McClelland and Tom Fitzgerald, who, Keating said, proposed a return to an old-fashioned re-regulated economy (Stretton); said that the cabinet was composed of 'Labor fakers' who lacked any entitlement to lay claim to the tradition of Chifley's light on the hill (McClelland); and claimed that the government, in a craven quest for deregulation, had needlessly laid bare its financial system to the rest of the world, which as a result was exacting an inordinate price for our balance of payments adjustment (Fitzgerald). He castigated the authors for appointing themselves 'umpires of Labor dogma, and in McClelland's and Stretton's cases, as self-appointed Labor torch bearers'. The thrust of Keating's dissertation was that far from selling out, the Hawke Labor government had kept the faith, squarely faced the issues, coped with the crises and instituted the type of reforms, such as capital gains tax and fringe benefits tax, which had made earlier governments quail.

Keating and Gough Whitlam would clash again before the year was out. After a public spat about Labor ideology, and the achievements of the two Labor governments, the two gladiators were persuaded, by the end of 1987, of the wisdom of calling it quits.

By late May momentum was carrying the government towards an election in July. The prospect of taking advantage of a divided opposition and going to the country while the outlook was still promising outweighed the negatives of a winter election that, should the numbers go against the government, would deprive Labor of its place in the book of political records. The risk was worth taking. Unforeseen events were to vindicate the decision to risk a July poll. Asking the country for an endorsement after the October sharemarket collapse, in which thousands of voters lost money, would have invited a thumbs-down from an electorate in need of a scapegoat.

Keating, who had been actively involved in discussions about the timing of the election, had flown to Sydney for a speaking engagement and missed the final meeting on Tuesday 26 May which determined the election date of 11 July. He had earlier argued for an early August poll, under the impression—which proved to be wrong—that an announcement of a double dissolution before 1 July would shorten the life of the next parliament and entail another early election. Hawke staffers joked that the real reason was that a July election would force Keating to cancel his proposed visit to Europe. He was due to leave Australia, with Anita, on Monday 1 June. He cancelled the trip on 28 May, the day after Hawke announced the 11 July poll. He forfeited his trip, but got the election he wanted.

Alan Ramsey wrote in the *Sydney Morning Herald* in August 1987 that the significance of Keating's argument for an August election was not in the loss of an overseas trip to market the government's policy. According to Ramsey, whose article started with the maxim that the best story in politics is often the story behind the story, the real point of interest was what Keating said when told of the July date. Lionel Bowen had told Keating that any double dissolution called before July would mean a half-Senate election before 1 July 1989. Keating's response was along the lines of: '*I* don't want to be fighting a Senate election in eighteen months' time.' Bowen's advice proved wrong but that was irrelevant—the story was in Keating's use of the word 'I'. To Hawke's staffers it was yet another sign of Keating's hardening ambition to step into the prime ministerial shoes. Ramsey commented:

> They [Hawke's staff] resent the massive publicity Keating gets as the chief architect of government policy. They are critical of what they see as his direct role in influencing some of the more senior opinion makers among political journalists. Hawke's staff are good at news management . . . but Paul Keating is better.

Keating threw himself into electioneering. Cheering news came with the results of an ANOP poll which showed that his popularity with the public had risen by 14 per cent to 50 per cent. Keating could afford to take a high profile in the election campaign. The press once again seized the now recurrent theme of the growing gap between Keating and his old Labor training-ground in Bankstown. The *Times on Sunday* found Keating's electorate still lukewarm about its local-boy-made-good, but even less impressed by the Liberal opposition. Asked about Keating's preference for wearing pin-striped suits, one local replied: 'Well, he can't go around in a pair of overalls and an open shirt, can he? You've got to dress the part.' The Liberals, counting on the fact that Keating was responsible for much of the government's credibility, threw themselves into re-igniting issues that could be damaging to the treasurer, particularly his controversial travelling allowance claim. Keating, though, survived that attack unscathed.

The election process threw up another irritation for Keating—an independent candidate named Paul James Keating, competing for the seat of Blaxland. The treasurer's electorate assistant, Michael Hatton, went white when he heard of the other Keating, whose name ranked alphabetically above Paul John's on the ballot paper. Treasurer Keating wrote to his constituents, advising them of the existence of Keating II: 'Another person by the name of Paul Keating is standing for election in an attempt to confuse and mislead voters,' he wrote. After the election, the unsuccessful second Keating disappeared from political view.

The election trail is gruelling. Keating crossed the country, giving talks and interviews. Photographs showed him stooping to chat to a pensioner in a retirement home, shaking hands with potential voters. Writing in the *Sydney Morning Herald* on 2 July 1987, Steve Burrell reported:

> On the whirligig of the campaign trail his wife, Anita, travels with him from time to time. Heading for yet another TV interview, he complains to her that viewers will see that he looks tired. 'Let them see that you work too hard,' she says, with just enough edge in her voice to suggest that she wishes he didn't.

But the hard work paid off. Labor won. On election night, Saturday 11 July 1987, Paul and Anita Keating were at the Bankstown Sports Bowling Club where the treasurer, as sponsor, opened the annual 'open fours' competition. His mother, Min, used to bowl there. Standing outside the club that night, Keating said of the election win: 'It restores your faith.'

The election was out of the way. Labor had been endorsed by the electorate for a record third term. Hawke was assured of his place as the longest-serving Labor prime minister. Keating was increasingly recognised as the backbone of the government, the treasurer whose economic policies gave the government credibility. The Hawke government had been returned on a platform of continued austerity, and the electorate had rejected the Liberals' promises of generous tax cuts. Labor's win despite a fall in real living standards had defied normal expectations of the electorate's behaviour and indicated how convincingly Keating had marketed his economic management.

But there was no time to rest on the laurels of the electoral victory. The results of the July poll had shown a move against Labor in several key seats, with swings of almost 8 per cent. The areas recording the most disenchantment with Labor were in New South Wales, around Sydney, Newcastle and Wollongong. Keating's own electorate of Blaxland had recorded the second highest swing against Labor of 7.4 per cent, a level beaten only by Fowler, in Sydney's south-west, where the swing was 7.9 per cent (but leaving its Labor member with 62.4 per cent of the vote). The Hawke government had lost votes but gained seats. Labor could ignore these messages at its peril—but the party was confused about what, exactly, the Australian electorate had been signalling. Keating took a brief holiday before knuckling down to work on the budget. The annual budget, normally held on the second Tuesday in August, had been postponed until 15 September to allow time for preparation after the election, but even that imposed a tight work schedule.

Amid the pre-budget pressure, though, Keating the passionate politician found the time to pursue his other great passion—art and antiques. He accepted an invitation to address a gathering at Canberra's National Gallery on 27 August. The gallery's press release, billing the treasurer as an 'arts connoisseur', was greeted with cynical snorts by political journalists who were more used to hearing Keating abusing the opposition in the House than delivering a learned and eloquent lecture on neo-classical art. Keating drew an audience of several hundred. His address was a mix of scholarly work and unmistakable Keatingspeak. Talk of the 'aesthetic, simple, classical grandeur of the ancients' was interspersed with phrases such as 'eternally smart'. There was a hint that the self-possessed Keating was slightly nervous in this role. He said he would rather be talking about the current account, difficult as that had been, than discoursing on neo-classical art. But he showed his knowledge of art and history, taking his audience through the evolution of the neo-classical style and the philosophies of the late eighteenth century that it represented. He wove in some political points, referring to the new order that emerged from the French Revolution, and the failure of the 'saleroom snobs' to understand the 'enormous political significance of the [neo-classical] objects—the huge powering force that led to the remodelling of Europe, the reshaping of America, the political systems that came from the drive of the philosophers and those interested in ancient ideals'. He talked of the liberal setting of the gallery and threw in: 'Liberal that is, of course, other than by reference to the remnants of our own failed establishment . . .' Keating might have been there to give a speech about art and history, but he is a politician to the soles of his mirror-polished black shoes, and never misses a chance to fire a shot at the enemy.

Keating had brought a couple of pieces from his own collection as examples of the neo-classical style, a pair of *torchères* and candelabra that were used to light an eighteenth-century room. He told the audience they were from a design by Thomas Hope, who had laid the foundations of the style known today as English Regency, and which until 1930 was known as English Empire. He went on to describe them:

> The candelabra are interesting because they are from a period of transition. They are on the turn from one style to another. They bear the last remnants of the *ancien régime* of Louis XVI. In the candle-branches, you might also notice the swag drape around the grease pan which is a classic Louis XVI motif. The base or feet are broad to give them stability on a *torchère*. The lion's paw feet are evocative of the full Empire style then emerging. But what is particularly interesting is the Egyptian figure which is the centrepiece of the design. The Egyptian figure probably came from the renewed interest in Egypt at that time.

Explaining his fascination for French empire *objets d'art*, Keating continued:

> I collect these things not only because I like the look and style of them, but because they represent something which I think is so significant in history. It is the force of history behind them which makes them so interesting. And in terms of their smartness; well, as one of my colleagues says, they are the buffer at the end of the station, and you can't go any further. They are eternally smart.

The connoisseur-treasurer told his audience there was a common misconception that he had a 'Napoleonic hang-up'. He said: 'If I was to nominate any particular person of the period I admire it would have to be [Thomas] Jefferson. He is without a doubt a model of the Enlightenment. He took an active role in developing neo-classicism in America . . .' He ended his speech by declaring neo-classicism the 'last great style', saying: 'A few devotees soldier on. Those of us who still get twitchy over a temple pediment and shun the cubist legacy keep the fires of aesthetic purity burning for another Renaissance. In the meantime we collect what's left. Tonight's offerings are but a remnant, but you would walk a long way to find smarter.'

Keating's lecture at the National Gallery received prominent newspaper coverage, mostly reflecting surprise that the treasurer had made a favourable impression as a connoisseur of art, at least that of the period of his choice. What fuelled speculation was his decision not to allow television or radio coverage of the speech. His critics said that his appearance was at the same time an attempt to broaden and soften his image as a future prime minister, and an event that he did not want broadcast to the wider community because it would smack of the elitism often said to distance him from Labor electors.

His lecture on art drew scathing comments from Jim McClelland, a lawyer, a minister in the Whitlam government and a newspaper columnist. McClelland, himself dubbed 'Diamond Jim' because of his cultivated and stylish image, has confused observers with his criticisms of Keating's style and his well-tailored Italian suits. Writing in September 1987, McClelland praised Keating for his skills and achievments but savaged him for his dogmatic style: ' . . . Paul, the tone which you adjudge to befit your attacks on Wilson Tuckey is not appropriate to your campaign to sell yourself as a Renaissance man. In the field of art, dogmatism and exclusiveness are marks of the limitations, not the breadth of your learning.' McClelland recounted meeting Keating in Canberra and said they became friends 'not because we were philosophical soulmates but each of us found the other entertaining and we provided each other with some comic relief from the *longueurs* of that mostly boring place'.

But McClelland was generous with his compliments. So was his wife, Gil. She told her husband, some ten years ago when she first encountered Keating, that he was the most brilliant politician she had ever met. McClelland wrote that he agreed with her, and still does—but queried whether brilliance was enough, or the most important quality in a leader. The chief accusation he levied at Keating was narrowness. McClelland wanted Keating to be more than just clever; he wanted evidence of depth and intellect and compassion.

> [Keating] succeeded in demonstrating that his self-acquired erudition in the field of the arts and history is as narrowly based as in the field of economics . . . the shallowness of his learning does not entitle him to the certitude that he pronounces and to the contempt he expresses for those who do not share them . . . the very narrowness of Keating's economic expertise, based solely on the advice of the currently fashionable value-free breed of positivist economists, precludes that scepticism and open-mindedness which are the hallmarks of the authentic cultivated human being . . . I have nothing but admiration for this acquisition, on the basis of very inadequate formal schooling, of the skills he has acquired in the fields of economics and the arts, but the crash-courses are no substitute for genuine erudition, which provides the best inoculation against the illusion that you—or anyone else—know all

> the answers and that critics can be written off as sentimental fossils. It will be a pity if such a gifted human being cannot match character with intellect . . . his performance to date leaves a big question mark over his capacity to be anything more than clever. And that's not enough.

Keating was so incensed at McClelland's column, and to follow-ups in other media, that he rang up his former colleague. McClelland says the call came through early in the morning. Keating was on the line himself, not through a secretary. 'That you, Jim? Paul Keating here,' he began and then launched forth: 'Just because you swallowed a fucking dictionary when you were about fifteen doesn't give you the right to pour a bucket of shit over the rest of us.' Keating the externaliser lets people know what he is thinking. McClelland pointed out that Keating's reaction confirmed his point—there is more to debate than smacking down the opposition. But to Keating the slightest show of dissent equates to being the enemy. McClelland took the chance to chide Keating for his open friendships with business people, for accepting their hospitality. He recalls Keating's reply: 'You know me, Jim. I love stars.'

McClelland has a great affection for Keating, and admiration for his abilities. But the admiration is qualified. He recalls their shared 'elitist contempt' for those around them. 'To my shame I fostered that,' he says and adds: 'Keating has a huge IQ but cleverness might not be enough. He has allowed jargon to take the place of real analysis—he risks becoming the "dessicated calculating machine" [the accusation flung at Hugh Gaitskell by the British Labour politician Aneurin Bevan]. He would do himself a favour if he dumped the jargon and let the world see the real Paul Keating who can, when he chooses, be a charming and entertaining person.' McClelland later buried the hatchet, endorsing Keating as probably the next Labor prime minister.

Keating the treasurer pulled a rabbit out of the hat in September 1987, announcing a balanced budget that sent financial markets into a euphoric spin and brought the treasurer laudatory headlines such as 'Keating in full command', in the Melbourne *Herald*, and 'Keating's brilliant budget' in the *Daily Mirror*. The *Australian* followed with 'Paul Keating: Apollo of the bourse?'. Reading his fifth budget speech to the House, Keating spoke of Australia turning the corner and of the government's wiping out the dismal legacy of a near-$10 billion deficit it had inherited in 1983 from the Fraser government.

He showed all the confidence that would be expected of a federal treasurer delivering Australia's first balanced budget in seventeen years, a result achieved through a combination of strong growth in tax receipts and $1 billion to be raised by the sale of government assets. The budget outcome was also predicated on stronger growth, falling inflation, lower interest rates and no rise in imports. Analysts seized on the arithmetic and complained that the $1 billion from asset sales was not a true saving. But that did not hinder the market momentum. Interest rates started to fall, the sharemarket soared and the Australian dollar began to climb. Financial analysts and economists could pull the budget numbers apart and dispute their validity but the emotional appeal of a balanced budget was unshakable.

An encouraging reduction in the August trade deficit added to the mood of triumph—but the budget had its critics. The former Treasury-secretary-turned-senator John Stone attacked the government for not cutting back further on expenditure; others called for measures to encourage savings and investment. The criticism that received most coverage was the knocking dealt to the budget by the finance minister, Peter Walsh. Addressing a conference of Labor lawyers in Perth, Walsh spoke more freely than his government would have wished. He criticised the budget's expenditure program and said that it was an insufficient response to Australia's serious problem of foreign debt. 'I can give you 200, a list of 200 bloody programs off the top of my head that can't be justified by social justice, equity or economic efficiency grounds and the reason we haven't abandoned them is because we don't have the courage to do so,' he told his audience. Walsh later said he did not know the press were present. Hawke and Keating made their displeasure very clear.

The balanced budget was a huge psychological advantage for Labor, and not least for Keating. His delight with the outcome was evident. Delivering an address to the Corporate Currency Club in Sydney's Intercontinental Hotel on 18 September, he smacked his lips with satisfaction as he ticked off the economy's good points. He later said:

> In the last six to eight months I feel people are beginning to see the place is just totally different, they appreciate and understand that. In a funny way I feel the balanced budget has had a big psychological influence, a big dark cloud has been taken off the horizon. But it happened over four or five years, it didn't happen overnight. It might not have been apparent but all that work, that work on the tax side, was all heading towards that, it all finally came together. And I do think that people believe that a rational tax system—capital gains tax, relief of double taxation of dividends—is

> going to produce a more dynamic economy. I think all that's coming home to a broader understanding of the conceptual framework. And I'm pleased about that. The month-by-month, quarter-by-quarter, year-by-year commentary on the economy is quickly forgotten—but what won't pass is the structural change—changes don't pass.

With the budget successfully out of the way Keating was gearing up for the annual IMF/World Bank meeting in Washington. His sensitive political antennae led him to keep well away from the Australia Card issue. The proposed identity card was an unpopular measure that Labor gratefully dumped when a retired public servant, Ewart Smith, found a minor but significant technical hitch in the proposed legislation. He gave John Stone the ammunition with which to kill the issue. Keating's trip was to include the Washington meeting and appointments in New York and Europe. But the months of uninterrupted work and pressure took their toll. Keating succumbed to a bronchial virus that threatened to turn into pleurisy. On doctor's orders the zealot was confined to quarters. The trip seemed off, but in the end was merely delayed and abbreviated. For once, though, Keating left the country with some work unfinished; the priority was to recover enough to get on with the budget-selling tour.

Keating returned to Australia in mid-October. Before he had time to settle into a regular routine of sleep and work, or to allow himself any post-budget complacency, came the worldwide sharemarket crash. New York's Dow Jones sharemarket index fell 22.62 per cent between the close of trading on Friday 16 October and the end of trading on Monday 19, a drop that in one trading day reduced the index to the level it had reached thirteen months earlier, in September 1986. What began as Black Monday on New York's Wall Street followed the sun around the globe to produce Black Tuesday in Australia. The all ordinaries index, the barometer of the Australian sharemarket, shed 24.3 per cent, one of the largest one-day falls. But even so, the index was only back to the level it had achieved months earlier, in February 1987. It was the speed, rather than the extent, of the sharemarket fall that sent traders reeling.

Australia's sharemarket performance in 1987 was different from that of other markets on two counts: in the three months before the crash the New York and London sharemarket indexes had shown a fairly stable trend, whereas Australia's all ordinaries had climbed by 21.5 per cent. And, whereas these other markets had stabilised fairly quickly after the losses of Monday 19, the Australian market kept falling and did not bottom out until 11 November, by which time the level of the all ordinaries index matched that of August 1986. Having wildly outperformed New York and London in a pre-crash burst, the Australian market then fell dramatically in October and took longer to settle.

The crash ended a worldwide boom that had lasted almost five years. Australia's new breed of financial entrepreneurs, who had dominated the business pages with their audacious and seemingly endless takeovers and backroom maneouvres, were brought to their knees. Some of these new money magicians—parvenu philistines as they have been labelled—were revealed as little more than paper-chasers with few tangible assets, and their artificial empires now demolished by the sharemarket crash.

The collapse illustrated an important point: that much of the fortune accumulated by Australia's new money men had been milked out of the sharemarket boom, not directly generated through opportunities created by government policies. It has been argued, though, that government could have imposed more stringent rules on, say, takeover activity. The fact that interest on borrowings remained a tax-deductible expense encouraged the entrepreneurs. But the broader-reaching financial deregulation—the floating of the Australian dollar, admission of foreign banks and deregulation of interest rates—did not itself create a new class of wealth. These steps were taken to encourage Australian industry and commerce to be competitive internationally. The relationship between a booming sharemarket and liberalisation of the financial system has been confused because the two coincided. They were separate events. Each could have happened without the other. And the general economy emerged relatively unscathed from the period of the crash, demonstrating that the health of the real economy is not governed by conditions in sharemarkets.

It was hardly suprising that the worldwide fall in sharemarkets revived the debate about the similarities between the 1980s and the 1920s. Parallels had been drawn before between the heady days of the 1920s and the affluent 1980s, with the rise of the yuppies, a booming sharemarket, easy credit and talk of return to protectionism in trade. Serious commentators pointed out significant differences between the 1980s and the 1920s, which argued against a repeat of the Great Depression of the 1930s. Important among these was the response by the central banks. In October 1987 they answered the crisis by pumping out money to keep the system liquid, instead of tightening credit as they had in 1929. The world economy was also generally in better shape in 1987, and company profits at a far healthier level than had prevailed in the late 1920s. A sharemarket collapse, especially one that had long been predicted and seen as long overdue, did not dictate a re-run of the grim 1930s. And, most important, for all the drama that went with 19 October 1987, the Australian sharemarket index fell merely to the level it had been at months earlier. However it was genuine panic that swept world markets in those couple of days when the indexes went into what seemed a free-fall, and many shareholders sustained real losses, particularly those who were late entrants to the booming market. But when the dust settled it was clear that what had been termed a collapse was really what has become identified by the euphemism 'major correction'.

Keating resisted pressure and calls for an immediate response from the government to the crash. He could see no wisdom in a knee-jerk reaction such as a rushed mini-budget. He was much criticised for this: a chorus of voices, mainly from the opposition ranks, demanded a mini-budget as evidence of government action. Others saw Keating's refusal to be pushed as a sign of his political maturity. He stuck to the view that the government was ready to make adjustments as they were needed. 'We've got all the bases covered,' he said.

The year 1987 was not to end without Keating seizing another opportunity to trumpet about the credentials and aspirations of the Hawke Labor government. On this occasion, 11 November 1987, he delivered an address to the Victorian branch of the Fabian Society—an intellectual socialist think-tank that is very much Gough Whitlam's homeground—in which he elaborated on the comparison of the problems confronting the Hawke government with those of the Whitlam period, and of the need for Labor to change so as to remain relevant. As in his earlier speech to the audience of Labor historians, he credited Gough Whitlam with bringing Labor out of the wilderness and into government. Whitlam's great achievement, he said, was 'to take the party by the scruff of its neck and drag it towards the contemporary reality and the real interests of the workforce'. But in language reminiscent of his earlier attacks on the Left, he took a shot at the 'romantics who choose to regard the 1972 Whitlam program as a purist application of high-minded Labor principle'. That, he said, was a highly selective view of the historical facts. 'The truth is the program was essentially about winning votes'. Keating went on to detail the Hawke government's four years of achievements in tax, health, social welfare and, particularly, occupational superannuation. The latter, he said, might not seem much to the comfortably middle-class, tertiary-educated attendees of some ALP branches, but for a factory-worker or a shop assistant who had only an old age pension to look forward to it was the start of a social change which would make most other so-called social reforms look limp by comparison. He stressed the government's record in reform and the complementary role played in this by the unions.

The swipe at the Whitlam era earned him the wrath of several former ministers in that government. Dr Jim Cairns, Gough Whitlam's former deputy and treasurer, said that if Hawke and Keating associated a little less with media tycoons they would win back greater Labor support. Jim McClelland said the problem was one of style—that he could not envisage Whitlam or Chifley acting like Hawke and consorting with millionaires. Whitlam later said that Keating would win neither support nor respect with criticism of the Whitlam government. 'I won't cop smart-arse remarks about my government,' he thundered. Whitlam stands as one of the Grand Old Men of Labor. Keating, hell-bent on pushing the credentials of the Hawke government, emphasising the different challenges of the 1980s and the need to adapt to change, had trampled on cherished ideals. The Labor Party likes to protect its legends. It feels it is big enough to absorb an occasional heroic failure. Above all, the Labor party has learned how much damage could be wrought by internal dissension and public scrapping. Keating and Whitlam hung up their gloves.

Bill Kelty, secretary of the ACTU, injected a light-hearted diversion when, in the course of an address to the Master Builders Federation in Canberra in November 1987, he compared Keating to Dorothy, the heroine of the *Wizard of Oz*. Dorothy was carried along by a whirlwind from her home in Kansas, and finally made her way down the Yellow Brick Road to the Emerald City. Kelty said Keating, like Dorothy in the land of the Munchkins, was confronted with a host of problems but unlike Dorothy had no magic to protect him from evil. Keating was present at the lunch and seemed unfazed by the analogy—except to say that blue suede shoes (given his past involvement with a rock band) would be more appropriate than Dorothy's red shoes.

By December 1987 Keating had decided to silence the post-crash calls for action by announcing that a mini-budget would be delivered in May 1988. That showed that the government was doing something, but gave everyone time to think—a welcome hiatus, given that virtually two budgets had been constructed in 1987. It also meant that the federal government would not be introducing any unpalatable measures before the New South Wales premier, Barrie

Unsworth, went to his state's polls in March. The July federal victory had given Unsworth little cause for confidence. The NSW swing against Labor had been 2.6 per cent, against a national swing of one per cent.

Keating produced some good news when he and finance minister Walsh jointly announced the forward estimates of government spending for 1988/89 to 1990/91. They foreshadowed a budget surplus of $580 million for the 1987/88 financial year and a rein on spending that would be maintained in 1988/89 and beyond. The two jubilant ministers offered to autograph enlarged copies of a chart from the forward estimates. The next day's news extinguished their good spirits: the Australian Bureau of Statistics released corrected figures showing that private business investment in plant and equipment had not risen by 11.8 per cent in the September quarter but in fact had virtually stood still, with only 0.5 per cent growth. Keating had based a great deal of his enthusiasm and confidence on the initial erroneous figure. What made the news worse was that the sluggish growth had occurred before the October sharemarket collapse, so that any post-crash deterioration would begin from an already-weak base. Responding to a question in the Senate, Walsh admitted that he knew in advance of his and the treasurer's press conference that a revision to the September figures was in the wind but did not know its size. It was suggested that the treasurer knew of the revision and its magnitude.

For Paul Keating 1987 ended on a sunnier note than 1986. The government had been re-elected for a third term, giving him the chance to see through the wide-ranging reforms he had spent so much time and energy introducing. It had been a year of punishing hours—on the expenditure review committee for the May statement, in a gruelling round of electioneering leading to the July federal election and then the demands of the annual budget. The burden of ERC work had forced him to cancel a trip to attend the interim meeting of the International Monetary Fund in April, and a bout of illness in September dealt him out of the annual IMF/World Bank meetings. The final months of the year had been dominated by speculation about the extent of economic damage that might yet surface following the sharemarket crash.

But there were bright spots: he had produced a balanced budget and had every expectation of taking the next budget into surplus. The Australian dollar had recovered from its earlier doldrums. Interest rates were declining. There was evidence of an improvement in the current account deficit. He could afford to relax a little, to succumb to the diversions of the silly season. He had been named as the first Australian Irishman of the Year at a $250-a-head inaugural dinner of the Ireland Fund of Australia, an accolade that prompted him to admit that like most Irish, he is 'sentimental to the last teardrop'.

Hawke encouraged his ministers to take a long and restful break during the summer recess from parliament. On Christmas Eve Keating was still in his office. Then he, too, recognised that the year was over and headed for the beach with his family.

15 Boy with a baton

We are all given the [field-marshal's] baton in the knapsack when we get our preselection. I got mine then and it is still tucked away.

PAUL KEATING

GOOD ECONOMIC news introduced 1988 to Australia and to treasurer Keating. The current account deficit fell significantly in January, to $428 million, well below the December level of $700 million and the previous January's $1.4 billion. It was the smallest monthly deficit since April 1984. Commodity prices were on the rise, particularly wool, which heightened the feeling of optimism. The Australian dollar strengthened and interest rates and inflation were coming down. The property market was booming. The all ordinaries index was weaker, reflecting a downturn in share prices, but the bad news seemed to be confined to the sharemarket.

Keating won points in January with the resources industry by removing foreign investment restrictions on new oil and gas projects. The move would encourage exploration for oil and gas in Australia. In the same month he announced a wide-ranging program of inquiries to be conducted by the Industries Assistance Commission, which had come under his wing in July 1987. The inquiries, into areas such as tourism and travel and food processing, would be part of a program aimed at increasing the speed of structural adjustment in the economy. The objective was to improve industry efficiency across the board.

Keating left for Europe immediately after the Australia Day

Bicentennial celebrations, on a trip that included delivering an address in Davos, Switzerland, to the World Economic Forum. An international audience of world leaders in finance, trade, investment and government heard him describe the change that had taken place in Australia, a change that he called 'an economic transformation the like of which has no parallel in our recent history':

> The story of the Australian economy today is about an economy shaking off its past complacency, of an economy becoming more dynamic and entrepreneurial and, most importantly, about the fact that the Australian people have shown they have been prepared to put in a sustained effort to break our dependence on a hitherto narrow economic base. This change has come about after the most traumatic and destabilising economic period for our nation since the Great Depression.

Keating spoke of Australia evolving from an inward-looking people to a more outward-looking economy. He praised the Accord for its role in facilitating wage restraint. He assured his international audience that Australia was not resting on its laurels. The problems of the external account, the high current account deficit, still had to be solved. But progress was being made.

In contrast to the progress being made on the economic front, Labor stumbled through a series of political crises in the early months of 1988. This brought accusations that the Hawke government had fallen victim to an arrogance and carelessness symptomatic of complacency after five years in office. The prime minister wrong-footed on the issue of timed local telephone calls and a by-election in the seat of Adelaide on 6 February turned into a stunning blow: Labor lost a hitherto impregnable seat. The resignation of the former minister for immigration, Mick Young, following a blunder over the party's use of campaign funds, and subsequent revelations that the prime minister had tried to help Young into a new job, brought mounting criticism on Hawke. Young's departure followed the earlier resignation of the former minister for tourism, John Brown, after accusations that he misled parliament. These setbacks, disastrous as they seemed at the time, paled when on 19 March Labor was swept out of office in the New South Wales election. It was deprived of government in the state which had been the party's traditional power-base.

Labor had held the seat of Adelaide since 1966. The poll results showed a 9 per cent swing against the ALP and pushed Hawke into killing off the notion of timed local calls. The concept was only the start of a series of micro-economic reforms planned on the basis of the 'user-pays' principle. The practice of timing local calls is common in many countries; it was inadequately explained in Australia so that the superficial and immediate assumption was that everyone would be worse off. Little time was given to explaining that users who made brief calls would pay less. Instead the critics leapt to the assumption that the timed calls would inevitably be an additional burden on those who could least afford it. The opposition made mileage out of the issue, and community, consumer and union groups all protested.

But Labor's problem went beyond timed local calls. No-one was fooled into believing Labor had lost Adelaide simply on the timed calls question. Rather Labor was increasingly accused of having lost touch with its traditional supporters, of having lost sight of what voters wanted and needed. Keating, in his renowned speech to the Fabian Society, had alluded to Labor's need to woo back its blue-collar base. Implementing reforms, even those that are sympathetic to the needs of the electorate, loses some of its political value if the electorate cannot see the benefits of these reforms.

Ross Gittins, economics editor of the *Sydney Morning Herald*, wrote on 8 February that 'we will look back on the Adelaide by-election and see it as a turning point in the battle for micro-economic reform. The economic rationalists' cause took a beating on Saturday.' And the political commentator Max Walsh, writing in the same issue, backed up this view: 'The telephone issue symbolised the choice between a rational economic policy and political exploitation through fear. Hawke's response was a sad capitulation to political philistinism and provincial populism.' Walsh pointed out that the issue was never debated on its merits but 'simply used by the Liberals . . . to frighten the ill-informed'.

Back in Australia in time for the opening session of parliament in mid-February, Keating kept a low profile during the commotion that surrounded Mick Young's departure and the accusations of 'terminal mateship' that were flung at Hawke for his indiscretion in trying to help Young find a job. Keating prudently kept his head down and distanced himself from what was increasingly seen as Labor—specifically the prime minister—losing its political grip. Labor had to pull its socks up. That much was obvious. What exactly to do was less clear. The government did not want to tamper with the economic policies that had won it credibility and, so it was believed, a third term in office. But the setback in Adelaide was an unwelcome reminder of some less comforting aspects of the July federal win—the unpalatable but undeniable truth that while Labor had won more seats it had not won more votes. In fact, it had lost ground in a number of safe seats.

The verdict was that Labor had lost touch with its base. Barrie Unsworth, fresh from a state election defeat, made cracks about Hawke being seen too often in a dinner suit, cigar in hand, with his business mates. Keating later retorted that the same film footage had been shown 100 times. Hawke vigorously rejected accusations that his government had lost touch and dismissed criticism of his mixing with the wealthy as an 'inverse form of snobbery'. In defending the government's relationship with business Keating has often talked of the Hawke's government's success being in 'building business into the equation' instead of seeing business as the enemy, to be feared, distrusted and beaten. Labor voters want reassurance that they, too, are built into the equation. Keating stresses that they are, that the reforms and adjustments the government is implementing are aimed at enhancing conditions for all. Economic efficiency, he told a press conference just before Christmas 1987, was the name of the game. Sending people down to the social security office was not looking after them:

> By the end of next year we will have created a million new jobs since 1983. Now I reckon that's looking after the people we're supposed to look after. One of the things I said out in Bankstown—someone said: What are you doing for us?—and I said I can't look after Bankstown unless this government's credible in its policies. If we're not, the interest rates the world will impose on us will drive us into recession. And the people out there, who just survive in the ebb and flow of the economy, will just be wiped out. That's what I think keeping the faith's all about. It's just a matter of doing what really has to be done. Well, we're doing it.

In late February the expenditure review committee—a remarkably stable core of men in the Hawke government—had started preparation for the May mini-budget. The members in the review committee had hardly changed since it was first established in 1983. In some respects the government might seem to have lost its stability but the ERC held firm and did not panic.

March had brought the Hawke government its fifth anniversary in office—a fitting time to look back with satisfaction on the achievements. But the recent turmoil and challenges ahead left little time for indulgent reminiscences. The privatisation debate was a running sore that threatened to split Labor ranks. Opposition to privatisation was strong from the Left, and from Hawke's own right-wing Labor Unity faction in Victoria. Selling public sector organisations—the property of the people—into private hands is anathema to many in the ALP. Foreign minister Bill Hayden, speaking on Channel 9's *Sunday* program on 6 March, summed up the difficulties when he said the issue of privatisation hit at the 'psyche' of the Labor Party. He said many people shared his resistance to selling off government enterprises, especially the Commonwealth Bank. 'I have strong feelings,' he said. 'It's in the history, in the psyche of our party, and if there's going to be any debate, all these things must be handled very tenderly in respect for the feelings and history of our party and its traditions.'

Privatisation is regarded as a means of improving efficiency. Its supporters argue that taking organisations into the private sector and making them accountable to shareholders and a bottom line produces leaner, hungrier, profit-oriented enterprises. The UK trail-blazed privatisation and New Zealand followed with a wide-ranging program of corporatisation, converting public enterprises into companies and selling all or part of their equity into private sector hands. Considerations of efficiency aside, a strong incentive to take organisations out of government hands and into the private sector is that it removes or reduces their need for government funding. Opponents of privatisation point out that while the government no longer has to budget to provide funds for publicly-owned organisations it also loses any revenue brought by those public enterprises that make a profit.

A number of government-owned institutions in Australia support the idea of privatisation as a means of raising the capital they need without putting pressure on the public purse. The capital expenditure of, say, Qantas or the funds needed to expand the capital base of the Commonwealth Bank would strain the budget and threaten government spending programs on social welfare; far better for these organisations to tap the private sector for funds.

Privatisation is part of the Hawke government's program for restructuring which has been widely implemented in the private sector. Improving efficiency, though, is not restricted to the private sector; the public sector has its turn. ALP philosophy has been commonly identified with public ownership and the nationalisation of industry, rather than privatisation. But, as Gough Whitlam points out in his book *The Whitlam Government*, nationalisation has scarcely been revived since the failure of the Chifley government to nationalise the private banks in 1949. 'Nationalisation became more a symbol of ideological purity than a positive commitment to practical social reform . . . The commitment to nationalisation had become a useless sacred cow within the ALP,' Whitlam wrote.

Nationalisation might have been dumped from ALP thinking but privatisation remains a divisive issue.

Keating had sensibly maintained his distance from the factional party infighting of early 1988. In the midst of the uproar surrounding Hawke's moves on Young's behalf and the warring over the national ALP secretaryship (following former secretary Bob McMullan's move into parliament), Keating called a press conference to remind the press gallery and the country that economic policy at least was on track. The conference was called ostensibly to discuss the February balance of payments. But as the treasurer rarely bases a conference on the trade numbers it was clear that Keating had decided to try to divert attention away from government fumbling and on to more successful aspects of policy. Keating had already been anointed as Hawke's successor. Asked about his ambitions, he replied: 'We are all given the [field-marshal's] baton in the knapsack when we get our preselections. I got mine then and it is still tucked away.'

The Hawke government, and particularly those on the expenditure review committee, faced a crowded agenda. Work for the May economic statement had been delayed until the NSW state election was over, leaving a tight program to be devised in two months. The economic statement, delivered on Wednesday 25 May, bore out predictions of radical changes to the superannuation industry and foreshadowed a budget surplus of at least $3 billion for 1988/89. Keating delivered his fourth May statement—the last of its kind to be read in the old Parliament House—with confidence and conviction. The program included tariff reductions, sharp cuts in corporate tax, the end of a number of business tax concessions, a proposal to end the foreign tax credits system and promises of personal tax cuts ahead. It maintained the attack on sacred cows that had been started in May 1983 when the Hawke government's first mini-budget raised the tax rate on lump-sum superannuation payouts. Keating had delivered another significant instalment in the saga of tax reform.

Silence reigned in the House of Representatives as Keating read out the far-reaching reforms that ended the tax-free status of investment returns from superannuation funds. The aim of the change was to spread the effects of dividend imputation and bring the superannuation funds within the tax net. The intention was to encourage the superannuation funds to buy shares in Australian companies, to achieve franked dividends, thus promoting domestic investment. The second change affecting superannation was the decision to tax employer contributions instead of employee lump-sum payouts. This brings revenue forward to the government and, according to government sums, does not cut into the benefits of fund members.

The complexity of the changes, which represented months of work by Treasury officers, by Keating and his tax advisers, was such that superannuation managers as well as the general public were confused. While everyone was examing the fine print of the micro-reforms the foreign exchange traders and sharemarkets reacted exuberantly, pushing the Australian dollar to its highest value in years and sending the sharemarket's all ordinaries index to a level not seen since the 1987 crash.

Within days speculation was widespread that the promised personal tax cuts would be structured with a top rate to match the new corporate rate of 39 per cent. Corporate tax had been cut by 10 percentage points, in what Keating called 'one big bang'. He likes the impact of that. And the new corporate tax puts Australian companies on a more equal footing with their overseas counterparts. The proposal to drop the foreign credits tax—which had not been foreshadowed—will end a system which levied the Australian company tax rate on dividends remitted from abroad to Australia. Keating's new system proposes a more rigorous method of taxing foreign-sourced income which will end the attraction, for individuals and companies, of using any of the 60 low-tax areas, such as Hong Kong, Monaco and the Cayman Islands. The reduced personal tax rates would be the final touch in Keating's strategy of achieving lower tax rates and broadening the tax base. In his words, he has 'run past consumption tax, gone the harder route and fixed direct tax'.

The 1988 May economic statement brought a high point in the mounting speculation about Keating's claim to The Lodge. The *Bulletin* boldly proclaimed 'Prime Minister Keating' on its cover and ran a long article discussing how, when and what kind of prime minister Keating would be. Columnist Jim McClelland gave his endorsement of his former colleague, saying: '. . . Keating already is for all practical purposes the leader of the government . . . Whatever you think of him, he's the best prime minister on offer'. A Morgan Gallup Poll carried out for the magazine showed increasing support not only for Keating as treasurer but also as a clear successor if Bob Hawke decided to step down. Hawke scored more points as friendly and likeable but Keating rated as more positive, less prone to changing his mind and less influenced by big business and the trade unions.

And what kind of prime minister would Keating be? 'He'll be the same kind of prime minister he is now,' was a backbencher's comment.

Keating underscored his own credentials for leadership when he delivered a searing attack on the opposition in the House on the day after his economic statement:

> You were in office from 1949 to 1983, bar three years . . . And you left everything the way you found it. The place got old and tired and worn out, just like you are . . . You didn't bother with the detail, that was for the public servants . . . you never ran the policy. You never ran the place. Well, let me tell you this. We run the place. We run the departments, we run the policy. We comprehend. We know.

Keating reeled off the changes made by the Hawke government and continued his blistering assault on the 'born-to-rule mob':

> Where you all come a gutser is, over here, we think we're born to rule YOU. And we're going to keep on doing it. And let me tell you this: it's been ingrained in me from childhood, I think my mission in life is to run you. And the prime minister thinks his mission in life is to run you. And let me say, the Labor movement thinks its mission in life is to run Australia.

Stirring stuff. No-one can match Keating for sheer parliamentary theatre. His faction loves it, the Left acknowledges it and the opposition has to suffer it.

Keating maintained the momentum and flair in June 1988 when he launched the party's new economic policy at the ALP national conference in Hobart. He gave a forceful performance that demonstrated his ability to inspire his followers. In a crisply delivered speech he cemented contemporary economic practices into the ALP platform. They included a number of firsts for the party's platform, among them the explicit recognition that Australia forms part of the world economy, that the country's chief problem is its external debt, and that Australia's is a mixed economy. In the past Keating had fought to impose changes on the platform. This time, with the changes already in place, he simply adjusted the platform to agree with his brand of economics. Keating, triumphant, was in his element. He described the new platform as

> a contemporary document. It actually tells the reader what the government is doing, intends to do and why . . . it's shed much of the waffle and compromise in language which not only made it unreadable in the past but actually made it irrelevant. No Labor government, no Labor conference, has ever had such a contemporary and relevant draft platform placed before it . . .

Keating brushed aside the Left's calls for more interventionist and less market-oriented policies. Just as he had successfully turned the Left's arguments back against them on the issue of foreign banks, he now mocked their calls for increased regulation as 'a romantic trip back down the time tunnel to the days of regulation . . . stepping back . . . to the 1960s and 1950s, to the politics of John McEwen, Malcolm Fraser and John Stone.'

Keating did not dally at the conference. He arrived, said his piece, and left. He had made his mark on the conference and on the party. And he knew it.

Index